The
National Physical Laboratory
A History

Edward Pyatt

Foreword by Dr Paul Dean

Adam Hilger Ltd, Bristol

British Library Cataloguing in Publication Data.

Pyatt, Edward
  The National Physical Laboratory: a History
  1. National Physical Laboratory—History
  I. Title
  539'.0720421   TA1

  ISBN 0-85274-387-4

Published by Adam Hilger Ltd,
Techno House, Redcliffe Way, Bristol BS1 6NX

The Adam Hilger book-publishing imprint is owned by
The Institute of Physics

Typeset by Macmillan India Ltd, Bangalore
Printed by J. W. Arrowsmith Ltd, Bristol, England

Contents

Foreword

The history of the National Physical Laboratory is very much a history of the growth of scientific activity in the United Kingdom in the twentieth century. The modest beginnings of the NPL, with Royal Society control and private donations to supplement a meagre government grant, through the long period of growth, the changes of the War years and the influence of DSIR, to its modern role as a Research Establishment of the Department of Industry—these all reflect the changing attitudes and patterns of organisation of science in this country. In this sense the story of the development of the NPL is more than just the story of a single major laboratory.

As Mr Pyatt shows, the historical threads that relate to the NPL go back a very long way, some three hundred years, to the establishment of the Royal Society and the (unrelated) building of Bushy House. In the late nineteenth century the need became clear for a public institution for measurement standards, calibration and related physical research, and from the endeavours of a number of far-sighted individuals the National Physical Laboratory was born. One of those individuals, Richard T Glazebrook, was to be its first Director. His tireless efforts strengthened the Laboratory in its early years and set the pattern for the growth and diversification that was to continue for over half a century. Many of our modern technologies and industries have developed from the resulting NPL programmes.

A crucial aspect of NPL activity has always been its work on standards and metrology. A modern state needs standards and measurement methods for its industries, for health and safety purposes, and for numerous functions of central and local government. The role of the NPL in this sphere is vital for the well-being of the country, and yet it is a largely unseen role that is not widely understood. The developing thread of standards and measurement activity is clearly identified in Mr Pyatt's history as one of the central aspects of the Laboratory's work, of no less importance than the research that has led to major new industries.

We are grateful that Mr Pyatt has risen to the challenge of Hadow's remarks (cf page ix) and written this history. I know that the task has not been easy. There are always problems in unravelling the complexities of historical records and in understanding attitudes and motivations. Whilst we accept that in any historical work there will be room for disagreement on detail or interpretation this, in itself, provides no reason for evading the challenge. The alternative would be no record, and we should all be the poorer.

P DEAN

Preface and Acknowledgments

John Hadow, who during his Secretaryship made many contributions to the history of the Laboratory and its site, wrote in 1969:

'It does not seem wise to attempt a comprehensive history of the Laboratory. The load would be immense and the opportunity for conflict over the contents would be extensive, while the authority and usefulness of such a publication would be at best limited'.

The irresistable challenge of these words led to the writing of this book. Whether he was right, or not, only the future can tell. But there has been considerable entertainment in the doing. Interpretations and opinions expressed are those of the author.

My service at NPL covered the period 1947 to 1977—certainly the most changeful years of its history. Part of my duties in the later years involved the assembly of the Laboratory archives, researching the history of Bushy House and the setting up of an NPL Museum; these activities facilitated the production of the present work. Among the many contacts who helped to formulate the views of the Laboratory and its organisation set out herein, I single out for special mention the following.

Dr Paul Dean, the present Director, whose interest and encouragement throughout the writing have been specially valued, and who contributes a foreword.

A E Bailey, my last Superintendent at NPL, who played a vital part in the closing stages of the project.

Friends and former colleagues, who have read chapters or parts of chapters, and whose comments and criticisms have been greatly appreciated—G Booth, W E Carrington, J A Champion, D W Davies, J Dawson, G D Dew, S C Ellis, J W C Gates, R W F Gould, S Grant, A Horsfield, R J King, A J D Mackenzie, B Petley, H Pursey, G H Rayner, D W Robinson, B Swindells and D M Yates. (Nevertheless, they cannot be blamed for any errors which may remain; these must result from wilfully ignoring their advice.)

D S Sutcliffe, who took over charge of the Museum and Archives when I retired and who has subsequently made everything in them available to me for study.

Miss J Johnson for considerable help with illustrations.

The Laboratory Library staff for unfailing courtesy and help.

My wife has given continuous encouragement throughout the course of the work. She has typed some manuscripts from my execrable handwriting and finally rounded off the book by the preparation of a substantial index.

All pictures, except where otherwise acknowledged, are Crown Copyright.

Edward Pyatt
Hampton
1981

Part I

The Founding of NPL

The Threads of History: 1651–1896

In October 1651, following the Battle of Worcester, King Charles II escaped to the Continent, a beaten fugitive harried from the land by his Parliamentarian enemies. In May 1660 he returned once again to his country and began a triumphal progress from Dover towards London. After the bitter fratricidal battles of the Civil War and the austerity of the Commonwealth, after all the troubles and anxieties of the last two decades, he was welcomed as a bringer of peace and prosperity. The King was well fitted for the role; shrewd and cynical in political manoeuvring, brave, sport and pleasure loving, there was something in him for everyone to respect or admire. Though possibly a secret Catholic (and certainly one on his death-bed), he ruled sensibly over an extremely Protestant country, which he held together in a period when the monarchy might well have failed again.

In the early years of the Restoration two entirely unrelated actions set in train chains of events which were to combine many years later to produce the National Physical Laboratory. In 1662 King Charles granted a charter of incorporation to a group of scientists and philosophers, who thereupon assumed the title of the Royal Society, destined to play a leading role in the founding of NPL more than two centuries later. In December 1663 he signed a memorandum:

> We have commanded Our Servt Edward Proger, One of ye Grooms of our Bedchamber to build a lodge for our service in one of our Parks att Hampton Court called North Parke[1], And to make a faire walke or laine there in such maner as We have directed.

This was the building which would later house the infant NPL and which continues even today to embellish the heart of the site.

The Civil War and Commonwealth years had seen the emergence of the new, so-called experimental philosophy; the belief that systematic obser-vation and experiment were the proper means for investigating and understanding natural happenings. Until then classical philosophy, which held that the Greeks (and particularly Aristotle) had said all there was to say about science, had dominated all facets of learning. Gatherings of these new philosophers had been held in London and Oxford. In 1659 they were meeting in London at Gresham College in Bishopsgate (where Christopher Wren was at that time Professor of Astronomy). After the Restoration the meetings became more regular and it was soon decided to form a 'Society for promoting Physico–Mathematical Experimental Learning'. The interest of the King was aroused and he gave the first charter in 1662. The following year a second charter granted a coat-of-arms with the motto '*Nullius in Verba*'.

The broad purpose of this new body was 'to enlarge knowledge by observation and experiment'. However the earliest members were by no means all scientists—the poets Dryden and Waller belonged, as did Samuel Pepys. Prominent among the scientists were Christopher Wren and Robert Hooke; the latter was appointed curator with the task of performing demonstration experiments at the meetings. In 1671 Isaac Newton was elected and four years later the Society played an active part in the foundation of Greenwich Observatory, where Flamsteed was appointed Astronomical Observer.

Edward Proger was born in 1621, the son of a Welsh courtier. He became a Page-of-Honour to King Charles I and, after a distinguished career in the Civil War, was made Groom-of-the-Bedchamber to the Prince of Wales. After the execution of Charles I in 1649 he followed the new King into exile

1   Edward Proger. Drawn by S Harding from a painting by Sir Peter Lely. Reproduced by permission of the Trustees of the British Museum.

and, continuing in his service until the Restoration, was awarded a lodge in the Park by Hampton Court as a reward for lifelong services. Within easy ride, or even walk, from the King's riverside palace it was within comfortable commuting distance for a valued servant or for a King wishing to escape temporarily from the affairs of State. It is probable that Proger's office entailed a certain involvement in the monarch's amorous adventures; it was even said that Proger's eldest daughter bore a close resemblance to the King, but all this is now mere speculation.

The design of the lodge in the Park can be attributed with a fair degree of certainty to William Samwell (1628–76) who, along with Hugh May and Roger Pratt, formed a coterie of gentleman architects at the Court[2]. The building cost £4000, a tremendous sum in those times, which was paid by Proger himself. In the ensuing years he devoted considerable effort, only partially successful, to recovering this money from the Treasury. It is probable that the building consisted simply of the present main block, with only two full floors above the basement, surmounted by a true attic floor with dormer windows. It was approached on the east side along an avenue of trees from the present-day Chestnut Avenue in Bushy Park across what is now the NPL sports field. There still exists in the grounds a Spanish chestnut tree said to have been planted by the King himself.

Occupation of the new lodge carried with it the office of Keeper of the Middle Park, which Proger held for the best part of half a century. On the death of Charles II in 1688 he relinquished his post at Court and retired to his house in the Park. Above Proger, holding the office of Keeper of all the Hampton Court parks, was General George Monck, Duke of Albemarle, the chief engineer of the Restoration. He was succeeded by the Duchess of Cleveland, one of the King's mistresses. In 1708, the Keepership (or Rangership) was purchased from her by Charles Montagu, Lord Halifax (later Earl of Halifax). He was granted the post conditional upon repairing a second lodge in the Hampton Court parks—that in Bushy Park (which name in those days was applied only to that part of the parks lying close to Hampton Hill). This, so-called Old Lodge (or Upper Lodge), became his home, while Proger continued to reside at the New Lodge (or Lower Lodge) a kilometre away in the Middle Park, until his death on 13 December 1713 at the age of 92.

Charles Montagu was born in 1661 and became MP for Maldon in 1689. He rose rapidly; as a Treasury Lord in 1692 he first raised the loan now called the National Debt; he established the Bank of England in 1694 and the following year appointed his friend Isaac Newton Master of the Royal Mint with the task of reorganising it.

Here the threads of our story come together again, for from 1695 to 1698 Charles Montagu was President of the Royal Society. In 1713 this office passed to Isaac Newton who held it until his death in 1727. These two men were very close as Catherine Barton, Newton's niece, is believed to have been married to Montagu in his later years. After Proger's death Charles Montagu attempted to bequeath the Rangership to the lady in his will, but as he only held it by Royal Patent it was not his to give. (In 1953 the authorities at Kew presented the Laboratory with a graft from Newton's apple tree. This was planted between Buildings 2 and 3 close to the wall of Bushy House garden and has since fruited).

Renovation work now began on Lower Lodge, but Charles Montagu himself died in 1715. The Rangership was granted to his nephew, George Montagu, who became Earl of Halifax of the 'second creation'. He continued and completed the repairs and extensions to Lower Lodge which his uncle had put in train, casing the existing structure in contemporary brickwork, converting the attic floor to a main third floor and later adding wing buildings to enhance the grandeur. It is probable that Catherine Barton continued to occupy Upper Lodge until her marriage in 1717 to John Conduitt, who succeeded Newton at the Mint.

By this time the distinction between Bushy Park and Middle Park was disappearing, since the fence between them was gone by 1700. The whole became known as Bushy Park, as it is today.

Lower Lodge remained in the Halifax family for three generations before passing in 1771 to Lord and Lady North. Lord North is unjustifiably saddled with responsibility for the loss of our American colonies (his solution to their problems arrived too late to save a situation already irretrievably lost by the generals in the field); Lady North was cunningly appointed to the Rangership by King George III when it was realised that

2   Bushy House in 1797. A reconstruction drawn by R D Treble.

her husband was constitutionally forbidden from holding an office of profit under the Crown while serving as Prime Minister. Extensive works were carried out on their behalf by the Office of Works in 1773–74. Lord North died in 1792 and Lady North in 1797.

On the death of Lady North the Rangership passed to the Duke of Clarence, third son of George III. Born in 1765, he seemed at this time sufficiently far down the line of succession to have no prospect of ever becoming king. After a brief naval career, he was created Duke of Clarence and then, at the age of 24, faced the usual aimless yet confined existence of lesser royalty. Within a short time he became infatuated with the famous comedy actress, Dorothy Jordan; the attaction was mutual and soon they were to all intents and purposes man and wife.

The Duke and Mrs Jordan set up house together in the Lower Lodge in Bushy Park, the Duke for many years playing the part of a country squire and farming the land around the House. Their liaison was accepted by the King and Queen and by the Duke's royal brothers, all of whom visited at some time or other. Ten children were born to the couple—all taking the name FitzClarence.

Their association finally broke up in 1811, for reasons which are unknown to this day. It is impossible to find a human explanation of the Duke's

3 'La Promenade en Famille'. The Duke of Clarence and Mrs Jordan setting out for Bushy House. Cartoon by James Gillray. Reproduced by permission of the Trustees of the British Museum.

conduct, for it would seem that he just cast off an old mistress because of her failing earning power and began to look around for a rich wife.

This was the period of the Regency. The Prince of Wales was ruling the country while George III, confined to Windsor, became increasingly mad as he grew older. In 1817 the Prince Regent's only child, Princess Charlotte, died in childbirth, leaving her uncles next in the line of succession. It became necessary for the Duke of Clarence to marry into royalty and the choice fell on Princess Adelaide of Saxe-Meiningen. They were married in July 1818 and settled down to a life of domesticity at Bushy House; two daughters died in early childhood, but Princess Adelaide mothered the FitzClarence children, and at the same time competently managed the Duke's financial affairs. Additions to the building during this period included the two large rooms on the east face and a servants' wing on the north side, all destined to have a future laboratory function.

King George III died in 1820 and the Prince Regent became King George IV. Then in 1827 the death of the Duke of York left the Duke of Clarence as direct heir to the throne. At 6.00 am on 6 June 1830, the Duke was called from his bed to meet messengers from London in the Main Hall of

4   The Duke of Clarence (later William IV), by Sir Thomas Lawrence.

Bushy House; his brother was dead and at the age of 65 he had come at last to the throne (as William IV). (The Duke is said to have closed the interview by telling his visitors that he must return to bed as he had always wanted to sleep with a queen.) The new King and Queen left immediately for Windsor, but retained the use of Bushy House by the appointment of Queen Adelaide to the Rangership. The seven years of his reign were stormy, great issues rending the nation one after the other. King William was not particularly clever, nor was he devious. In spite of periods of unpopularity the monarchy grew in stature, setting a firm basis for its great stability and popularity during the next reign.

In the same year that King William IV ascended the throne, his younger brother, the Duke of Sussex, became President of the Royal Society, an office he held for the next eight years. At this time there were so many non-scientists among the members that he was able to secure election in preference to Sir John Herschel, the noted astronomer. In many respects the Society was little more than an ordinary club—a state of affairs which disturbed its more scientific members. A number of contemporary papers drew attention to this problem[3]. As a result a movement was launched which resulted in the foundation of the British Association for the Advancement of Science in 1831.

The prime mover of this new Association (which was based on the Deutscher Naturforscher Versammlung) was Sir David Brewster. He said of it:

> The Royal Society still embodies in its list every name which stands high in British science; it still communicates to the world the most important of our discoveries, it still crowns with the most coveted honours the ambition of successful talent and, when the public service requires the aid of philosophy, it still renders to the nation the ablest assistance and the soundest counsel. Nevertheless, it must be admitted, that the Royal Society no longer performs the part of promoting natural knowledge by any such exertions as those we now propose to revive. As a body, it scarcely labours itself, and does not attempt to guide the labours of others.

He went on to point out that as specialised bodies take over the promotion of small sections of science they tend to separate from the main body, which thus progressively loses its integration. The British Association aimed to maintain that integration.

It is interesting to note here that the word 'scientist' was coined by William Whewell as late as 1840. Previously he had been described as a 'man of science' or a 'cultivator of science'.

When King William IV died in 1837 and was succeeded by the young Queen Victoria, the Dowager Queen Adelaide retained the Rangership of Bushy Park and used Bushy House as one of her official residences. Certain

developments and refitments, such as the Orangery, date from this time.
There is an excellent engraving of her at this period standing in front of iron
stairs and the vehranda, easily recognisable as part of the present-day scene.
Locally she was highly popular—a substantial contributor to charities. The
House and its gardens were beautifully sited and maintained.

5   Queen Adelaide at Bushy House. The iron staircase and the veranda can still be
seen at Bushy House. Reproduced by permission of the Trustees of the British
Museum.

In 1841 the Government decided that it could no longer support the
Observatory and Museum at Kew and the contents were dispersed to other

museums. The first telescope had been set up there in 1725 when Kew House belonged to Samuel Molyneux FRS. Later Frederick, Prince of Wales, son of George II, leased the house and the Princess of Wales, mother of George III, resided there; the observatory became disused. King George III, finding that the transit of Venus in 1796 could not be observed there, caused an Observatory to be erected in the Old Deer Park. Thereafter the King often visited, taking a close interest in the instruments and collections; his sons in their turn did likewise.

In 1841 the Royal Society applied for the building; it was accordingly made over to them, but soon relinquished. An application was then made in the name of the British Association as a site for the verification and trial of old and new patterns of magnetic and meteorological instruments, and the buildings were assigned to them in 1842. Until 1872, when the Royal Society once again took charge, the BA spent £12 000 there. In the period 1854–69, 11 000 thermometers, 2000 barometers and 2500 hydrometers were verified and a number of standard thermometers constructed (the basic standard was supplied by M. Regnault, the noted French physicist).

6 The Kew Observatory today.

After the death of the Dowager Queen in 1849 Bushy House became a gift of Queen Victoria. It remained empty, in the care of a housekeeper and some servants and gardeners, until 1865 when it was loaned to the Duc de Nemours, second son of the exiled King of France. The King and his family had occupied a number of houses in the Thames Valley since leaving their country in 1848. After 1871 the Duc was allowed to return to France and did so at intervals while retaining a considerable ménage at Bushy House in case of need. During this period the House was maintained substantially weather-proof, while the gardens were not allowed to become a wilderness.

Meanwhile the Park outside gradually developed as a place of public recreation. On the death of the Duc in 1896 the House passed to his son, the Duc d'Alençon, who returned it to the Crown the following year. Once again it became the gift of Queen Victoria and all was poised for a startling change in the use of this already historic house.

Nineteenth Century Science: 1868–1900

The first moves towards national support for scientific research in Britain came from Lieutenant Colonel Alexander Strange FRS (1818–76), who retired in 1861 after serving in the Indian Army on the Indian Trigonometrical Survey. In a paper read to the BA in 1868 entitled '*On the necessity for State Intervention to secure the progress of Physical Science*' he stated:

> There should be established a system of national institutions for the sole purpose of advancing science by practical research, quite apart from teaching it; that such institutions, provided with extensive appliances and skilled operators, should be presided over by a governing body constituted with reference solely to the scientific eminence of its members, or, which would be better, by a single chief, directly responsible to a Minister of State.

This was a most unusual attitude for the time and stamps Strange as 'a natural scientist with revolutionary ideas about the role of science in society and the correlative duties of society towards science'[4].

Arising from this suggestion a committee[5] was appointed by the BA to consider the questions:

(*a*) Does there exist in the UK sufficient provision for the vigorous prosecution of physical research?

(*b*) If not, what further provision is needed? and what measures should be taken to secure it?

After interviewing many UK scientists the committee finally recommended that a Royal Commission be set up.

A new scientific journal, *Nature*, which first appeared in 1869 under the editorship of N Lockyer, took up the cudgels on behalf of State sponsorship of science and continued to work for it during the remainder of the century.

7   Colonel Alexander Strange. Reproduced by permission of the
National Portrait Gallery.

In April 1870, Strange read a paper on the '*Relation of the State to Science*' at the Society of Arts, drawing attention to the lack of system and method in the allocation of funds to scientific projects of national importance. A year later he produced more detailed suggestions in a paper at the Royal Service Institution—'*On the Necessity for a Permanent Commission in State Scientific Questions*'. A national approach was called for, he said, to the application of science to defence, telegraphy, meteorology, astronomy, ventilation, sewerage, public hygiene and surveys. A Science Council and a Minister for Science should be appointed.

Later in 1871, when the BA met in Edinburgh, Strange again returned to the charge with a further paper '*Government Action on Scientific Questions*'. In this year Sir William Thomson was President and in his general address he lent his weight to the arguments:

The success of the Kew Magnetic and Meteorological Observatory affords an example of the great gain to be earned for science by the foundation of physical observatories and laboratories for experimental research, to be conducted by qualified persons, whose duties should be, not teaching, but experimenting. Whether we look to the honour of England, as a nation which ought always to be foremost in promoting physical science, or to those vast economical advantages which must accrue from such establishments, we cannot but feel that experimental research ought to be made with us an object of national concern, and not left, as hitherto, exclusively to the private enterprise of self-sacrificing amateurs, and the necessarily inconsecutive action of our present Government Departments and of casual committees.

A Royal Commission, the Devonshire Commission[6], began its work in 1872. The final outcome[7] advocated State laboratories, increased research grants for private scientists, and recommended that a Ministry of Science and Education be formed with a Council of Science to assist.

Cardwell[4] summarises the influence of Alexander Strange on all these events as follows:

> He saw very clearly, what relatively very few saw at that time, the possibilities of, and the necessity for, a developed system of applied science . . . . He bent all his energies to realising his objectives and it is a testimony to his judgement that practically everything he called for has, today, been realised. It is astonishing what he achieved in so few years and it is a sad commentary on the state of science in England at that time that it was an Indian Army officer and not an academic, a civil servant or an industrialist who saw so clearly what the defects were and what the remedies should be.

Unfortunately the bright hopes of the early 1870s were not realised. A long period of apathy ensued and it was not until 1891 that the subject of State science was raised once again at the BA.

In the meantime the Association did actively undertake the organisation of some parts of electrical science. In 1861 at the suggestion of Sir William Thomson a committee was appointed[8] to consider the subject of standards of electrical resistance. At the time there was no coherent system of units or standards and several alternatives were considered. Finally the system proposed by Weber, which expressed all units in terms of the fundamental mechanical units—length, mass and time (CGS system) was adopted. This committee derived all units in these terms and published the results in a paper by Clerk Maxwell and Fleeming Jenkin in their Second Report at the Newcastle-on-Tyne meeting in 1863.

The committee also undertook to convert the definitions into working standards. Resistance and current were taken as fundamental units and Clerk Maxwell, Fleeming Jenkin and Balfour Stewart took on the work of realising the ohm, which they described in their report for 1863. The work continued until the Committee was dissolved in 1870.

Elsewhere in the world the question of international agreement on units and measurement of physical quantities was receiving earnest consideration. Some of the earliest moves came from the French, who had adopted a metric system as early as 1793. International meetings took place in Paris in August 1870 and again in September 1872 (when Great Britain was represented by Sir George Airy—Astronomer Royal, H W Chisholm—Warden of the Standards and W H Miller FRS—Professor of Mineralogy at Cambridge).

A number of committees began work on detailed policies for the construction of international prototypes of the metre and the kilogram and for the establishment of an international bureau of weights and measures. A Diplomatic Conference was called in Paris in 1875 to consider the recommendations and the so-called Convention du Metre was signed there on 20 May 1875 by the representatives of 17 nations. Great Britain for political reasons did not sign until nine years later.

This established the Bureau International de Poids et Mesures (BIPM) at Sèvres, maintained by the signatory states:

> The task of the Bureau is to ensure worldwide unification of physical measurements by establishing the fundamental standards and scales of measurement of the principal physical quantities, and maintaining the international prototypes. The Bureau is also responsible for making comparisons of national and international standards and carrying out or co-ordinating determinations relating to the fundamental physical constants[9].

This function has continued to this day.

Meanwhile other policy-moulding events were taking place further afield. Immediately after the Franco–Prussian War a great expansion of industry took place in Germany with the full backing of scientists of the calibre of Helmholtz and Siemens. As a result a national laboratory, the Physikalische–Technische Reichanstalt, was established during the period 1883–87 at Charlottenburg, a suburb of Berlin. Helmholtz became the first Director.

Doubts as to the validity of the BA Ohm derived from the earlier studies led to the reconstitution of the BA Committee in 1881 and the work continued, Lord Rayleigh[10] taking a leading part. They organised the systematic testing of resistance coils, the work being carried out in the Cavendish Laboraory at Cambridge by R T Glazebrook, a young protégé of Rayleigh's.

The idea of a national laboratory was next aired in 1885 when J A Fleming read a paper '*On the necessity for a national standardising laboratory for electrical instruments*' to the Society of Telegraph Engineers and Electricians[11]. He urged the setting up:

> . . . in the neighbourhood of London of premises fitted with the usual arrangements of a physical laboratory . . . in telegraphic communication with the observatories of Greenwich and Kew.

Staffed with 'experimentalists and mathematicians', equipped with a range of standard measuring apparatus, he envisaged the laboratory as taking over the provision, maintenance and dissemination of standards and their determination in absolute terms, the testing of materials and the general supervision of fair trading in the electrical field. On the thorny question of finance his observations are still relevant today:

> . . . any broad ill-defined scheme of endowment of research is an unpractical thing . . . there is too much danger that endowment of research in this fashion would simply degenerate into research after an endowment.

The money, he thought, should be derived from the fees accruing to the State from many thousands of electrical patents each year. Action should be taken by the Society of Telegraph Engineers and Electricians in conjunction with the British Association.

The ensuing discussion involved many famous names. G M Whipple of Kew Observatory advocated the setting up of such a laboratory at Kew. R E Compton on behalf of industry said:

> the need for such a standardising establishment is so great that, if the Government does not move in the matter, we, as English manufacturers, must of necessity combine and do the work ourselves.

This was brave talk. Standards work was already in train under the aegis of the BA Committee, but nothing further happened until 1890 when a Board of Trade Committee on standards of measurement for the electrical industry was set up[12]. The standards recommended by the BA Committee became the legal standards for the Empire and a Board of Trade Laboratory was established for the verification of instruments.

The 1891 meeting of the BA was held at Cardiff and in his Presidential address Sir Oliver Lodge drew attention to the work of the PTR in Germany. He wished, he said:

> to call attention to the fact that the further progress of physical science in the somewhat haphazard and amateur fashion in which it has hitherto been pursued in this country is becoming increasingly difficult and that the quantitative portion especially should be undertaken in a permanent and publicly supported physical laboratory on a large scale.

He referred to the work being done at Kew and in the new Board of Trade laboratory, and continued:

> But what I want to see is a much larger establishment erected in the most suitable site, limited by no speciality of aim nor by the demands of the commercial world, furnished with all appropriate appliances, to be amended and added to as time goes on and experience grows, invested with all the dignity and permanence of a national institution, a physical laboratory in fact comparable with Greenwich Observatory and aiming at the very highest quantitative work in all departments of physical science.

He emphasised that the need was for a laboratory to carry out routine work of high accuracy, the maintenance of standards and long period experiments. He did not visualise a programme of research and thus, we presume, not one of improvement and refinement of standards and methods. Another committee was set up, but this one never met.

It can be seen that the conflicting needs of pure physical science and its application in industry were already in need of some accommodation if both were to be served in one national laboratory.

8   Sir Douglas Galton.

In 1895 Sir Douglas Galton[13] was President of the BA and when addressing the annual meeting that year at Ipswich, he said:

> There could scarcely be a more advantageous addition to the assistance which Government gives to science than for it to allot a substantial annual sum to the extension of Kew Observatory in order to develop it on the model of the Reichsanstalt. It might advantageously retain its connection with the Royal Society under a Committee of Management representative of the various branches of science concerned and of all parts of Great Britain.

In a further paper he suggested reviving the 1891 committee to report on:

(*a*) the functions which an establishment of this nature should fulfil,
(*b*) the system which should be adopted for its control and management.

This Committee[14] was therefore appointed to consider:

> . . . the establishment of a National Physical Laboratory for the more accurate determination of physical constants and for other quantitative research, and to confer with the Council.

It will be noted that there is no mention at this stage of standardisation and testing or of the needs of industry.

The Committee reported to the 1896 meeting of the BA in Liverpool in favour of the establishment of such a laboratory, recommending that the definition of functions and management should be placed in the hands of the Royal Society and immediate executive and initiative power should rest in a Director. 'We recommend', they went on,

> that an annual grant, in addition to the sum already expended at Kew Observatory, of £5000 per annum, and an additional expenditure of £30 000 for building and equipment, would do all that is essential to carry out the scheme in a wise and worthy manner.

In February 1897 a deputation from this BA Committee waited on the Prime Minister, Lord Salisbury. He received them sympathetically and subsequently a Government Committee[15] was appointed to consider whether standardisation and other work already undertaken partly or wholly at the public cost could fitly be associated with a new institution.

The terms of reference of this new Treasury Committee were:

> To consider and report upon the desirability of establishing a National Physical Laboratory for the testing and verification of instruments for physical investigation, for the construction and preservation of standards of measurement and for the systematic determination of physical constants and numerical data useful for scientific and industrial purposes—and to report whether the work of such an institute, if established, could be associated with any testing or standardising work already performed whether wholly or partly at public cost.

It is noteworthy that standardisation and testing now occupy a prominent place in the brief.

The Treasury Committee reported[16] on 6 July 1898; their conclusions were:

(*a*) That a public institution should be founded for standardising and verifying instruments, for testing materials, and for the determination of physical constants.

(*b*) That the institution should be established by extending the Kew Observatory in the Old Deer Park, Richmond, and that the scheme should include the improvement of the existing buildings, and the erection of new buildings at some distance from the present Observatory.

(*c*) That the Royal Society should be invited to control the proposed institution, and to nominate a Governing Body, on which commercial interests should be represented, the choice of the members of such Body not being confined to Fellows of the Society.

(*d*) That the Permanent Secretary of the Board of Trade should be an ex-officio member of the Governing Body; and that such Body should be consulted by the Standards Office and the Electrical Standardising Department of the Board of Trade upon difficult questions that may arise from time to time or as to proposed modifications or developments.

The enquiry was protracted and detailed occupying 11 whole days in the winter of 1897–98; 30 expert witnesses contributed their views and visits were made to the Reichsanstalt and Versuchsanstalt in Berlin and the Magnetische Institut at Potsdam.

The Board of Trade Standards Department and Electrical Standardising Laboratories were painstakingly investigated. These were considered capable of carrying out their statutory duties, but were unable to undertake the necessary continued refinement of methods and improvement of standards, nor were they in a position to assess the accuracy to which their standards represented the absolute values. There was no legal obligation to establish new and improved data and that which was used was often derived from the BIPM in France. There was no opportunity to work towards the legalising of new standards, when these were called for, while the only electrical measuring instruments[17] tested were those for which there was a legal requirement.

The witnesses included Sir Douglas Galton, who continued to press his views; in particular he stressed the importance of research back-up for a standardising laboratory. R T Glazebrook (Secretary of the Electrical Standards Committee of the BA) described his work at the Cavendish Laboratory on standards of resistance, capacitance and voltage; there he charged for calibrations, issued certificates and carried out intercomparisons with other standards laboratories. The proposed new laboratory would operate similarly. H J Chaney and Major P Cardew (respectively Superintendent of Weights and Measures and Head of the Electrical Department at the Board of Trade) told how their standardising function had necessarily to depend on physical constants and numerical data derived from the best research available, often therefore from sources abroad. They welcomed the prospect of a national laboratory to provide this vital information. Representatives of major industries, nominated by the leading scientific and engineering institutions, testified to the importance of the proposed laboratory for the solution of a wide range of general manufacturing problems; an almost overwhelming selection was put forward, including the behaviour of metals under alternating stresses, the strength and durability of metals as influenced by alloying and the pressure of wind on surfaces of different areas and shapes. As Carey Foster said, 'we can take it for granted that the advancement of science means in the long run the advancement of industry.'

In view of the great controversy which was to break out some ten years later, it is interesting to quote the Report on the subject of the testing of materials:

> It would be neither necessary nor desirable to compete with or interfere with the testing of materials of various kinds as now carried on in private or other laboratories, but there are many special and important tests and investigations into the strength and behaviour of materials which might be conducted with great advantage at a laboratory such as is contemplated.

On 7 October 1898 the Report was sent to the Royal Society by the Secretary to the Treasury, saying that the Government supported the four conclusions and asking if the Society would be prepared to undertake a controlling role. On finance:

> . . . Her Majesty's Government would be prepared to ask Parliament to vote an annual sum of £4000 for five years certain as a grant in aid of the expenses of the proposed institution. As regards buildings the existing Kew Observatory would remain available for its present or for similar uses, and, in addition, Parliament would be asked to make a grant not exceeding £12 000[18] in all towards the erection of suitable buildings.

Correspondence followed between the Treasury and the Royal Society; a mutually agreed draft scheme was drawn up and in March, 1899, this received the approval of the Government.

'Thus', wrote Glazebrook later,[19] 'the Laboratory was started.'

The National Physical Laboratory Founded: 1900–1902

The National Physical Laboratory, thus created, was to be controlled by a Governing Body consisting of a General Board (comprising President, Treasurer and Secretaries of the Royal Society, a Vice-Chairman (who was also Chairman of the Executive Committee), the Permanent Secretary of the Board of Trade and 36 ordinary members—24 from the Royal Society and two from each of six technical institutions) and an Executive Committee (comprising President, Treasurer and one Secretary of the Royal Society, the Chairman of the Executive Committee, the Permanent Secretary of the Board of Trade and 12 ordinary members).

The first Executive Committee[20] was appointed by the Council of the Royal Society at a meeting on 4 May 1899. It met for the first time on 16 May 1899 when the scheme of organisation agreed between the Treasury and the Royal Society was laid on the table. Soon afterwards the Directorship was offered to R T Glazebrook and he was appointed from 1 January 1900 (see Appendix 1).

9   Richard Tetley Glazebrook, first Director of the NPL.

In the ensuing months sub-committees were put to work to consider suitable programmes:

> . . . drawing up a series of suggestions as to work which might be most usefully carried out in connection with the following branches of science or industry, viz., mechanics and engineering, electricity, optics, chemistry, meteorology, terrestrial magnetism, thermometry. Meteorology and terrestrial magnetism constituted the Kew branch of the work, and at a rather later date Dr Chree, Superintendent of the Kew Observatory, became Superintendent of the Observatory Department of the NPL. The other subjects later formed the nucleus of the Departments in which the work was ultimately organised.

The Treasury Committee Report contemplated the establishment of the Laboratory at Kew, but alternative sites at Eltham, Oxshott and Hainault Forest were also considered; finally an area of about 15 acres in the north-east corner of the Old Deer Park at Richmond was accepted. Soon afterwards a site in Bushy Park, Teddington, was briefly considered, but the original plan was adhered to and planning went forward. Designs were prepared for suitable buildings, while the Pagoda in Kew Gardens was offered for the housing of a tall mercury column for use as a pressure standard. The first design showed:

> . . . buildings of an ordinary Laboratory type with several storeys. Colonel Compton strongly pressed the advantages for workshop and engineering purposes of a single storey building, top-lighted with a saw-tooth roof. As against this, for physical experiments, a constant temperature is in many cases essential, and in such a single storey building this is difficult of attainment. Eventually the difficulty was solved by the proposal to erect a top-lighted building 80 ft × 50 ft in area for the engineering work and a three storey building 80 ft × 42 ft with a basement containing constant temperature rooms for Physics[21].

However, the Kew plans soon came up against a substantial snag. Some environment-conscious objectors in Richmond opposed the Old Deer Park scheme so forcefully that the authorities had to think again. Richmond Town Council resolved, 'The proposal to erect a large physical laboratory and engineering shop in the Old Deer Park is highly objectionable.' We owe them a debt of gratitude since the NPL would sooner or later have outgrown the Kew area, enforcing a further move or a fragmentation destructive of its essential unity. Once more Bushy House came under consideration, now as the most favoured site.

Since the departure of the Duc d'Alençon in 1897 the House had remained empty. Though the office of Ranger seems by now to have lapsed, it was still a gift of the Queen, though actually an embarrassment for which there was no obvious use. One of her advisers expressed the opinion:

> Its proper destiny is occupation by some South African magnate who desires to breathe the atmosphere of Wolsey and the Bourbons.

In fact its 'destiny' was a great deal more lofty. In London there were properties (nos 77 and 78, Pall Mall) held by the Commissioners of Woods and Forests and at present leased to Lord de Vesci which, close to Buckingham Palace, would make ideal grace and favour establishments. An exchange between the Crown and the Commissioners was therefore proposed. The negotiations were protracted, since among other things the Crown insisted on approving the use to which the House would be put in view of its proximity to the public park. In the meantime studies of its suitability for the task in hand were undertaken. E G Rivers of the Ministry of Works wrote on 29 August 1900 to Glazebrook:

It is very substantial and the ground floor has great rigidity—in fact you can obtain firm bases for instruments from the brick groining at any point. Of course there is more room than you will require, but on the whole I think that the Royal Society will be wise in accepting the offer—there are advantages beside the disadvantages.

In the ensuing months plans and costings were prepared for alterations to the House and for the construction of an engineering building[22] and a power house. The cost was estimated to amount to £14 000 instead of the £13 000 estimated for the Kew site.

In the latter half of the year (1900) things moved slowly, but inexorably, towards their final form. Early in October the Treasury in an informal note on behalf of the Queen expressed willingness to assign the House; the Executive Committee placed all the details in front of the Royal Society:

> . . . a reasonably satisfactory National Physical Laboratory can be provided on the Bushy site, and they do not recommend the Royal Society further to oppose the arrangement which the Treasury, with the approval of Her Majesty, have adopted.
>
> They cannot, however, conceal from themselves that it will be very difficult for them to maintain and administer a National Physical Laboratory on the Bushy site for the amount annually allowed by the Treasury, and they fear that it may be necessary for them to press in the near future for an addition to that allowance.

At the beginning of November a formal offer from the Treasury was placed before the Executive Committee. At the same meeting the Director was informed that he should reside in the upper floors of Bushy House, paying rent for the rooms so occupied (a practice followed by all subsequent Directors). The Office of Works was given charge of the site.

A formal offer on behalf of the Queen was forwarded from Windsor on 24 November 1900:

> My dear Akers-Douglas,
> I am desired by the Queen to inform you that Her Majesty by her Grace and Favour agrees to hand over to the Commissioners of Works the House and Grounds at Bushey [sic] as defined upon the map, a copy of which will be placed on record in your office—the House and Grounds to be used by the Royal Society for the purpose of a Physical Laboratory.
> In consideration of Her Majesty's act of Grace and Favour it is further agreed that the Government will place the De Vesci House in Pall Mall, rent free and in order for occupation, at the disposal of Her Majesty, to be appropriated as a Grace and Favour residence under the usual conditions as Her Majesty may think fit.
>
> Yours very truly,
> Arthur Bigge.

All the agreed conditions were set down in formal letters to the Royal Society from Lord Esher of the Office of Works dated 22 December 1900

Nov. 24th 1900

My dear Akers-Douglas.

I am desired by The Queen to inform you that Her Majesty by Her Grace and Favour agrees to hand over to the Commissioners of Works the House and Grounds at Bushey —

as defined upon the map, a copy of which will be placed on record in your Office. — the House and Grounds to be used by the Royal Society for the purposes of a Physical Laboratory.

In consideration of Her Majesty's act of Grace and Favour

it is further agreed that the Government will place De Vesci House, in Pall Mall, rent free and in order for occupation, at the disposal of Her Majesty, to be appropriated as a Grace and Favour residence under the usual condition as

Her Majesty may think fit ——

Yours very truly
Arthur Bigge

P.S.
I conclude that your Office will inform the Lord Chamberlain, with other arrangement &c

10   The letter giving Queen Victoria's permission for the use of Bushy House by NPL.

and 22 January 1901 and these provided the basis for final acceptance by the Society on 18 February 1901. As Glazebrook remarked: 'In spite of its somewhat aristocratic history it will make an admirable laboratory building.'

Teddington at this time was a small riverside town with a population of some 14 000. Round about there were waterworks, market gardens and houses and estates occupied by lesser gentry, of which Bushy House was among the largest. Nearby were the Palace of Hampton Court, the wide sweeps of Bushy and Home Parks and an attractive large loop of the River Thames dominated by its last and largest lock.

The railway from London had been opened to Kingston via Teddington in the early 1860s, with a branch soon afterwards extending from Strawberry Hill to, Shepperton, while by 1871 Kingston had been linked with New Malden on the LSWR main line.

11   Queens Road, Teddington in the early 1900s. The present Main Gate of NPL is on the left at the bend in the road. The building on the corner, Elm Lodge, is still standing.

Trippers arrived by the railway to see and enjoy the amenities of the river and to partake of the splendours of the royal Bushy Park. They came to see the Chestnut Avenue at blossom-time, to ride, to shoot (forbidden after 1892), to cycle (a great centre for bicycle rallies), to picnic and to play various sports.

Soon the electric tram was on its way, the NPL Annual Report in 1902 remarking that 'tram lines are already laid in Teddington and the cars will be running shortly'. They came on 2 April 1903, when Stanley Road Junction (already reached by an extension from Twickenham) was linked to Hampton Court by way of Teddington and Hampton Wick. Two days later a 'loop' was completed from Hampton Court by way of Hampton and

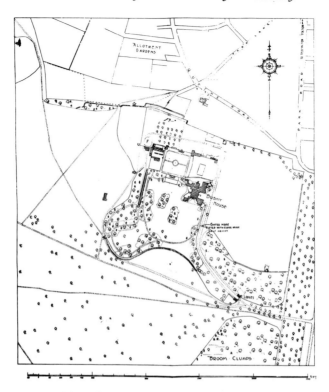

12   Plan of the site when the NPL took it over.

Hampton Hill back to Stanley Road Junction. London United Tramways invested considerable sums in road widening and improvement; as the *Daily Telegraph* (1 April 1903) said of its efforts:

> There are those that think that the very sleepiness of Teddington and Hampton Wick is part of their charm. So it is, but nobody cares to eternalise narrow and nearly impassable lanes, and in broadening and straightening the roadway the company has done a permanent service. . . . To be gifted by Nature and not allowed to enjoy Nature's gifts is a crabbed contradiction from which the electric fairy is going, in part at least, to save us.

The new lines and the road improvements not only greatly increased the numbers of visitors, but also served to open up the town to industry and commerce. The NPL in particular could now draw its staff from a wider area and communicate so much more easily with its surroundings. There had been some bus services—notably a horse omnibus which carried visitors from Teddington Station through Bushy Park to Hampton Court, but never the sort of regular service offered by the new tramways.

The big new double lock, opened on the Thames at Teddington in June 1904, made the local reaches of the river an even greater attraction for visitors. The entertainment could at times be spectacular, for instance, during an exceptionally high tide in March 1906 a tug was carried through the lock without the gates being opened.

The 6 inch Ordnance Map of 1899 (and the official plan accompanying Lord Esher's correspondence) show the Estate lying entirely within the Park wall, which ran through the heart of the present NPL site to the right-angled corner of the Park behind the present ship tanks. Portions of this wall remain between the Admiralty laboratory site and NPL sports field and west of Bushy Road on the NPL site. Beyond the boundary of the original Estate it still separates the Park from the present NPL site on the west side. The Estate was bounded on the east by Glazebrook road. The Cannon Gate giving onto the Park was then the main entrance and there was no considerable outlet towards Teddington. Further west the Estate and the Park were separated by a ha-ha on the edge of the House lawns, so that the main rooms on this side commanded an extensive unbroken view. Beyond that the boundary was much as it is today. On the Teddington side of the Park wall were allotments and the gardens of North Lodge, Elm Lodge,

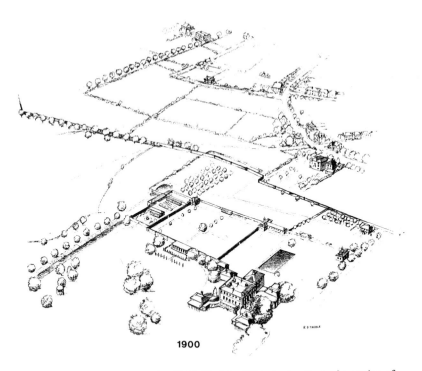

1900

13　The NPL site 1900, by R D Treble. This is the first of a series of drawings throughout the book, showing the NPL site at various stages of development.

14   Interior of the engineering building workshop.

Victoria House and so on. A path from the site of the present main gate led from Queens Road direct to the Park via a gate in the wall, which can still be seen behind No 2 Tank.

West and south of the House were parkland areas with lawns and trees, much as today. The house itself was surrounded by formal gardens. Of particular note are a round pond near the west boundary, a rectangular pond on the site of the present Building 5 and two identical clockhouses, which probably formed parts of stables, symmetrically placed relative to the back of the House. One of these has recently (1976) been restored, the other was built into (and can still be detected below) the present Building 10. The more easterly of these clockhouses was used as a residence until 1913, while Queen's Cottage nearby continued in domestic use until the 1930s.

The modification of the House and the construction of the new buildings were now authorised. Tenders invited for the engineering building produced quotations between £2830 and £3777. The second lowest—by Campbell, Smith and Co Ltd—was accepted in March. The turbogenerator, purchased from Messrs Parsons and Co. and installed in the power house, was many years later transferred to the Science Museum in South Kensington.

Certain areas of standards work—thermometers, barometers, watches, chronometers, sextants etc—had been handled for many years previously at

15   The Parsons' turbo-generator (left) installed in the power house.

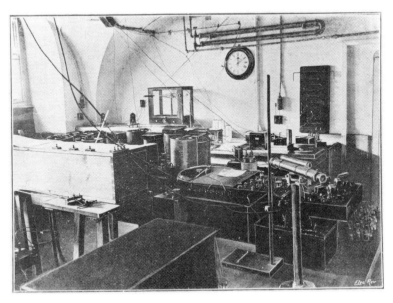

16   The electrical standards room in Bushy House, showing the arrangement for testing standard resistances.

4 *The National Physical Laboratory.*

The basement and ground floor of Bushy House have been transformed into a Physical Laboratory, while the upper floors form offices and a residence for the Director, in whose salary a corresponding reduction has been made. The basement is covered with a brick groining on which the main building rests, but the more important Laboratories are in four large wings, one at each corner, and these have no basement below : thus steady supports are everywhere possible.

One wing, containing the original dining-room and library, has been fitted as an electrical and magnetic laboratory. All iron has been, as far as possible, removed from the structure, and, with a view of preventing a stray magnetic field from any currents which may be used, concentric wiring has been employed for all large currents, while the wires for smaller currents have been twisted.

In this room will be placed the Lorenz apparatus which the Drapers' Company have recently with great generosity given to the Laboratory in memory of the distinguished services to science and to education of the late Principal J. V. Jones, F.R.S., of Cardiff.

Along with this there will be other apparatus for the absolute measurement of current and of electromotive force.

Another wing has been fitted for thermometric work. A special study will be made of high temperature thermometers, and the Laboratory owes to the generosity of Sir A. Noble the means for installing a number of electric ovens for testing thermopiles and other instruments for the measurement of temperature up to 1000° or 1200° Centigrade.

In a third wing a metallurgical laboratory has been fitted in which to continue the work begun at the Mint by Sir William Roberts Austen and the Alloys Research Committee. For this purpose apparatus for cutting and polishing sections, and further photo-micrographical examination, has been obtained. The Committee have to thank Mr. Stead for his assistance in arranging this.

The fourth wing is fitted as a chemical laboratory.

In the basement are a number of constant temperature rooms.

Sir Andrew Noble's fund, referred to in the last report, has provided a measuring machine, a dividing engine, and a comparator which will be placed in some of the basement rooms. In an adjoining room the resistance measurements of the B. A. Committee will be continued, while in another apparatus for the production of liquid air is being set up.

The testing of pressure gauges will form an important branch of the work, and for this a mercury column some 50 feet in height has been erected in one corner of the house.

Gas and water have been laid on freely throughout the building—also electricity. A 100-volt circuit is connected to the main dynamo and battery in the power-house, and supplies light. Numerous plug points enable a supply to be taken off for lights for experimental purposes or for small motors. For experimental work a special battery of fifty-five cells has been installed. This is divided into groups of five. Wires run from the switchboard to the various rooms in such a way that one or more of these groups can be switched on to any circuit. Thus voltages between 10 and 110 volts can be obtained as required.

The house is heated on the Webster low-pressure system by steam from a Lancashire boiler in the boiler house at a distance of about 100 yards.

17 Description from the NPL Annual Report (1901) of the arrangements in Bushy House.

Kew Observatory[23]. This work now fell under the aegis of the new NPL, but the team remained at Kew as 'the Observatory Department of NPL' under the superintendency of Dr C Chree FRS. They did not move to Teddington for another decade. Dr J A Harker, already working on thermometric standards at Kew, was appointed to the Teddington staff. Glazebrook's electrical standards work was transferred from the Cavendish Laboratory on loan from the Electrical Standards Committee of the BA.

The NPL Annual Report (1901) records the first division of Bushy House for scientific purposes (figure 17). Initially it would seem that work was confined to the wings and the basement. The other ground floor rooms were progressively taken over as the Laboratory expanded. Glazebrook's own office and associated clerical functions were accommodated on the first floor, approached by the minor stairway on the left of the main hall.

Glazebrook at this time was engaged in active propaganda at every opportunity. In *Nature*[24] he wrote:

> The first aim of the Laboratory is to assist in promoting a union which is certainly necessary if England is to retain her supremacy in trade and in manufacture, to make the forces of science available for the nation, to break down by every possible means the barrier between theory and practice, and to point out plainly the plan which must be followed unless we are prepared to see our rivals take our place.

After he had expounded his aims at the Royal Institution in May, the *Electrician* commented that the idea was experimental and Glazebrook could not expect more funding until the Laboratory proved its worth:

> The favourite amusement of the scientific professor, of chasing indeterminate equations through remote labyrinths of physical uncertainties, is not a sport which the Director and staff of NPL can indulge in with impunity.

During 1901 the staff shown in table 1 (*see over*) were appointed for Bushy House. The remunerations were modest, and of them Glazebrook was later to remark:

> The salaries were small; the *Electrician* pointed out that the remuneration is not extravagant, no doubt the duties will be equally light. The staff did not so regard their duties; they had opportunities for research and the advancement of natural knowledge, and devoted themselves heartily to the development of the Laboratory. It will be noted that of the scientific staff of eight, four became Fellows of the Royal Society, while three have been honoured by the King.

Moseley[25] has pointed out that the high calibre staff were prepared to come and work for low salaries because of a general lack of job opportunities for physicists, now being turned out in ever increasing numbers. The demand for scientists by industry did not pick up until after World War I.

Table 1   The first staff and salaries at the NPL.

Superintendent (Eng. Dept)	£400 p.a.	Dr T E Stanton	October 1901
Assistants (Phys. Dept)	£250 p.a.	Dr J A Harker	March 1901 (temporary since January 1900)
	£200 p.a.	A Campbell	October 1901
	£200 p.a.	Dr H C H Carpenter	October 1901
Junior (Phys. Dept)	£100 p.a.	B F E Keeling	October 1901
Assistants	£100 p.a.	F E Smith	June 1901
(Eng. Dept)	£100 p.a.	C Jakeman	October 1901
	£100 p.a.	S W Melsom	January 1902

Four mechanics and engineers
Clerk and accountant   G E Bailey

The Observatory Department at Kew comprised Dr C Chree (Superintendent);
T W Baker (Chief Assistant); E G Constable, W Hugo, J Foster, T Gunter and
W J Boxall (Senior Assistants); E Boxall and G Badderley (Junior Assistants) and
eight other assistants.

Around this time enquiries were made on behalf of the Institution of
Naval Architects as to the possibility of erecting a ship testing tank at the
Laboratory. Nothing came of this immediately but (as we shall see in due
course) this project did at last go ahead within the next decade.

By October 1901 the Glazebrooks were in residence on the upper floors of
Bushy House. During the winter of 1901–02 the alterations at Bushy House
were completed at a final cost of £19 000 (in place of the original estimate of
£14 000) and all was now ready for an official opening.

The opening ceremony was performed on 19 March 1902 by the Prince
and Princess of Wales (later King George V and Queen Mary). It took place
in the large bay of the engineering building, where there is a commemorative
plaque to this day. HRH, carrying out his first duty as an FRS, said:

> I believe that in the National Physical Laboratory we have the first instance of
> the State taking part in scientific research. The object of the scheme is, I
> understand, to bring scientific knowledge to bear practically upon our
> everyday industrial and commercial life, to break down the barrier between
> theory and practice, to effect a union between science and commerce. This
> afternoon's ceremony is not merely a meeting of the representatives of an
> ancient world-renowned scientific society for the purpose of taking over a new
> theatre of investigation and research. Is it not more than this? Does it not show
> in a very practical way that the nation is beginning to recognise that if its
> commercial supremacy is to be maintained, greater facilities must be given for
> furthering the application of science to commerce and industry?

18   The Opening Ceremony, 19 March 1902, being addressed by the Prince of Wales.

He stressed the superiority in world markets of some German goods which resulted from the substantial scientific backing of the PTR. With a strictly orthodox view of the function of the monarchy he accepted the unwillingness of the Government to spend corresponding sums here:

> . . . it is to the liberality of the public that we must look, not only for money, but for presents of machinery and other necessary appliances.

As a sailor, he welcomed the projected setting up of a ship testing tank. Finally: 'I have great pleasure in declaring the National Physical Laboratory open.'

Notes

1   In those days also sometimes called Middle Park.
2   Samwell's interiors were laid out in characteristic arrangements of square rooms. None of his better known designs has been preserved (Eaton Hall, Cheshire, has been demolished; the Grange, Hampshire, has been submerged in more recent building and is now very much of a ruin; however the plans of both are on record), so that the lay-out of his house in the Park near Hampton Court, still beautifully preserved in the grounds of NPL, is the finest example of his work remaining in the country. There is one small ceiling remaining which can be positively identified as late 17th century.
3   Babbage C 1830 *Science without a Heart* etc.
4   Cardwell D S L 1957 *The Organisation of Science in England*: (Heinemann)
5   The committee members were Strange, Thomson (later Lord Kelvin),

Tyndall, Frankland, Stenhouse, Mann, Huggins, Glaisher, Williamson, Stokes, Jenkin, Hurst, Huxley and Balfour Stewart (later augmented by Tennyson, Playfour and Lockyer).

6   The committee members were: the Duke of Devonshire, Huxley, Stokes, H J S Smith, Kay-Shuttleworth, Lord Lansdowne, Samuelson, Sharpey, Miller, Lubbock and Lockyer.

7   *Report of the Royal Commission on Scientific Instruction and the Advancement of Science* 1872–5 4 vols (London).

8   This committee consisted of Thomson, Williamson, Wheatstone, Miller, Matthiessen and Fleeming Jenkin; to whom were added a year later Bright, Clerk Maxwell, C W Siemens, Balfour Stewart, Varley, Carey Foster, Latimer Clark, Forbes, Hockin, Joule and Esselbach.

9   Swindells B 1975 *A Commemoration of the Centenary of the Metre Convention 1875–1975* (National Physical Laboratory)

10   The part played by the Rayleighs in the history of NPL is summarised in a paper by H Barrell in *App. Optics* **3** (1964) 1125.

11   Fleming J A 1885 *Proc. Soc. Teleg. Engrs.* 488–521

12   The Standards Department of the Board of Trade was set up originally to carry out the provisions of the 1866 Act. Initially it concerned itself mainly with weights and measures.

13   Sir Douglas Strutt Galton (1822–99) was one of those scientists/technologists with wide ranging interests who did so much for progress in Victorian England. He was commissioned in the Royal Engineers in 1840 and thereafter worked on railways, water supply, sewerage, sanitary science and so on. After 1860 he continued these tasks at the War Office, transferring in 1869 to the Office of Works as Director and finally retiring on a pension in 1875. He was a Secretary of the BA from 1871 to 1895 and then President. It was in this post that he worked unceasingly to further the idea of a national physical laboratory.

14   The committee members were: Sir Douglas Galton, Sir H Roscoe, Lord Kelvin, Lord Rayleigh, Lodge, Ricker, Clifton, Carey Foster, Schuster, Ayrton, Anderson, Thorpe, F Galton and Glazebrook.

15   The committee consisted of Lord Rayleigh, Sir Courtenay Boyle, Sir James Wolfe Barry, Sir Alexander Noble, Chalmers, Siemens, Rucker, Thorpe and Roberts-Austen.

16   The Report cost $1\frac{1}{2}$ d, the Minutes of Evidence 1 s.

17   There is a private note in the NPL archives which contends that the Board of Trade did not announce its readiness to undertake the testing of electrical measuring instruments until two months after the Treasury Committee began its deliberations.

18   The Report also states, '. . . at the Reichsanstalt the cost of the buildings and equipment amounted to £195 000 and the annual expenditure is about £15 000, of which only a small part is covered by fees'.

19   Glazebrook R (1933) *Early Days at the National Physical Laboratory* (a lecture)

20   The Executive Committee consisted of Lords Lister and Rayleigh, A B Kempe, Sir Courtenay Boyle, Professor Rücker, Captain Abney, Captain Creak, Professor Carey Foster, F Galton, Professor Perry, Sir R Strachey,

members of the Kew Committee; Sir J Wolfe Barry, Sir E Carbutt, A Siemens, Sir W Roberts-Austen, G Beilby, Sir N Barnaby, representatives of the Technical Societies; Professor Clifton, Professor O Lodge, Sir A Noble, Professor Schuster, Sir J J Thomson, Dr Thorpe, representatives of the Royal Society.

21 The single storey design, called 'weaver-shed', was subsequently adopted when the buildings were finally constructed on the Bushy House site. Glazebrook's worst fears were unfounded, since this very commendable design continues even today to provide a satisfactory housing for modern science.

22 Exactly to the design prepared already for the Old Deer Park site — a north light construction, 80 ft × 50 ft.

23 Barrell H (1969) *Meteor. Mag.* **98** 171 'Kew Observatory and the National Physical Laboratory'. Up to the foundation of the NPL rather more than 400 000 instrument verifications had been carried out at the observatory.

24 Glazebrook R T 1901 *Nature* **64** 290

25 R Moseley 1975 *PhD Thesis* University of Sussex *Science, Government and Industrial Research; The Origins and Development of the NPL (1900–1975)* unpublished

Part II

Early Development of NPL

A Role Developed: 1902–1908

A noteworthy feature of the Laboratory finance in this period was the large number of donations of cash, equipment and facilities from a wide variety of sources—industry, learned societies, private individuals, all combining, as the Prince of Wales had suggested they should, to set the new organisation on its feet.

In 1895 the Drapers' Company had offered £700 to Principal Viriamu Jones of University College, Cardiff, for a Lorenz apparatus[1]. Following his premature death in 1901 this sum was placed at the disposal of the NPL and F E Smith began to elaborate the design.

There were generous donations, too, of apparatus and cash from many quarters[2]. For the year therefore there was a profit of £79 9s 7d (receipts £9314, expenses £9235).

During 1902 the staff at Teddington was augmented by the transfer of W Hugo (Senior Assistant) from Kew to join Harker in thermometry and the appointment of F W Skirrow (Junior Assistant), whose stay however was short. Miscellaneous test work eventually got under way—the Engineering Department making 40 tests and the Physics Department 229 (including 31 electrical instruments, 38 thermometers, 12 metrological instruments, 22 glass vessels and 94 sets of weights). The test work income was £69 2s 8d.

A 1902 decision of the Executive Committee to grant to a Japanese student sent by his Government the privilege of working at NPL for a time, had far reaching consequences. This policy has been actively pursued right up to the present day, enabling many generations of foreign scientists to work there and, in exchange, many from NPL have gone to work with their counterparts abroad.

The bumper year of 1903 saw the new laboratory really get into its stride. New recruits included E H Rayner to the Electricity Division (a future Superintendent of the Electricity Department), F J Selby to Optics and Tide Prediction (a future Secretary), C C Paterson to Electrotechnics and Photometry (who went on to a distinguished career with the GEC) and W A Caspari to Chemistry.

This year saw the construction of a further new building—a lathe house to accommodate a Whitworth standard screw-cutting lathe. This was a building within a building, with very close temperature control, and it served until the construction of the Wernher Building in 1913. It was then

39

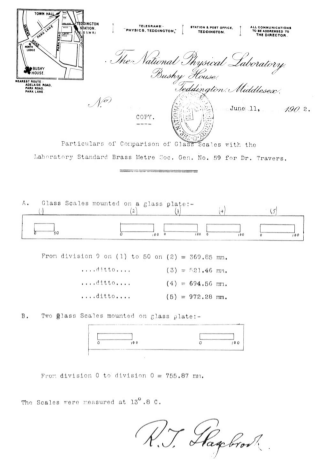

The National Physical Laboratory
Bushy House,
Teddington, Middlesex.

June 11,   *190* 2.

COPY.

Particulars of Comparison of Glass Scales with the
Laboratory Standard Brass Metre Doc. Gen. No. 59 for Dr. Travers.

A.   Glass Scales mounted on a glass plate:-

From division 9 on (1) to 50 on (2) = 369.85 mm.

....ditto....   (3) = 521.46 mm.

....ditto....   (4) = 694.56 mm.

....ditto....   (5) = 972.28 mm.

B.   Two glass Scales mounted on glass plate:-

From division 0 to division 0 = 755.87 mm.

The Scales were measured at 13°.8 C.

19   An early test certificate.

incorporated in this new structure and the Lathe was transferred to a new site in the Metrology Building. Tide predicting equipment belonging to the Indian Government was transferred to the north extension of Bushy House, behind the north facing portico, and thereafter was operated by NPL.

One of the first tasks undertaken by the Engineering Department was a study of the magnitude and distribution of wind forces on structures such as bridges and roofs. Following the Tay Bridge disaster of 1879 the Wind Pressure Commission of 1881 recommended that structures should be designed for wind pressures of 56 lbs per sq ft corresponding to a wind speed of 140 mph, but there was no actual measured data to back these guesses. Stanton first tested models in a vertical wind tunnel, two feet in diameter; later a 50 ft tower was erected in the grounds to study larger scale models in

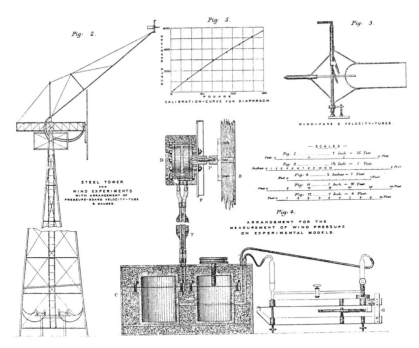

20   Diagram of the steel tower for wind experiments.

natural wind. The results suggested that the forces on a large structure could be deduced from laboratory experiments on a model—a discovery with far reaching implications. The work was later extended to structures occupying an extended area by the erection in 1909 of two 18 m towers 100 m apart.

Test work expanded to 1330 tests producing an income of £350 8s 4d, while another £536 10s was paid for commissioned researches. However, in spite of this the annual accounts showed a deficit of more than £100, while essential purchases had reduced the capital in hand by some £1400[3].

Towards the end of 1900 there had been a proposal by the London United Tramways Co. to electrify lines running close to the Kew Magnetic Laboratory. Tests and discussions took place and finally it was decided to move the Laboratory to a part of the country remote from any likelihood of electric traction services. During 1903 Glazebrook undertook the task of finding a new site and 'with a bicycle, spent an interesting time in many out of the way parts of England and Scotland'. Ultimately the choice fell on Eskdalemuir in Scotland[4] and building commenced there the following year.

By now it was becoming obvious that some increase of grant had to be made if the NPL was to stay viable. The original allocation of £4000 p.a. was due to end in 1904 and some new and (hopefully) extended provision had therefore to be made for the future. In November 1903 Lord Rayleigh, on behalf of the Executive Committee, advanced this view to the Treasury; they indicated in reply that, while there was no question of reduction or removal of the grant, any pleas for its increase would be carefully scrutinised. The Laboratory authorities decided to prepare a memorandum on future expansion and by February 1904 this document was available for consideration.

21   The power house, in the early 1900s, with Bushy House beyond and the engineering building on the left. The power house was demolished in the 1950s. Note the weaver-shed roof on the engineering building.

One of its major points concerned the costs of similar organisations in other countries. The Reichsanstalt in Germany and the Versuchsanstalt in Prussia had cost £200 000 and £137 500 respectively and received annual grants of £16 000 and £15 000. At the National Bureau of Standards in Washington, £115 000 had been spent on buildings and equipment with an annual grant of £19 000. The Laboratoire d'Essais in France had received £47 000 capital grant and £5500 annually. The corresponding figures for NPL were £19 000 and £4000 annually.

Table 2 shows the new capital expenditure, on buildings and equipment, that was estimated. The increase in annual expenditure, including provision

Table 2   Estimated new capital expenditure in 1904

Engineering Dept, including a new large testing machine		£14 200
Physics Dept,		
Electrotechnics	£7500	
Metrology	£5500	
Optics Equipment	£ 500	
Chemistry	£1000	
		£14 500
		£28 700

for new apparatus, was put at £6000 to be reached in the course of four years. The scientific staff and scale of salaries to be attained when the additions were working are shown in table 3.

For the time being this was turned down by the Treasury, but after a deputation had been received by the Prime Minister the Treasury at length agreed to ask Parliament to increase the annual grant to £5500 in 1905–06 and to £6000 the following year. Capital increases would have to be spread over a number of years, but an additional grant of £5000 for 1905–06 and an equal amount for the next four or five years might be provided. As a result salaries were revised, Laboratory hours were fixed at 9.30 am to 5.30 pm, but staff still had no pension rights.

The NPL Annual Report for 1904 records 2006 tests with a test fee income of £975 19s 8d and £1497 19s 1d receipts from special researches. The lathe house and the Engineering Department's tower were completed and put into service, and the first telephone was installed in Bushy House.

Numerous donations continued to come in from all manner of private sources. The increased capital grant was to be spent on new buildings to house the Metrology and Electrotechnics Divisions of the Physics Department. During 1905 tenders for the latter from Messrs Mowlem for

Table 3   Staff numbers and salaries proposed in 1904.

1	Superintendent	£500–£700
10	Principal Assistants	£300–£500
4	Assistants	£200–£300
4	Junior Assistants	£100–£150
4	Student Assistants	£ 50–£100

£5791 (another generous gift, since this was cost price) were accepted, while the former was temporarily shelved. About this time the Indian Engineering College at Coopers Hill, where testing for Indian Railways was carried out, was being closed down. The plant could be transferred to the NPL on condition that the same service would continue to be offered. Thus the Laboratory would acquire a tensile testing machine, which in the event was exchanged in part payment for a new 100 ton machine from Messrs Buckton.

B F E Keeling, who had done much to establish the Metrology division of the Physics Department, left to take up an appointment with the Survey of Egypt; his place was subsequently taken by H H Jeffcott.

1905 continued the rapid burgeoning of the new Laboratory, as programmes of research and of international intercomparisons of physical standards, now well under way, produced rising pressures for extensions of both equipment and accommodation. A notable new recruit to a permanent post in the Engineering Department was L Bairstow (destined to become a major figure in aeronautical research), who at first joined Stanton in the work on wind pressures and on the alternating stressing of metals.

These two items formed a large part of the Engineering Department's programme at this time, but in 1905 the wind pressure investigation received a set-back since a lack of winds left only ten days suitable for outdoor observation.

Ten widely different iron and steel specimens made up in a range of forms were subjected to 800 alternations of stress per minute in specially designed apparatus. From the data it was possible to determine the limiting range of stress for a million reversals.

In the meantime C Jakeman in the same Department was measuring the specific heat of steam at different pressures and temperatures.

In the Physics Department F E Smith completed the work on the current balance, a BA sponsored concept for the absolute determination of current designed by W E Ayrton and T Mather, in which the force between two coils carrying current is measured by balancing it against physical masses in a conventional mechanical balance system. The error of this fundamental determination was considered unlikely to exceed a few parts in 100 000. The balance continued to be used in more or less the same form for the next 70 years.

There are a number of records during the year of intercomparisons of standards of resistance between NPL and the German standards laboratory, the PTR, involving a series of measurements at both. Similarly the Photometry Division was engaged in comparing flame standards and electric secondary standard lamps with PTR and with the New York Electric Testing Laboratory, in order to reach agreement on an international value for the Candle.

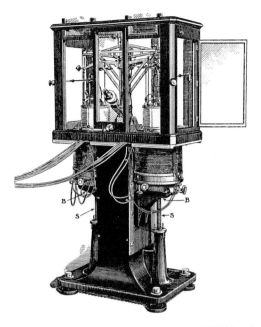

22   The first design for the current balance. This has been continuously modified and used until recently.

In the Thermometric Division Dr Harker determined the melting point
of platinum as 1710 ± 5°C, agreeing closely with a PTR value.

The Metrology Division was working largely for the Engineering
Standards Committee, a national body aiming to standardise engineering
work, a technological advance vital for many expanding and potentially
competitive industries. A lengthy investigation of shafts and holes was
carried out at NPL and in engineering works all over the country. Errors in
workmanship depended on the class of work, increasing in each class with
increase of diameter—for example, in gas engine manufacture errors of
0.002 in were found in shafts and of 0.003 in in holes. The average errors
over the whole of the industry were 0.0016 for shafts and 0.0018 for holes.
Similar studies were made of bolt heads and nuts revealing errors up to
0.020 in. As a result an all round improvement in methods was slowly set in
train. The standard leading screw lathe in the lathe house was now operating
with an error not exceeding 0.0003 in over a length of 36 in.

In 1905 the test work income reached £4358 14s 0d and the total earned
income £5957 4s 0d. The staff—scientists plus auxiliaries—now numbered
65. The first volume of *Collected Researches* was published, reprinting
papers by Laboratory members which had originally appeared in the

journals of learned societies. This earned the occasional adverse comment such as the letter to *The Electrician* which read:

> If there is anyone who does not realise that the mercury standard ohm is merely a ponderous academic joke this paper is not without its use. If he reads it he will now realise it fully.

In June 1905 a meeting of MPs was called to consider additional state grant to the Laboratory:

> The National Physical Laboratory at Teddington is only partially a State institution. We give it a very small annual grant—just about the tenth of what the Germans give to their corresponding institution, and much less than what the United States and France give. It has a splendid staff, and it is doing valuable work in aid of our industries. But it is starved, and little interest is taken in it. In Germany this kind of institution is regarded as a necessary part of the executive brain. Here we ignore it.

The meeting took place on 4 July 1905 and as a result a Memorial with 150 signatories was prepared and presented in October to the Chancellor of the Exchequer asking for a grant of £30 000 for buildings and equipment and that the annual contribution be gradually raised to £10 000. An appendix emphasised once again the importance of a standards laboratory to back industrial science, to back the Board of Trade's legal standards work and to operate an ever increasing number of governmental standards procedures, such as the verification of gauges, templates etc for the Engineering Standards Committee, the War Office standard leading screw lathe, and so on. The NPL Annual Reports are conspicuously silent regarding the outcome of this particular approach, but undoubtedly the financial position did continue to improve as the years went on.

The first sizeable building project, the new Electrotechnics Building, was completed during 1906 and opened by the Right Honourable R B Haldane, Secretary of State for War, on 25 June. The ceremony was followed by an inspection of the Laboratory and a garden party in the grounds of Bushy House. The total cost of the building itself was around £7600 and another £1800 was authorised for its equipment. The main block, 120 ft × 50 ft, was divided into two bays with top-lighting (in accordance with what became an almost standard design for the site). To the east was a two storey wing, 100 ft × 25 ft, for photometric work[5] and to the south an annexe, 100 ft × 20 ft, for workshops, stores and offices. Immediately after the opening one generous benefactor, Sir John Brunner, donated £5000 towards equipment.

Soon afterwards an extensive building programme was put in train with a total contract value of £11 600[6]. This was completed and the buildings in use within the next twelve months. Some of the costs came from the Government (£10 000 for 1906–07), while numerous private individuals and organisations donated cash, materials, services or equipment.

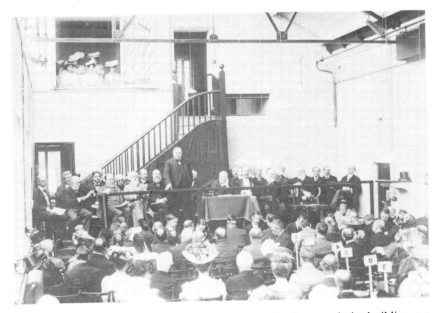

23   The Right Honourable R B Haldane opening the electrotechnics building, 25 June 1906.

24   Garden party at Bushy House on the occasion of the opening of the electrotechnics building. The iron staircase and veranda are those shown in the picture of Queen Adelaide (figure 5).

There were organisational changes at this time too. Carpenter and Caspari both left the Laboratory and then, some time later in the year, W Rosenhain was recruited to become Superintendent of a new Metallurgy and Metallurgical Chemistry Department.

The big programmes of research and standards continued in all departments, many involving international intercomparisons. Notable amongst these was the first design of a calculable mutual inductance by Campbell, a device which could, in conjunction with a suitable AC bridge network, enable the absolute value of the unit of resistance to be determined[7]. The Weston cell as a stable voltage source and the silver voltameter to standardise current were being extensively investigated.

The Metrology Division approved and retained a set of tram, bull-headed and flat-bottomed rail templates for checking commercial productions; pipe flange templates were made similarly available. The investigation of tolerances necessary for screw threads continued (see for example table 4). The tremendous influence of all this work on general engineering standards in the country's manufacturing industries cannot be underrated.

Table 4 Results of an interchangeability test in which nuts and bolts nominally the same size were screwed together in all possible combinations.

Number of combinations tested	1207
Good fits	46%
Slack fits	25%
Engaging sufficiently to allow screwing up with a spanner	8%
Not fitting	21%

In July of this year matters came to a head in a long controversy over chemical tests of materials at the NPL. It happened in this way, as described afterwards by Glazebrook:

> In May, 1903, a request from the London, Brighton and South Coast Railway for an analysis of some steel rails led to a discussion as to the desirability of coupling chemical analyses with the work, and it was agreed that such analyses might be proceeded with. . . .

By April, 1905, a marked increase in the number of chemical tests had taken place and the matter was discussed with the Executive Committee. The current test pamphlet provided that: 'the Chemistry division undertakes work in connection with materials sent to the Laboratory for other tests . . .'

and this statement was usually submitted to enquirers. An earlier pamphlet had contained the more general statement that the Laboratory would: 'undertake all such tests on machines, instruments and materials as its equipment will permit. . . .' These statements would appear to define the Laboratory's terms of reference more or less in accordance with the guidelines laid down by the Treasury Committee of 1898. However, Glazebrook continued:

> The President of the Society of Public Analysts wrote in June, 1905, complaining that certain cases had been brought to their notice in which the Laboratory appeared to be competing with professional chemists, to which Lord Rayleigh replied that the Committee have no wish at present to depart from the practice as stated in the Test Pamphlet.

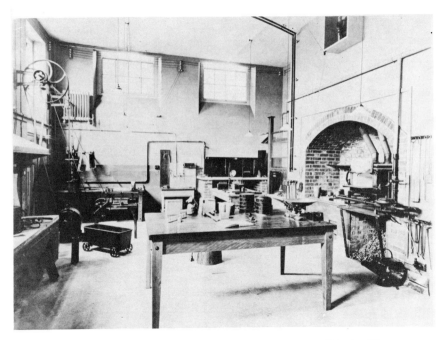

25   The first metallurgical laboratory in the kitchen of Bushy House.

In July a deputation from the Society of Chemical Industry, led by Sir William Ramsay, visited NPL. The Institute of Chemistry, which up to that time had not been represented on the General Board of the NPL, became involved; their President was later appointed to NPL Executive Committee. A question was raised in Parliament and, as a result, the Government appointed a small Committee[8] to consider the matter.

The selection of the committee aroused considerable controversy, since one member was Lord Rayleigh's brother-in-law, while two others were members of the NPL Committee. As the *Electrician* said of it:

Self examination is not what is required, and an enquiry into the methods of the NPL by a committee drawn from that institution could only be considered as worthless.

The brief of the committee was to study:

(*a*) The character of the mechanical, physical and chemical tests undertaken there,

(*b*) The possibility of their interfering unduly with the business of other agencies,

(*c*) The desirability of publishing the results of all such testing work, and to report

(i) whether, having regard to the industrial interests of the country generally and to those of private agencies, any change is desirable in the scope of the work of the Laboratory,

(ii) on what lines any further development of the business should proceed.

The committee sat all through 1907 and consulted a large number of interested witnesses.

In their Report (11 December 1907) they confirmed that the Laboratory terms of reference did include 'the standardisation and verification of instruments, but also, under proper restrictions, the testing of materials'. They distinguished between contractual testing (the ordinary testing of materials to ascertain whether their quality and behaviour are up to contract) and investigatory testing—to place restriction on which would be to hinder the advance of knowledge. As a general rule the Laboratory should be barred from contractual testing, but with important exceptions, e.g. where there are no other places adequately equipped, for Government purposes, or for reference purposes. The restrictions did not apply to the testing of instruments or of their component parts. Subject to these observations, continued the Report:

. . . we do not consider that any alteration is required in the scope of the work of the National Physical Laboratory as defined by the Committee of 1898. The conclusions of the Committee were, with minor exceptions, generally accepted by the witnesses who appeared before us, and we have not thought it necessary to do more than recommend certain slight modifications and a more precise determination of some doubtful points of detail.

To some extent the Laboratory had been forced into this situation by the parsimony of the Treasury. They encountered considerable opposition in the technical press, e.g. in the *Times Engineering Supplement*:

. . . are they [the Laboratory's staff] merely men of academic distinction who seem to imagine that all industrial difficulties can be solved at Teddington? [Circumstances did in fact force them towards such arrogation.] . . . What is required is a little more common sense and less talk, less self-advertising and a concentration of the energies of both the Director and staff on the scientific work for which the Laboratory was instituted.

The Treasury approved the Report in a minute of 1 February 1908; and Glazebrook was able to comment: '. . . so we received our second charter and were free to develop in accordance with the recommendations'.

Years of Expansion: 1908–1914

The evidence for the 1905 Committee was largely prepared by Selby, who in the course of this work collected the statistics quoted in Table 5 showing how the staff were dividing their time. The averages working out at Care of apparatus 29 %, Research 49 % and Tests 22 %. Expenditure had increased from £10 306 in 1903 to £14 252 in 1906, receipts usually staying just ahead. Fees for work done grew from £3162 in 1901 to £5796 in 1906, but a high proportion of this was still being earned by the extensive test facilities being operated in the Observatory Department at Kew. The expenditure on buildings over the years is given in Table 6.

Table 5 Statistics collected in 1905–08 showing the division of staff time at the NPL.

	Care of apparatus (%)	Research (%)	Tests (%)
Bairstow	0	100	0
Campbell	50	25	25
Carpenter	10	75	15
Caspari	20	60	20
Harker	15	50	35
Jakeman	15	70	15
Jeffcott	30	30	40
Melsom	25	10	65
Peterson	50	30	20
Rayner	30	60	10
F E Smith	5	90	5
Stanton	50	40	10

Table 6   Expenditure on buildings in the NPL from 1901 to 1906, together with the source of money.

	1901	1902	1903	1904	1905	1906
From						
Government ($£$)	14 000	5000			5000	10 000
Donations and						
Subscriptions ($£$)		976	1124	2313	2056	1910

In addition a total of $£11\,950$ had been given towards equipment, plus many valuable gifts of actual apparatus.

Selby, in addition to taking charge of the Optics Division of the Physics Department and of the tide prediction work, was also responsible for the Library. He served as assistant to Glazebrook in many administrative matters and it is no surprise to find that some four years later he became Secretary of the Laboratory, that is head of the Administration and Clerical Department.

In 1907 T Smith was recruited to assist Selby in his various tasks; the Optics Division expanded rapidly to the testing of lenses, binoculars etc. Among the new 'boy clerks' at Kew were two lads who were to have a long association with the Laboratory, continuing beyond World War II— R R Strand and J G Durham.

Outstanding papers on the Ampere balance (by Ayrton, Mather and F E Smith), the silver voltameter (by F E Smith, Mather and Lowry) and the Weston cell (by F E Smith) appeared during the year—a big step forward in electrical standards. Work began on the Lorenz machine, while the construction of the standard mutual inductance was completed. And, the shape of important things to come, the Laboratory was asked by the Post Office to investigate methods of measuring oscillation frequencies in wireless telegraphy.

With the departure of Metallurgy and Metallurgical Chemistry to their new building certain of the original laboratories in Bushy House became vacant. The testing of mercury thermometers at high temperatures was moved into the south-east wing, formerly a chemical laboratory and once the chapel, while a new furnace room was constructed by roofing over a yard adjacent to the north-west wing.

A diverse range of metrological work continued with the twin goals of helping industry and of deriving and maintaining absolute standards; at the same time the taking over and equipping of the new Metrology Building went on apace. In the Engineering Department work continued on the effect of wind pressure on structures, the resistance of materials to impact, the

26   The Lorenz machine.

specific heat of steam and the elastic limits of materials under alternating stress. The Metallurgy and Metallurgical Chemistry Department was still working on a tremendous range of copper–aluminium alloys, while themselves also busy settling into a newly finished building. All Departments continued their test work producing a total test fee income for the year of £9324 1s 3d.

During 1907 an interesting new line of work was opened up resulting from a request by HM Commissioner of Police that the Laboratory should test the accuracy of construction and working of taximeters. At this time motorised and horse-drawn cabs were operating side by side. The work involved type approval and a number of designs were rejected and had to be modifed before they were considered acceptable. Test methods and apparatus were devised at Teddington and the following year an official testing station, under the control of the NPL, was opened at Lambeth in London, where it continued to operate for the next half century.

In 1908 the Treasury grant was raised to £7000. A new test pamphlet was issued and the following scales for staff were approved: Principal Assistants £300–£500, Assistants £200–£300, Junior Assistants £100–£150, Student Assistants £50–£100. The first Principal Assistants were Campbell, Jeffcott, Paterson, Selby and F E Smith.

The idea of a ship testing tank had first been mooted in 1901 and referred to by the Prince of Wales in his speech at the official opening the following year. Now, at last, the Council of the Institution of Naval Architects received a firm offer from Alfred Yarrow of £20 000 towards its erection and equipment. Work began along the western edge of the site bordering the Park. The out-stations at Eskdalemuir and Lambeth (where eight designs for motor cabs and nine for horse cabs were accepted during the year) were opened. The Metrology Building was finally brought into use, leaving behind in Bushy House only those activities requiring very close control of temperature, which the basement there had been proved to provide.

27   The ship tank under construction, 1910.

The NPL *Annual Report* for 1908 summarised the building fund expenditure of the great expansion between 1905 and 1908 (see table 7).

Following an extensive programme of standards work in many countries an International Conference on Electrical Units and Standards was called by the Government in October. Meetings were held at the Royal Society but the delegates found time to visit NPL and inspect the work in progress. Real advances were made towards unanimity resulting in the defining of the

Table 7 Building fund expenditure 1905–08 (taken from the NPL
Annual Report 1908).

	Building ($£$ s d)			Equipment ($£$ s d)		
Electrotechnics building	7593	2	3	3192	5	0
Engineering laboratory additions	3042	6	1	394	1	1
Metrology building	7827	5	3	1282	11	1
Metall. Chem. building	4299	6	8	1243	8	4
Transformer house	332	6	4	165	16	0
Additions to engine house	314	0	0	864	8	2
Thermometry Division	428	19	1	177	14	4
Eskdalemuir				472	1	4
Engineering building (new lavatories)	133	8	2			
Lathe house heating	22	1	4			
	23992	15	2	7792	5	4

With a general expenditure of £1557 3s 2d this gave a grand total of
£33 342 3s 8d to offset against an income from Government grants and
private donations of £33 650 0s 0d over the same period. The test fee
income for 1908 was £13 088 18s 5d at the end of the year the staff
numbered 109.

International Electrical Units, which held sway for many years and were not
in fact superseded until World War II. Details of the decisions were
conveyed by the delegates to their various governments. As a result an Order
in Council in January 1910 revoked that of 1894, replacing its provisions by
those agreed at the Conference. By now international intercomparisons were
taking place world-wide and the *Annual Report* records the travels of a
Weston cell from Teddington to Washington, then on to Tokyo and to
Berlin by way of Siberia and so, eleven months later, back to Teddington. Its
EMF had decreased by 3 parts in a million.

The Wright Brothers made the first powered flight at Kitty Hawk on 17
December 1903; Alberto Santos Dumont made the first public flight in
Europe in 1906; the Wright Brothers exhibited their aeroplane in Europe in
1907–08. Now in 1909 came two important and interconnected events in the
history of aviation. The first aeroplane crossing of the English Channel by
Louis Bleriot, demonstrated our vulnerability to air attack in time of war,
and caused the Right Honourable R B Haldane, the Secretary of State for
War, to suggest the setting up of an Advisory Committee for Aeronautics.
On 5 May the Prime Minister, Mr Asquith, announced in Parliament:

With a view to securing that the highest scientific talent shall be brought to bear on the problems which will have to be solved in the course of the work of the two departments (the Admiralty and the War Office), the National Physical Laboratory has been requested to organise at its establishment at Teddington a special department for continuous investigation—experimental and otherwise—of questions which must from time to time be solved in order to obtain adequate guidance in construction.

The Committee, presided over by Lord Rayleigh and chaired by Glazebrook, included among its members representatives of the Armed Services, and also Professor J E Petavel, a future Director of NPL. The Government was faced by three tasks:

(*a*) The scientific study of the problems of flight, with a view to their practical solution,

(*b*) Research and experiment into these subjects in a properly equipped laboratory, with a trained staff,

(*c*) The construction and use of dirigibles and aeroplanes, having regard mainly to their employment in war.

The Committee would deal with (*a*) and determine the programme for (*b*), which would be the work referred to the Laboratory. (*c*) would remain with the Service Ministries.

28   'The Aeronautical Department gets to work'. Glazebrook (second left) arriving at, and Lord Rayleigh (right) leaving, the first meeting at the War Office.

An Aeronautical Division was therefore set up in the Engineering Department at NPL, with L Bairstow in charge reporting to Stanton. Two bays were added to the Engineering Building and a 4 ft tunnel installed; a 25 m square shed was built to accommodate a whirling table and two new 18 m towers erected 100 m apart to enable studies to be made of lateral variations of wind pressure.

Another important body founded during the same year was the Advisory Tank Committee to oversee all aspects of the ship testing tank now under construction. They appointed G S Baker of the Royal Corps of Naval Constructors as Superintendent to commence his duties on 1 March 1910.

Wide ranging investigation of the properties of alloys continued in the Metallurgy and Metallurgical Chemistry Department, of the effects of alternating stresses and the strength of welded joints in the Engineering Department and of gauges in the Metrology Division of the Physics Department. The latter completed the installation of the mechanically complex Blythswood machine[9] for the ruling of gratings.

G W C Kaye, a future Superintendent and compiler of Kaye and Laby's *Tables of Physical Constants*, was recruited by the Physics Department, while T W Baker completed 50 years service with the Observatory Department at Kew.

1910 saw work begin on the extension to the metallurgy and metallurgical chemistry building, while the ship tank (initially called the National Experimental Tank, and later the William Froude[10] National Tank, No 1 Tank, or the Yarrow Tank after the donor of the building funds) was completed and filled during September. It held 5000 tonnes of water with a centre depth of 3.75 m; it is 150 m long by 9 m wide. Immediate checks were put in hand of deformation, subsidence and cracking, but the structure proved commendably sound. The official opening ceremony was conducted by Lord Rayleigh on 5 July 1911.

In July 1910 the magnetic and meteorological work of the Observatory Department transferred to the Meteorological Office. This had been suggested the previous year by Sir William Napier Shaw, while the remainder of the test work on thermometers, watches, barometers, hydrometers and so on should be transferred to the Bushy site and remain the responsibility of the NPL. A new building programme was needed to accommodate the extra work and staff. At first the move was held up by lack of funds and the test work continued to be done at Kew. However in due course the Government made a grant of £5000 in the estimates for 1911–12 and erection of a new administration and optics block was begun at Teddington; this was designed to conform architecturally with Bushy House and was opened in 1913 by the Right Honourable A J Balfour. The transfer of work and staff from Kew was thereupon completed[11].

The extension in 1910 to the Metallurgy and Metallurgical Chemistry Building was helped considerably by a generous donation of £10000 from

29   Interior of No 1 Tank.

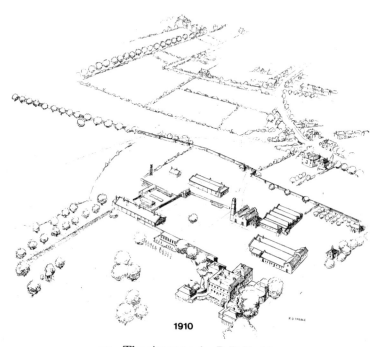

1910

30   The site 1910, by R D Treble

Sir Julius Wernher, for whom it was subsequently named. It was completed the following year. It incorporated within its structure the special lathe house of 1903, the standard screw-cutting lathe being transferred to new quarters alongside the new Metrology Building.

Another new building in 1911 was that for testing roads and road materials in a new programme being carried out by the Engineering Department for the Road Board. A circular testing machine with eight wheels was accommodated in a room 13.75 m square, the specimen road being laid in a circular track 75 cm wide with a mean diameter of 10 m. It was estimated that:

> . . . for a tar-macadam road, solid steel wheels running at 16 km h $^{-1}$ would in 24 h continuous operation represent one year's wear on a typically heavy trafficked road.

31 The road testing machine, 1911.

During 1911, the *Annual Report* records that HM Office of Works granted NPL the use of a portion of the field east of Bushy House as a sports ground and contributed £100 towards the cost of preparation. On this side of Bushy House is the front door, which was approached along an avenue of trees from the Chestnut Avenue in Bushy Park. The line of this approach avenue across the field can still be detected today in aerial pictures by depressions, parch marks or similar.

On returning from a mountaineering trip in the Alps in the autumn of 1911, Glazebrook developed typhoid. The attack was serious and only assiduous care and attention by his doctor and his wife's untiring and devoted nursing made recovery possible. He did not resume work until the early summer of 1912, Stanton meanwhile acting as Director. To celebrate his return the staff made a presentation and a group photograph of the whole Laboratory team was taken; unfortunately no really large prints of this remain.

32   Thomas E Stanton.

In the latter half of 1912 another awkward administrative hurdle had to be cleared. NPL carried out some work, amounting to type approval, on ships' lights for the Board of Trade and, on presenting their bill, had it referred to the Treasury. The Treasury view was that, since they had already made a general grant of £7000 (over and above building grants) to NPL in 1912–13, this sum should be expected to cover the cost and no more cash would be forthcoming. The original terms of reference of NPL had stated that. ' . . . fees for standardising or verifying instruments . . . should be paid by Government departments as well as by private individuals.' The Treasury held that this present work was rather ' . . . special researches undertaken to ascertain the principles to be carried out in future . . . '. However they then folded and accepted the liability. Thus another principle became established.

In the years after 1910 the London and South-Western Railway was proceeding fast with the electrification of its suburban network. When they threatened to convert the line through Teddington a clause was inserted in the Act by which the Company undertook that magnetic disturbances produced thereby at the Laboratory should not exceed their present value (due to background and trams) by more than 20 %. F E Smith was given the task of assessing the effect and a non-magnetic hut[12] was erected for the measurements in 1913 in the Director's garden adjacent to the Park, ready for the coming of the electric trains in 1916.

In 1913 the British Radium Standard (21.1 mg of radium chloride) was placed in the charge of NPL. This had been purified and standardised by Professor Stefan Meyer of Vienna and compared with the International Standard by Mme Curie at the BIPM.

It is interesting also to learn that this long ago radio time signals were being regularly picked up at Teddington from Paris and Norddeich on an aerial 250 m long and 7–12 m high. It was noted that the Greenwich signal arrived on a land line 0.2 s later than the others.

When the War, inevitable in the highly charged atmosphere of the time, finally came in August 1914 the staff of the NPL numbered close on 200. By this time the Laboratory was playing a significant role in helping with the problems of industry, in measuring and maintaining standards of physical quantities and in international cooperation in scientific matters. However, shocks were in store for the nation's science which, when cut off from contacts with Germany, had suddenly to face many new and unexpected challenges.

World War I: 1914–1918

As soon as commercial links with Germany were severed in August 1914, a wide range of shortages became apparent. There was a manifest disparity between the industrial capabilities of the two countries due almost entirely to the superior organisation of German science in training, in research and in the application of science to industry. Only 40 firms in Britain were employing graduate scientists; the annual output of honours graduates in mathematics, science and technology was just over 500 and none of these were trained in research; the corresponding figure for Germany was some ten times greater with around 3000 engaged in full-time research. Vastly increased programmes for training in science and for the utilisation of scientists were urgently needed.

Items previously supplied almost entirely from Germany, and for which virtually no manufacturing facilities existed in this country, included dyestuffs for uniforms, acetone for explosives, optical glass for range-finders, magnetos (then a Bosch monopoly) and a range of chemicals for drugs. Immediate action was needed to supply these deficiencies and many others.

Research for the war effort fell to the relevant ministries—the War Office and the Admiralty, to which was added in 1915 the Ministry of Munitions. At this time the National Physical Laboratory, with its well developed departments of physics, electricity and metrology, engineering and aerodynamics, metallurgy and ship design, was by far the largest organisation of its kind receiving a measure of government support. Some of its normal functions were perforce laid aside and a tremendous load of routine work progressively taken on, the staff expanding from 187 in July 1914 to 532 in March 1918. Senior staff were in great demand in various advisory capacities, some indeed were seconded to the Inventions Department of the Ministry of Munitions, where they dealt with a range of problems far beyond their original fields of expertise at the Laboratory.

In the early part of the War certain general scientific bodies were actively campaigning for expansion of the role of science in industry. These included the British Science Guild (founded in 1905 by Sir Norman Lockyer to promote the spread of the utilisation of science, after he had failed to persuade the BA that it should extend its activities in this direction), the Institute of Industry and Science (an association of scientists and industrialists founded in 1915 as a direct result of the needs of war) and the Royal Society. Early in 1915 the Government set up the McCormick Committee to report on the scientific manpower situation and this led to the setting up under the Board of Education of an Advisory Council[13] (of the Privy Council Committee for Scientific and Industrial Research) with the wide ranging tasks of:

(*a*) Instituting specific researches,

(*b*) Establishing or developing institutions or departments for the scientific study of problems affecting particular industries,

(*c*) The establishment and award of Research Studentships and Fellowships.

To these ends £25 000 was available initially and £40 000 in the following year.

Thereafter the Advisory Council promoted a wide range of research projects, in the laboratories of professional institutions, in academic and private laboratories and at NPL. As the need for continued expansion of investment into ever widening research programmes became more and more appreciated, some coordinating tasks were placed in the hands of specialised standing committees. Finally the function of the Advisory Council broadened so far beyond the bounds of the Board of Education that the Government was pressed to set up a separate department and, in December 1916, the Lord President of the Council announced the intention to found a Department of Scientific and Industrial Research. However the NPL did not come directly under its charge until after the end of the War.

By March 1915 the *Annual Report* already listed 50 members of staff on active service. The service pay of married men was made up to their Laboratory salary, while unmarried men were made up to half salary. Posts were to be kept open for returning servicemen, whose military service was to count towards promotion. An Active Service Organisation was set up to maintain contacts and circular letters were produced regularly until April 1919 (the first eight numbers duplicated, the remainder printed). Forty-two staff members became special constables, two constables patrolling the grounds four times per hour between 6 pm and 6 am each night.

In June 1914 the Parker Committee on Research in Telegraphy and Telephony (of which E H Rayner of NPL was Secretary) had suggested the setting up of a National Research Laboratory at NPL under the direction of the Director of the NPL. However the onset of war prevented formal action by the Government and, though research on wireless telegraphy continued throughout the War and long afterwards, line communications work was eventually carried out elsewhere.

The War put a stop to much of the international collaborative work on standards, though Drs Giebe and Schultze of the Reichsanstalt were working at Teddington on standards of electrical resistance as late as July 1914.

The heat section of the Physics Department acquired a liquid air plant, while the watch rating section brought into regular use the comparator chronograph used for comparing test timepieces with the standard Morrison clock presented to NPL by Lady Douglas Galton. This year also saw the installation of an experimental rolling mill in a new building facing

33   The Morrison clock, now in the NPL museum.

the Wernher building. This would enable bars and sheets to be made from experimental alloys, large numbers of which were by now being produced in the various programmes of the Metallurgy and Metallurgical Chemistry Department.

By March 1916 the Ministry of Munitions was in full swing, with Glazebrook serving as Scientific Adviser on Physical Questions, and a number of researches devolved on NPL; perhaps the most important and far reaching in its consequences was the testing of gauges required in the manufacture of fuses and shells. A special staff was recruited under J E Sears Jnr, head of the Metrology Division of the Physics Department, to carry out this work and among them were numbers of young women, the first to be employed in the Laboratory in any capacity. Miss B Runge joined the staff in

34 Gauge testing in the metrology building.

July 1915 and by March 1916 there were 47 females. The work expanded rapidly taking over all available space in the Metrology Building. Finally serious interference with other work began to be felt and a new building (15 m × 43 m) was constructed in 1916 at right-angles to the older building along the west side of Bushy House garden. The following year a gauge workshop was added for the manufacture of special items and the training of industrial personel. During the year 1916–17, 277 350 gauges were tested and a final rate of 9000–10 000 per week, that is half a million per year, was attained.

These were not the only items to produce startling test figures. In 1917–18, 148 694 clinical thermometers were tested, as well as 13 306 telescopes, 13 734 binoculars and 16 437 luminous dials.

In 1916 a piece of land was purchased on the north side of the site, destined to provide a new approach from Teddington and its railway station, which, at long last, was reached by electric traction. The instruments for measurement of magnetic interference, already installed at the Laboratory, came into use and detected a level of interference in excess of that promised by the specification. The issue between the Railway and the Laboratory went to arbitration; the assessor found in favour of the latter, but the eventual outcome is unclear.

35   Testing a mine during the World War I.

36   Tests on a spectrometer

The considerable expansion of research in aerodynamics in the War years resulted in a massive building programme to house the new facilities. A 7 ft tunnel was added in 1915, followed in 1916 by additional 4 ft and 7 ft tunnels. A third 7 ft tunnel was installed in 1917, followed by the $14 \times 7 \text{ ft}^2$ 'Duplex' tunnel completed shortly after the end of hostilities. The earlier tunnels were accommodated in new buildings adjacent to the whirling shed behind, and to the east of, the new extension bays of the engineering building. The Duplex tunnel was housed in an entirely new building on the north edge of the site.

Swiss watches were still being tested and special arrangements were made with the Customs authorities not to charge duty on such test items provided that they were re-exported within three months. Home-made Porcelain products, previously imported but now being made in this country, indicate a shouldering of this sort of burden by home manufacturing organisations, with NPL playing its part in assessment.

The growth of cracks in the fabric of the buildings of the Tower of London was among investigations carried out by the Engineering Department. One station close to the river detected movements which suggested an effect due to the rise and fall of the tide.

At March 1917 a staff total of 420 was recorded, nearly a quarter of them women. Land adjacent to the Laboratory was taken over for allotments and, in view of the imminence of air raids, arrangements were made to put out all lights on receipt of notice from the authorities—blacking out all the weaver-shed roofs was deemed impracticable. In this same year, in the first really big reorganisation, three new Departments were created, each with its own Superintendent—an Electricity Department under F E Smith, a Metrology Department under J E Sears Jnr and an Aerodynamics Department under L Bairstow. At the same time F J Selby became Secretary of the Laboratory. However, almost immediately Bairstow resigned to take up a post with the Air Board and Stanton resumed the Superintendency for the next few years. The new Electricity Department remained the joint responsibility of Smith, Campbell and Paterson until April 1918 when the former was formally appointed, Campbell retired and Paterson left to join the GEC. Rayner then became Principal Assistant.

North Lodge, a double-fronted Victorian house in Queens Road on the Teddington side of the site, was acquired in 1918 (purchase completed in 1921 for £2455) and used initially as a men's canteen. The women's canteen, specially set up for the gauge testers, was a small temporary building elsewhere on the site. Elm Lodge, also in Queens Road, was acquired in 1919 for £1150 and used as a temporary housing for glass vessel testing. Next door, the massive Victoria House was purchased during 1920 for £3050, to become the home for many years of thermometer testing. These miscellaneous dwellings, taken over as temporary expedients, could not be replaced

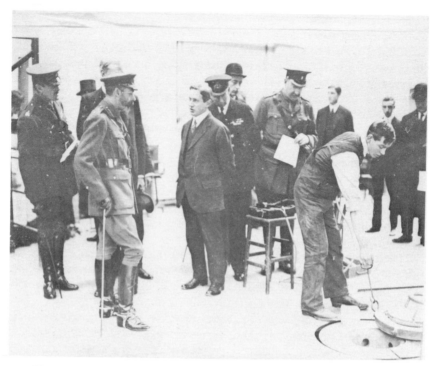

37   King George V talking to W Rosenhain during a visit to the Laboratory during
World War I. The furnace (bottom right) was still in use in 1963.

in the times of financial stringency in the 1920s and 1930s and have
continued to serve various scientific purposes up to the present day.
Meanwhile further new buildings, arising from War needs, were under
construction; these included glass testing, gauge workshop and a big block
to house the Duplex tunnel for the Aerodynamics Department. All became
available during 1919.

In April 1918 the financial responsibility for NPL passed out of the hands
of the Royal Society[14] to the Government's new creation—the Department
of Scientific and Industrial Research (DSIR). Scientific control however
remained with the Royal Society. The main conditions for future operation
were laid down as follows:

1. The name of the Institution shall be 'The National Physical Laboratory'.
2. The scientific control of the Institution shall be exercised by the President
and Council of the Royal Society in the manner provided for in sections 3–13 of
the original scheme as modified by these provisions.
3. The property of the National Physical Laboratory shall be vested in
the Imperial Trust for the encouragement of Scientific and Industrial
Research.

THE NATIONAL PHYSICAL LABORATORY,

TEDDINGTON, MIDDLESEX.

Visit of His Majesty The King,

NOVEMBER 23rd, 1917.

Programme.

10.45. Reception at Main Entrance, Administration Building, by the Director, SIR RICHARD GLAZEBROOK, C.B. Proceed to

10.50. GAUGE TESTING DEPARTMENT.—*Superintendent, Mr. J. E. Sears.*
Indexing of Gauges before and after Test. Tests of miscellaneous Gauges of general types for Gun Ammunition, Submarine Mines, Aircraft, etc. Measurement of Screw Gauges. Projection apparatus for Screw and Profile Gauges.

11.15. WILLIAM FROUDE NATIONAL TANK.—*Superintendent, Mr. G. S. Baker.*
Experiments to illustrate the new Otter Sweep for mines, which is being developed under instructions from the Mining School, Portsmouth. Model of a new Standard Ship having straight frames throughout its length. Model Cutting Machine Apparatus for testing models of Aeroplane Floats.

11.35. DEPARTMENT OF METALLURGY AND METALLURGICAL CHEMISTRY.
—*Superintendent, Dr. W. Rosenhain.*

Experimental Foundry.—Furnaces for very high temperatures used in research on Refractories. Furnaces for study and production of Alloys, chiefly Aluminium and Magnesium Alloys for Aircraft. Furnaces for research on Optical Glass.

Workshop and Testing Room.—Tests at high temperatures on special light Aluminium Alloys for use in the Pistons and Cylinders of Aeroplane Engines.

Main Hall.—Specimens of light Aluminium Alloys. Specimens illustrating work on Steel and other Alloys.

Chemical Laboratory.—Main room for Chemical Analysis of Steel.

11.55. ENGINEERING AND AERONAUTICS DEPARTMENTS.—
Superintendent, Dr. T. E. Stanton.

Engineering Workshop.—Method of machining Wings of Model Aeroplanes in Aluminium. Test of Railway Coupling. Wear Test of hardened pins for joints, etc.

Aeronautics.—7-foot Channel with complete Model of B.E. 2 C. Aeroplane under test. Exhibition of Models of R. E. 8 Aeroplane and of rigid Airship No. 33. Kite Balloon Model. Model Screws, Wings, Bodies, Struts, Tailplanes, Bombs, etc. Whirling Arm for propeller testing.

12.20. Return through GAUGE STORE to Administration Building.

38 Programme for the visit of King George V.

4. The income of the Laboratory, including receipts from fees, will be vested in, and shall be under the control of, the Committee of the Privy Council for Scientific and Industrial Research.

5. The Executive Committee shall be responsible for the management of the Institution in accordance with the scheme of work and estimate of expenditure referred to below, and shall appoint and dismiss the officials, except the Director. In the case of the clerical staff it may be found convenient to take advantage of the ordinary Civil Service methods of appointment.

6. The Executive Committee shall present in December in each year to the General Board a Report on the work of the National Physical Laboratory for the current calendar year, and a statement of the work which it is proposed to undertake during the ensuing financial year.

7. The Executive Committee shall submit to the Committee of Council for approval, not later than January 1 in each year, a Report on the work of the previous calendar year, together with a scheme of work and an estimate of expenditure, and they shall carry on the work of the Laboratory in accordance with its provisions.

8. The Director of the Laboratory will in future be appointed and may be dismissed by the Committee of the Council, but before making any appointment the Committee will invite the President and Council of the Royal Society to nominate some person suitable for the position, and will consult them as to the appointment to be made. Before making their nomination the President and Council of the Royal Society will consult with the Executive Committee of the Laboratory.

9. The arrangements for finance will be those usual in a Government Department.

10. The Committee of the Council will be responsible for any legal proceedings which it may become necessary to institute or defend.

11. The Advisory Council for Scientific and Industrial Research will be the Visitors of the Laboratory.

These were to be the guidelines for the next forty years. Ever since the foundation of NPL a dual system of standards had been maintained by it and the Electrical Standards Laboratory of the Board of Trade, with accurate intercomparisons carried out from time to time. The Board of Trade had long had special national responsibilities assigned by Parliament for the custody and maintenance of primary electrical standards and testing of electrical instruments used as secondary standards, while the NPL had enjoyed a detached and semi-private status. Now that it was to come under more direct control of the Government it seemed appropriate that it should take on this function in future. The necessary arrangements were duly made with the Treasury, and the Board of Trade standards were handed over to the NPL in the course of the next year or so.

By now the Director's salary was £1500 p.a. The 1917–18 *Annual Report* reveals his tremendous involvement in outside committees—the NPL having its fingers in all manner of technical pies[15]. The Superintendents (now earning £800–£1000 p.a.) and senior scientists also carried out such tasks in addition to their supervision of the NPL research programme. In general the salaries of the scientists had long been considered inadequate and there had been no arrangements for pensions; now a comprehensive structure was adopted with a pensions scheme under the Federated Superannuation Scheme for Universities.

During 1918 a Committee of the Institution of Electrical Engineers was appointed to consider the setting up of a National Electrical Proving House 'to examine and test within ordinary commercial limits all classes of electric appliances to approved specifications and generally to test electrical materials and products'. It was suggested that this might form part of the Laboratory. However, after careful consideration the Advisory Council of the DSIR concluded that 'the routine testing of ordinary commercial products is not, and ought not to be, within the functions of either the National Physical Laboratory or of this Department, though the research necessary to the establishment of suitable tests for these purposes would properly rest with the Laboratory. . . '. This decision was of far reaching importance to the future development of NPL. Nevertheless a certain amount of routine testing continued to be done.

Another event of 1918 draws particular attention to this—the Clinical Thermometer Order of the Ministry of Munitions, which stipulated that all clinical thermometers offered for sale must be tested at NPL. The staff for this work was enlarged to 40, eight baths enabling 20 000 items to be tested each week. These numbers soon rose to 30 000 per week and six more baths were added; the old accommodation in Bushy House no longer sufficed and part of the new glass testing building had perforce to be taken over. During the first nine months of 1919 1 047 700 thermometers were tested and 90 assistants were employed. One firm sending 9000 had 28 % rejected and, since there was no outlet for the rejects, this could have proved a serious matter for them.

Radio valves, destined to play a significant yet transient role in physical research, began to come into use. Experiments involving valves had been mainly the concern of the Electricity Department during the War years, but now we find them coming into more general use, for example in the setting up of a powerful new oscillator 'using a large audion (kathodic valve) with the associated inductance coils and condensers.'

By November 1918 NPL and its scientists had become firmly established in the scientific life of the nation by their numerous and diverse contributions to the war effort. Now they had to turn their efforts to the problems of peace in a world badly hit by the ravages of the previous four years.

1919 was in many ways a sad year for the Laboratory. On 30 June Lord Rayleigh died. He had been associated with the whole idea of a national laboratory from its formative days in the 1890s, first as Chairman of the Treasury Committee of 1898, then as Chairman of the Executive Committee, in which his contacts throughout the worlds of science and of politics had been of inestimable help to NPL. He saw it through many a crisis and through many a leap forward in its functions, notably the wrangles with industry resolved by the 1907 Committee, the foundation of the Advisory Committee on Aeronautics and the utilisation of NPL's services in aid of the war effort.

Sir John Brunner, too, who had donated generously towards the equiping of the Electricity Department in the early days, died in this post-war year.

Now Sir Richard Glazebrook, Director since the NPL's foundation in 1900, reached the retiring age of 65. He left in September, having spent the last months of his career in a long and sometimes bitter struggle with government officials over the conditions of transfer of the Laboratory to

DSIR, fighting for and preserving many of the ideals he had always upheld. He dominated the first two decades of the NPL's history. As the Executive Committee wrote:

> Of his services . . . it is impossible to speak too highly. During his tenure of office, he raised the Laboratory, which commenced work on a modest scale, to a great National Institution of first-rate importance, and secured for it a commanding position among the great standardising laboratories of the world, to many of which it has served as a model. The Committee feel that its success is mainly due to his energy and organising ability, and to his wide scientific knowledge; and they desire to express their sense of the debt the nation owes to him for the strenuous services he has rendered in the application of science to industry in this country.

The occasion was marked by a special ceremony which has since become a tradition—the staff presented him with a portrait of himself in oils, painted by his cousin Hugh de T Glazebrook. (This was later handed back to the Laboratory and now hangs in Bushy House.) In addition there was a huge magnificently bound volume containing the signatures of every member of the current staff (this too now resides in NPL Museum). His scientific career was however far from finished. He continued to work with his large number of committees and indeed with other new ones; he continued to help and to use his influence on behalf of the Laboratory for which he had already done so much.

The new Director was Professor J E Petavel, Professor of Engineering at Manchester. The organisation of NPL into seven Departments, plus an Administration, which he took over, retained much the same form for the next 20 years, the only change being the formation of a Radio Department, breaking away from the Electricity Department in 1933. This was a period of solid, relatively unspectacular and continuously diversifying achievement, in which the NPL steadily advanced its standardisation role and research capability.

Notes

1   Used for absolute determination of the unit of electrical resistance, this called for precise and stable mechanical construction in which field he was expert.

2   Sir A Noble gave £1000 for miscellaneous purchases; Armstrong, Whitworth and Co. also gave £1000, followed by £200 p.a.; the Institution of Civil Engineers donated £500 p.a., the Iron and Steel Institute £200 p.a. and so on.

3   Receipts £10 200, expenses £10 306, capital in hand fell from £3822 7s 1d to £2379 9s 11d.

4   Ten miles from the nearest railway—'the diameter of a two shilling piece on Bradshaw's Railway Map'—was considered essential, but even so one

wonders why they had to go so far afield; for example Aberayron, St Davids or Hartland Point might have served. The possible presence of magnetic rocks among the local strata may have provided another limitation. Strangely these requirements can nowadays be met very much closer to London.

5   Their standard of luminous intensity at this time was the Vernon Harcourt pentane lamp, samples of which were certified by the Laboratory. It was replaced by incandescent lamp standards in 1909.

6   (*a*) The addition of two bays, each 80 ft × 25 ft, to the engineering building, both with north light 'weaver-shed' roofs to house the new 100 ton testing machine and other apparatus loaned by the Indian Government.

(*b*) A building for metallurgical chemistry, rectangular 83 ft × 47 ft.

(*c*) A building for the Metrology Division of Physics Department, designed for close temperature control with a double glass roof and a row of internal rooms; incorporating a gallery 50 m in length for the testing of long tapes and measures. Here too the outer shell had the 'weaver-shed' roof.

7   Refinements to the design continued for the next 50 years, until the advent of the calculable capacitor after Wold War II.

8   The committee members were the Right Honourable G W Balfour, Sir A Noble, Sir J Wolfe Barry, W J Crossley MP, R Chalmers and G C Upcott.

9   The result of 30 years work by Lord Blythswood, this was donated on a semi-permanent basis by his widow. It continued at NPL until 1957, when it was passed on to the Science Museum.

10   William Froude was the pioneer of ship testing in tanks. In 1871 he persuaded the Admiralty to finance the construction of a model towing tank in Torquay, which continued to operate for 15 years.

11   During the period when the Observatory Department formed part of the NPL organisation a further 394 000 instrument verifications were carried out, making a grand total of around 809 000 since Kew first began offering the service in 1853.

12   The hut was later moved to the sports field and became part of the pavilion complex.

13   Sir William McCormick was administrative chairman, and Lord Rayleigh was among the members (who were all FRS).

14   Sir Alfred Bray Kempe, the Treasurer of the Royal Society had been Treasurer also of the NPL since its inception at the turn of the century.

15   The Engineering Standards Committee and its sub-committees on Screw Threads, Limit Gauges, Standardisation Rules and Physical Standards; the Gauge Committee of the Ministry of Munitions; several DSIR committees including Glass and Optical Instruments and Cold Storage Research Board; Optical Properties of Glass; Civil Aerial Transport Committee, Air Inventions Committee and Reconstruction Advisory Council.

Part III

The Inter-War Period

NPL Between the Wars: 1919–1939

Professor (later Sir) Joseph Petavel who took over the Directorship from Sir Richard Glazebrook in 1919, continued in the post until his death in 1936. A bachelor with no close family, he left furniture and pictures etc to the Royal Society for continuing use in Bushy House, as well as a considerable sum of money, which up to 1977 enabled later Directors to entertain. He was responsible for planting the very large numbers of bulbs which brighten the surrounding gardens every spring. By taking a detailed interest in their experimental work he came to know all members of his staff, reinforcing his memory with a 'little black book' which he was said to carry around at all times.

39 Joseph Petavel, second Director of NPL.

After a short interregnum, when Sir Frank Smith (by now Secretary of the DSIR) took charge, Dr (later Sir) W L Bragg from Manchester was appointed Director in 1937. A year later, however, he accepted the Cavendish Professorship of Experimental Physics at Cambridge and Sir Frank Smith once again took over. In 1938 Professor (later Sir) Charles Darwin became fourth holder of the Directorship and he continued at the helm throughout the war years.

Traditionally the Director acted also as Superintendent of the Physics Department and Petavel continued in this office until 1922, when Dr W G C Kaye returned from a protracted war service. He then took over and continued in office until 1940. Other Superintendents of Departments who served the whole period between the wars were J E Sears Jnr (Metrology) and G S Baker (William Froude National Tank, which changed to William Froude Laboratory in 1932). Sir Thomas Stanton headed the Engineering Department until his retirement in 1931; he was replaced by H Gough who in 1938 gave way to S L Smith. Similarly W Rosenhain, Superintendent of the Metallury and Metallurgical Chemistry Department since 1906, retired in 1932 to be succeeded by C H Desch. After the departure of L Bairstow, T E Stanton temporarily resumed control of the Aerodynamics Department; this Superintendency passed to R V Southwell in 1920 and on in 1925 to E F Relf, who continued in the post up to World War II. In the Electricity Department F E Smith held office until 1920; for the next nine years E H Rayner acted on an officer-in-charge basis, sharing the duties with G W O Howe (1921), S W Melsom (1922–24) and D W Dye (1925–28); thereafter he became full Superintendent, continuing in office until 1940. The Radio Department was formed in 1933 from the wireless section of the Electricity Department and the Radio Research Station of the DSIR at Slough and at first came under R A Watson-Watt. When he left in 1937 to take his plans for radio-location to the Air Ministry, R L Smith-Rose became Superintendent. F J Selby, who had held the post of Secretary of the Laboratory and head of the Administration Department since 1917, retired in 1932 and his place was taken by W F Higgins, transferred from the Physics Department, who continued in office until 1944.

In thus listing the principal figures in the NPL story for the inter-war period we must not forget the very large numbers of senior and junior staff, whose work helped to build the reputation of the Laboratory. The success of an organisation of this size and complexity, working in the forefront of science and technology, demands a solid contribution at all levels from the Superintendents, through the working scientists, to the supporting staff in laboratory, workshop and office. Each one contributes to the success of every other.

Some scientists coming up for retirement in these years had given a lifetime of service. E G Constable, for example, joined the staff at Kew in 1873, transferred to NPL in 1912, and by the time of his retirement in 1925 had served for more than half a century. C Jakeman, one of the first recruits to the new organisation at the turn of the century, had served 35 years when retiring in 1936.

The position of women scientists in NPL also provides an interesting study. One of the first was Miss E M Keary of William Froude National Tank who, joining in 1915, had reached the rank of Assistant (then a reasonably high scientific grade) by the time of her retirement in 1929. Miss M L V Gayler (later Mrs Haughton) was awarded a DSc in 1924 and continued in the Metallurgy Department until World War II. Her contributions, both practical and theoretical, in the field of age hardening of alloys, made her one of the leading metallurgists of the inter-war years. In 1923 there were 13 female scientists (7 Assistants and 6 Junior Assistants) with more than 50 women of other ranks; the numbers of scientists fell rapidly so that by 1928 there were only four and at the end of the next decade a mere two. The numbers were however well maintained in the lower ranks. There seems to have been some hint of prejudice against them in Petavel's staffing policies.

The post-1918 purchase of properties beyond the northern edge of the original site for use as temporary accommodation for science has already

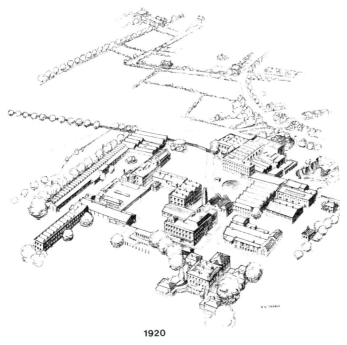

1920

40   The site 1920, by R D Treble.

been noted. These opened on to Queens Road, Teddington, and were separated from the Laboratory site by a right-of-way which led through the Clapperstile allotments directly into the Park. These allotments, occupying seven acres, were taken over piecemeal during the next decade; the right-of-way was deflected to the west and the original gate bricked up. Further north lay an extensive area of 27 acres called the Parks Estate. This was purchased in March 1921, almost doubling the area of the Laboratory site and ensuring space for development for many years to come. Most of the new buildings of the 1920s and 30s were erected on these extensions to the site, first of all close to the Park wall and the original Bushy House estate, spreading during World War II and afterwards to the remote north end of the Parks Estate. With the acquisition of this new property, the present Main Gates and Gate Lodge were set up and opened in 1925. Around this time the main roads inside the Laboratory received their present names—Rayleigh and Kelvin Avenues, Admiralty and Bushy Roads. (Other roads were later named after Glazebrook and Stanton.)

41   The first aerial view of site (1919) with No 1 Tank in the foreground and Bushy House on the right.

In spite of the financial stringency of the 1920s and the slump of the early 1930s the growing importance of NPL in the life of the nation was recognised by the construction of a series of new special-purpose scientific buildings on the site. Outstanding were those for High Voltage (1927), the

Physics Department (1931), the compressed air tunnel (1931), No 2 Tank (1932), acoustics (1933), photometry (1935) and the high speed tunnel (1938). In 1925, moreover, the DSIR initiated the construction on the site of a building for an intended parallel organisation—the Chemical Research Laboratory. This expanded and flourished as a separate body until amalgamated with NPL in 1965.

Under the DSIR the system of scientific control continued to operate much as it had always done, the Royal Society controlling and advising on the work through a General Board, of which the President of the Society, *ex-officio*, continued to act as Chairman. The board in turn appointed a selection of its members as an Executive Committee to take care of the details; membership of the latter often included 'old boys' of the Laboratory, such as R T Glazebrook (who was Chairman from 1926–32), L Bairstow, H C H Carpenter, C C Paterson. As science became progressively more complex, the Executive Committee in its turn appointed special committees to advise on particular sections of the work—a Research Committee, Electrical Units and Standards Committee, High Tension Committee, Advisory Committee for Metallurgical and Engineering Research on Materials, Joint Advisory Committee on Acoustics and so on. To utilise his vast experience, R T Glazebrook was prominently associated

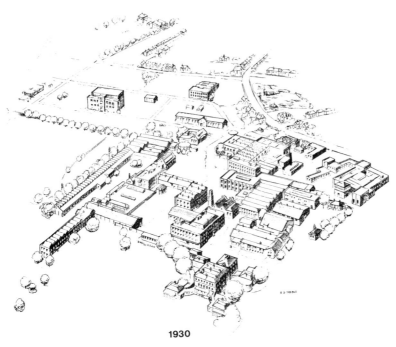

1930

42   The site 1930, by R D Treble.

with several of these. The applied science departments each had their own advisory committee—the Aeronautical Research Committee appointed by the Air Ministry for the Aerodynamics Department and the Advisory Committee for the William Froude Laboratory.

A special report by the Executive Committee in 1928[1] set down the exact position reached so far on the national standards which were the charge of the Laboratory (see Appendix 5).

Hereabouts in time the rapidly expanding scientific story becomes so diversified and complex as to require treatment by separate subject threads rather than a year by year coverage of the Laboratory as a whole.

By the 1930s the four main functions of the Laboratory had crystallised to be (*a*) assistance to industry in its immediate problems by advice and experiment, (*b*) research of longer range to open up new technical possibilities for industry, (*c*) the testing of instruments and (*d*) the maintenance of the standards on which all physical measurements depend—involving the continuous intercomparison of standards and methods with those of other nations.

The results of Laboratory researches were published widely in the proceedings of scientific societies, in technical journals and in the *Collected Researches*, 25 volumes of which appeared between 1905 and 1935. The *Annual Report* which appeared regularly until 1939 holds a wealth of

43   Bushy Road and the power house in 1932, taken from the same place as figure
21.

detailed information for students of any particular aspect of the laboratory's scientific progress. The *Journal of Scientific Instruments* was founded in 1922 as a joint venture by the Institute of Physics and the DSIR (the first editor was E H Rayner, followed by Dr J S Anderson) and remained the responsibility of the NPL until 1925. There were two attempts to produce a house journal in this period, both reminiscent of school magazines. *NPL Review* produced seven issues in 1919–20; later *Bushiana* ran to only five issues in 1932–33.

An important publication during the 1930s was the text of a lecture *Early Days at the National Physical Laboratory*, given by Sir Richard Glazebrook at the Laboratory on 23 March 1933. This has proved a valuable source of material for historians; quotations from it occur in some earlier chapters.

By 1939 the Laboratory had achieved a recognised niche in the scientific life of the country. The national standards laboratory with world-wide recognition, it was producing reliable scientific data and ideas having application in many fields—both industrial and academic; it was the keeper of scientific standards and the arbiter in any dispute over scientific accuracy; it was part of an international network designed to raise the standards of physical measurement on a global scale. To this end the foundation of standards laboratories in Empire countries had been powerfully promoted. These organisations in their turn have made great contributions to the international standards community.

Integration with the British world of science had been hastened by participation in extramural activities—committees, conferences and the solution of pressing national problems, also by participation in functions such as the British Empire Exhibition at Wembley in 1924.

Appreciation of the Laboratory's capabilities and contacts between its staff and their counterparts in the academic and industrial worlds were promoted by the annual Open Days. Beginning on an informal basis in the early days of Petavel's Directorship, these gradually turned into a formal annual event of great benefit to staff and visitors alike.

Thus when the grim clouds of war began to gather at the end of the 1930s the probable function of the Laboratory in the struggle ahead could, in contrast with the situation of 1914, be clearly seen.

Physics Department: 1919–1939

One of the original departments of the Laboratory, Physics had traditionally been headed by the Director. In 1922 the Superintendency was taken over by Dr W G C Kaye, who continued in office throughout the rest of the two decades.

At first most of the Physics Department was sited in the original state rooms and servants' quarters of Bushy House, though some of the thermometer testing was soon moved into the new building alongside the Administration block. A Victorian dwelling house at the Teddington end of the site, called Victoria House, was acquired in 1922 and the thermometry section of the Heat Division moved there as a temporary expedient (they stayed on until the mid 1950s!).

A special-purpose building uniting the whole Department under one roof was discussed and planned throughout the 1920s, but the erection was not begun until 1929. It was opened by Sir Gowland Hopkins on 23 June 1931. Two years later an acoustics building was added behind the other, but the grandiose concept of completing a whole Physics campus by joining these two to enclose a quadrangle never came to fruition. The Physics Department building, to which 'fair-faced brick' gives a depressingly 'warehouse' look inside, was characterised by high ceilings and huge supply ducts, high enough for a man to stand upright, with the mains feeders running along the walls as bare copper bars.

Dr Kaye is said to have maintained exceptionally high standards of tidiness, insisting that all small apparatus be cleaned up and put away in cupboards each night. Luckily for him and for his scientists his reign did not extend into the era of electronic experimentation! The occupation of this building left empty rooms in Bushy House; some were taken over by the Electricity Department, but the main drawing room, where Mrs Jordan and the Duke of Clarence entertained his royal brothers and where later thermometers were tested, was refurnished as a magnificent conference room. Petavel designed a special screen to shield the chairman's back from the roaring coal fire.

During these two decades the work of the Department was divided into four major divisions; Heat and General Physics, Radiology, Sound and Optics.

As long ago as 1911, Kaye had shared responsibility for the production of that famous scientist's 'bible'—Kaye and Laby's *Tables of Physical Constants*. Some physical data were known to be way out of date (going back in some cases, it is said, as far as 1850). The Physics Department in the course of its researches was obviously going to come up with more and more data of this sort and that is indeed what happened. In later years the task of updating this work, which reached its 14th edition in 1973, was undertaken by NPL[2], though nowadays the data are collected from all over the world.

The Heat Division was concerned with the thermal properties of materials—the specific heats and the thermal and electrical conductivities of metals and alloys at temperatures up to 1050–1100 °C and the thermal conductivities of refractories used in furnace construction and for heat insulation purposes. Specific heats of gases at high temperatures and pressures and the heats of combustion of gases were also included in the programme.

The Division included sections for thermometry and pyrometry, which carried out tests on all classes of instruments for measuring and recording temperature e.g. clinical thermometers, mercury thermometers of ordinary and precision types, deep sea thermometers, electrical resistance thermometers, thermocouples and optical and total radiation pyrometers.

Clinical thermometers always called for large scale effort. Immediately after the War in the year September 1919–Septermber 1920 no less than 1 500 000 were certified. In 1921 clinical thermometers for export were no longer required to be tested and numbers dropped to around half a million a year (40 000 per month), the staff being reduced correspondingly from 85 to 35[3]. During the 1920s 6000–7500 precision thermometers were certified each year, rising to 11 000–12 000 per year in the 1930s. Many of these were special-purpose thermometers, such as for example, the thermometers intended for the 1921 Mount Everest Expedition and for Shackleton's Polar Expedition.

44   Thermometer testing in Bushy House, early 1920s.

The Laboratory has contributed throughout its history to international discussions aimed at the setting up and maintenance of accurate standards of temperature. The absolute temperature scale, which is based on the gas laws, is difficult to realise experimentally and the aim had been to define an International Scale realisable with the common range of temperature measuring instruments—mercury in glass thermometers, resistance thermometers, thermocouples and spectral radiation pyrometers. In 1927 the proposal for an International Temperature Scale was put to the Bureau International des Poids et Mesures by the national standards laboratories of UK, USA and Germany and thereafter a considerable amount of correlating work was carried out in these countries. The NPL carried out accurate comparisons of the International Scale with the scale defined by primary standard mercury thermometers issued by BIPM and also determined the melting points of sulphur, silver, gold, palladium and platinum. Already early in the decade a new precision disappearing filament optical pyrometer had been constructed in the Laboratory, with carefully dimensioned sector discs to extend its range towards higher temperatures. This remained the standard until finally overtaken by photoelectric methods in the 1960s.

Many temperature measurements were carried out in industrial or other locations. Apparatus was designed in 1921 to measure the temperature of the air at various levels up to 150 ft as an aid to refraction studies in India. This was applied to the measurement of heights of mountains by distant

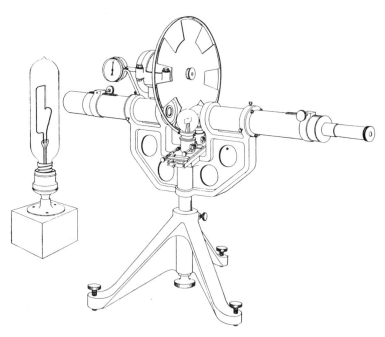

45   The standard disappearing filament optical pyrometer, in use from
1922 until the 1950s.

observation from the plains, where temperature gradients in the air cause refraction variations which call for considerable corrections. In the same year the national airship programme required a means of measuring the temperature difference between the gases in the envelope and the surrounding atmosphere, an important guide to the manipulation of gas and ballast. A valuable contribution to the country's steel industry came in the mid 1930s with the design of a quick immersion platinum thermocouple in a thin refractory sheath to measure the temperature of the melt in an open hearth furnace before tapping.

46   Measuring temperature in a steel works, using a thermocouple in a ceramic sheath.

For may years the Heat Division made substantial contributions to the work of the Food Investigation Board of the DSIR, examining refrigeration systems and heat insulating materials, measuring the heat properties of freezable foodstuffs and advising on instrumentation and measurement methods for use in cold storage. In 1923–24 the transport of apples from Australia received special consideration, a team from the Laboratory travelling in the refrigerated ships and making temperature, humidity and other studies. In 1929 the transport of meat from New Zealand was the subject of a similar investigation.

Another important piece of work undertaken by the General Physics Division was the production of an all-metal condensation type high vacuum pump, as invented originally by Langmuir. The first experimental versions were made of glass or silica, but it was the NPL metal models which marked the real start of high vacuum technology in this country. First a two-stage pump, comprising a jet pump and a condensation pump, was constructed; later the two were combined in a single unit.

The Radiology Division had charge of the British Radium Standard, renewed in 1934, and made measurements of the radium content of submitted samples. During the inter-war period radium valued at more than £1M was examined (it was estimated in fact that 20% of the world's supply had been tested at NPL). In addition the Division developed methods for measuring x-ray intensity and dosage, x-ray and gamma ray absorption and scattering, and for the efficient generation of x-rays. Techniques of using x-rays for the study of the internal structure of materials were developed in wide collaboration with other divisions of the Laboratory and with academic and industrial organisations outside. Metal crystals, magnet and trans- former steels, paints, tooth structure, pivots and jewels for industrial bearings, were some of the many subjects studied in this programme.

An x-ray protection service was offered to all users of x-rays, in hospitals and so forth, and an impressive advisory experience built up. Methods and standards were slowly evolved on an international basis.

The Sound Division was organised by Kaye in 1921, when some experimental facilities (which are in fact still there) were provided in the

47   Early radiological work.

basement of Bushy House. The acoustic properties of a large number of materials were measured.

48   Testing motor horns.

Noise was studied from such diverse sources as aircraft, motor horns, tube trains, motorcycles and air raid sirens. Methods of making acoustic measurements, in some cases embodied in instruments for commercial sale, were developed for the solution of a vast range of problems. An artificial ear (1933), providing an acoustic load simulating the characteristics of the human ear, was developed to make measurements on telephone receivers under normal use conditions. Methods of sound intensity measurement and frequency spectrum analysis were also studied and put into service.

The Division gradually accumulated an extensive experience in the acoustic design of new buildings and in the modification of old buildings to improve the acoustic properties. Among their responsibilities were a conference room in Whitehall (1921), the Ulster Parliament Buildings (1924), Melbourne Town Hall (1926), the Royal Albert Hall (1928) and the League of Nations Assembly Hall, Geneva (1938). Liquid ripple tanks (1926), shaped to provide a two-dimensional cross-section, were found to aid considerably the prediction of the internal acoustics of a building.

In 1933 a new acoustics laboratory of unusual design was erected close to the perimeter wall and Bushy Park and was thus free from traffic noise and vibration. Each experimental chamber comprised a room within a room, the two enclosures being nowhere directly connected. The inner room, with walls and floor 14 in thick, rested on concrete piers with an interposed slab of natural cork to damp out vibration. The outer walls were made nine inches

49   Measuring noise with a portable apparatus, 1932.

thick. All rooms were asymmetric in plan and elevation so that no two walls were parallel, nor were ceilings horizontal. Later a similar lagged room was added and a first floor room to enable floor structures to be tested.

The Optics Division was engaged principally on the design and measurement of the properties of the elements of optical instruments—refractive indices, curvature, prism angle, transparency, reflectivity etc. Tests were carried out on telescopes, binoculars, sextants, theodolites, photographic lenses and shutters (including those for the 1921 Mount Everest Expedition), polarimeters, saccharimeters and quartz control plates, colorimeters, meteorological radiometers and radiometric instruments in general. During 1919 in the aftermath of the Great War, 57 000 telescopes and 53 000 binoculars were certified, and in 1920 nearly 5500 sextants[5].

In 1921 studies commenced on a method of specifying colour in terms of three spectral colours and this, with some modification of detail, was adopted by the International Commission on Illumination in 1931. In due course it became possible to write colour specifications in scientific terms; the British Standards Institute issued such standards for some industries; colorimetric specifications were written for railway and road traffic signals, aerodrome and airway lights and so forth. Colour analysis instruments were developed at the Laboratory.

Ultraviolet and infrared spectroscopy and standard methods of radiation measurement were also studied. International intercomparisons were carried out between the scales of radiation maintained in different countries.

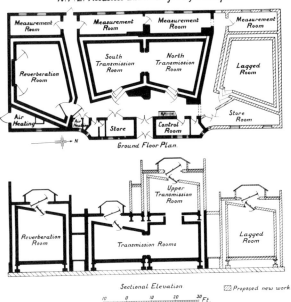

N.P.L. Acoustics Laboratory. Physics Dept.

50　Plans for the new acoustics laboratory, 1933.

In 1940 the work of the Optics Division was joined with that of the Photometry Division of the Electricity Department to become a new and independent Light Division.

Electricity and Radio Departments: 1919–1939

During World War I the Laboratory had worked on many electrical projects—signalling by earth currents, locating guns and planes by sound, detection of mines and submarines, measuring the speed of projectiles etc, while all switchboard and electrical instruments for the Navy had passed through on test. Now followed the challenges of peace time.

The Electricity Department calved off from the Physics Department in the middle of the war years; in its turn it made a substantial contribution to the foundation of the Radio Department in 1933. The NPL's electrical work had long been divided between a special-purpose building of 1907 and Bushy House, where the former cellars and servants' quarters in the basement provided stable temperature conditions, and some of the big wing rooms an iron-free environment suitable for precise work on magnetic and electrical fields. Here, under the charge of the Department, were those famous instruments for absolute measurements—the Lorenz machine, based on the work of Viriamu Jones, and the current balance of Ayrton and Jones, both of which had been modified and refined by F E Smith before the War. This was known as the Electrical Standards and General Measurements Division. The special-purpose electrotechnics building housed the Electrotechnics Division and the Photometry Division.

During the 1920s the rapid development of the transmission of electrical power at high voltage led to a demand for precise standards and measurements in these new elevated ranges. A special building was therefore designed and constructed on the Parks Estate, coming into use in 1927. Facing it across Rayleigh Avenue the Electricity Department acquired another extension in 1935, when a building for the Photometry Division was erected between the road and No 2 Tank. This released space in the electrotechnics building for the expansion of the measurements and standards work.

The Department did not have a regular Superintendent until 1929, when E H Rayner was appointed; previously the control had been divided between the Principal Assistants of the Department, of which Rayner had been one since the departure of F E Smith in 1920. The Radio Department was in charge at first of R A Watson-Watt, later of R L Smith-Rose.

The Electrical Standards Division devoted most of its effort to the maintenance and application of standards in electrical measurement. The

51   Historic mercury resistor (back), standard cells (left) and standard resistors (front right) in the NPL museum.

units nominally employed were the International Units as defined by an International Conference on Electrial Units and Standards, held in London in 1908. Due to the uncertainties of absolute measurement at that time it was deemed necessary to define the units in terms of certain concrete standards—resistance by that of a specified column of mercury and current by the rate of deposition (by the current) of silver from a silver salt solution. These definitions were maintained throughout the period between the Wars, though by the late 1930s sufficient confidence had developed in the measured absolute values to consider replacing International Units by Absolute Units; however the War delayed this move until 1947.

Ever since the foundation of the Laboratory considerable effort had been devoted to the realisation of all systems of units. The Lorenz machine and the Campbell Bridge method for absolute resistance determination (between the results of which there was no significant difference) were continuously improved, as was the current balance for absolute current. Working standards were produced by design and construction of standard resistors (still in use today), by wide ranging studies of the behaviour of Weston cells and by frequent intercomparisons with similar units produced in the national laboratories of other countries. The ingenuity of F E Smith and Albert Campbell had kept the NPL in the forefront of this field and their successors ably carried on the tradition.

The Board of Trade standards, passed over to the NPL in the 1920s, remained the British legal standards of the ampere (a somewhat simplified current balance), the volt (a precision electrostatic voltmeter) and the ohm (a resistance coil)[5].

The Division also developed a range of secondary standards for the measurement of derived electrical quantities, such as capacitance and inductance. The inter-war period saw a rapidly developing interest in radio standards for wavelength and frequency and for the impedance of components at radio frequencies. An important development of the 1930s was the Hartshorn–Ward dielectric test, which was operated over a wide frequency range. This was later exploited commercially and was extensively employed for many years afterwards.

D W Dye designed a multivibrator wavemeter which was extensively used for precise frequency measurement. It was based first on a stable tuning fork giving a few parts in 100 000 and later (1934) on a vibrating quartz ring oscillator giving one part in 10 million. An improved design of the latter, introduced by L Essen in 1936, achieved an even greater stability.

The transmission of standard radio wave patterns of the 'highest realisable stability' at specified dates and times began in 1924[6]. In the same year the *Annual Report* describes the use of the cathode ray oscillograph to compare frequencies by means of Lissajou's figures etc, and to delineate waveforms.

The Division was also responsible for a range of magnetic tests, including determination of the properties of permanent magnets, examination of

52   Board of Trade voltage standard.

magnetic steels, the measurement of energy losses in transformer iron, the investigation of materials under weak magnetisation and magnetic research generally. Of special interest were the horizontal and vertical (earth field) force magnetometers, built for Greenwich Observatory and installed in the magnetic observatory at Abinger in the mid 1920s. The former was based on an idea put forward by Schuster in 1911 and measured the horizontal field to a few parts in 100 000; the latter, an NPL design, measured the vertical field to a similar degree of accuracy. Both utilised carefully constructed Helmholtz coils of accurately determined dimensions, a current through which annulled the field component being measured.

During the 1930s an investigation was carried out which had profound effects on the safety of hospital operating theatres. Fatal explosions had often occurred when ether mixture was being used as the anaesthetic and these were traced to the build-up of electrostatic charges on the theatre equipment when the floor was insulated and the atmosphere warm and dry.

The Electrotechnics Division was responsible for tests on electrical measuring instruments of all kinds—ammeters, voltmeters, wattmeters, supply meters (responsibility for the type approval of which passed from the Board of Trade to the NPL in 1922), resistors, shunts, fuses etc, also for general investigation of electrical problems, such as the effect of heating and

53 Primary frequency standards: a valve maintained tuning fork (left) in use 1931–34, the Dye ring multivibrator (right) used 1934–36, and the Essen ring multivibrator which superseded it (centre).

of dielectric losses in power cables, the measurement of power losses in insulating materials, the AC resistance of cables and bus-bars, the earthing of electric circuits and studies of resistance materials, accumulators etc. The testing of circuit breakers gave rise to a national scheme somewhat on the lines later adopted by the British Calibration Service. The constituent firms of the Association of Short-Circuit Testing Authorities made available their test plant to other manufacturers at the request of the Laboratory, which then issued certificates of conformation to the relevant British Standard.

The design and commissioning of new facilities for measurement work at high voltages also fell to this Division. The building to house this work was completed in 1927 after the senior officers of the Department had thoroughly investigated similar installations in other parts of the world. Three identical transformers were provided, each capable of giving 375 000 V when supplied with power at 1000 V. They could be used in parallel, in three-phase or in series to give over a million volts, with power available up to 500 kW. The experimental area 120 ft × 60 ft × 45 ft high had an opening at one end to enable a high voltage line to be taken out of doors and provision was made for testing under artificial rain. Breakdown tests on insulators were done for manufacturers and methods of measuring effective and peak voltage in alternating circuits were developed. Yet another facility was an impulse generator capable of providing two million volts and a high voltage cathode ray oscillograph for investigating surge phenomena (i.e. lightning) and their effects on high voltage transmission line equipment. An experimental high voltage transmission line, similar to those used on the 'grid', was erected in the Laboratory grounds to facilitate these tests. This building added considerably to the power requirements of the site, which doubled between 1919 and 1926 and doubled again between then and 1931.

The Photometry Division carried the responsibility for the standards of light in Britain. The fundamental unit, the Candle, was maintained by a series of secondary standard incandescent lamps, frequently intercompared with those of other national laboratories. Later (1930) a primary standard of light was developed in the form of a black body operating at the freezing point of platinum. This was adopted internationally—its brightness being 60 candles per cm^2.

The Division made its biggest impact on the outside world by a range of illumination studies by daylight and by artificial light. Measurements were carried out and recommendations made concerning the lighting of factories, offices, picture galleries, coal mines etc, street and dock lighting, the effect of glare and the recovery of the eye after exposure to it, and special problems affecting types of work such as printing. During these decades advice was given to Buckingham Palace (so that debutants would look their best!), the National Gallery (1920–1), the Tate Gallery (1923) and on public buildings in general, often through the Illumination Research Committee of the DSIR. Advice given concerning the Pensions Ministry Building at Acton provides an early example of cost–benefit analysis. Four hundred lighting points were saved—an installation cost of £1000, an annual maintenance saving of £270 and an annual electricity supply saving of £100.

To aid the work a special shelter was erected at NPL in 1922— 60 ft × 30 ft × 17 ft high with a glass roof but no side walls—to house experimental models made of wood and canvas[7].

Investigation was also made on the design and proving of ships' navigation lights, railway and road signal lights, bicycle rear reflectors, and the standardisation of coloured glasses used in such lights.

Over the years the candle power of a range of light sources was determined from small electric lamps to lighthouses. Life testing of lamps provided a continuous and important study. Equipment for the measurement of luminous flux (i.e. the integration of the light emitted by a source in all directions) takes the form of a hollow sphere, whitened on the inside; emission from a viewing aperture at the side enables the luminous flux from an unknown to be compared with that from a standard. The earliest form, completed in 1921, was constructed inside a three foot diameter submarine mine case lined with concrete. By 1926 a ten foot diameter wooden sphere lined with zinc sheet was specially built for the measurement. Another

54   The 10 ft integrating sphere photometer, 1926.

feature of the period was the increasing use of photoelectric cells in many of the radiation methods.

The Radio Department, a separate identity after 1933, continued the work which had been in progress in the Wireless Division of the Electricity Department since World War I. During the inter-war decades fundamental researches were carried out into the propagation of radio frequency waves, first by a theoretical mathematical approach and second by experimental and observational work at long and medium wavelengths. Close studies were made of fading, of methods for field intensity measurement, of the mode of propagation of shorter wavelengths and of radio direction finding. Early work on direction finding included the development of receivers substantially free from errors due to spurious signals, of rotating beam transmitters (a permanent rotating beacon for marine navigation was installed at Orfordness in 1929), of directional aerial systems and so on. As early as 1922 a radio transmitter with a 450 ft aerial on masts 100 ft high and a counterpoise earth screen was designed and operated at Teddington for these measurements.

A programme of research into the nature and origin of atmospherics was directed towards the improvement of geophysical and meteorological

55   Measurement of signal strength, 1925.

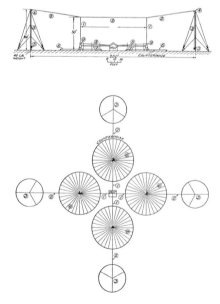

56   Adcock rotating transmitter aerial layout, 1930.

knowledge on the one hand and towards the mitigation of the most serious ultimate limitation on radio communication, as then known, on the other. This work involved simultaneous photographic recording of received signals at the Department's out-stations at Slough and at Leuchars, Fifeshire.

An investigation of the physical properties of the ionosphere, and of its effects on radio communication, carried out in cooperation with scientists outside NPL such as Professor E Appleton, involved the design of a 2 kW transmitter working over a wide range of frequencies and types of modulation (both continuous wave and pulse). One was installed at Teddington and used also for standard frequency transmissions, a second at Slough.

Studies were also made of the electrical properties of soil, of generation, utilisation and measurement of radio frequency waves of under one metre wavelength, of selectivity of receivers and of general electronic design principles. Work on life testing thermionic valves was begun as early as 1923. The mode of operation of high frequency oscillators of the Barkhausen and other types was probed; in 1932 came an early mention of the magnetron, a source with a future!

Techniques were developed for meteorological measurements by radio transmission from balloons. A 35 MHz oscillator in the balloon was modulated by varying fequencies in two different audio bands, the one recording temperature, the other pressure. Eventually the balloon burst and the equipment descended by parachute. Distances of 170 km and heights of 14 km were attained, the balloon's position being continuously determined by radio direction finding.

Antenna designs, both theoretical and practical, had to be carried out to support all this work, while an ever extending range of radio frequency measurement techniques was developed to handle problems as they arose.

There were non-radio problems too, such as the detection of larvae in timber by amplification of the sounds made in moving or gnawing.

The test work burden of the whole Department was considerable throughout this period—a total of 2000 to 2500 miscellaneous items, ranging from frequency meters and valves, through potentiometers and transformers, to lamps and signal glasses being tackled in each twelve month period. This produced a not inconsiderable income. Taken in conjunction with the basic standards work and the many special investigations successfully pursued, the work of the Department adds up to a substantial contribution to the electrical and allied industries of this country.

The radio work provided a sound basis for the development of the techniques of radar, the benefits of which were to be incalculable in the struggle to come.

Metrology Department: 1919–1939

The Metrology Department of the Laboratory separated from the Physics Department during the 1914–18 War at the same time as the Electricity Department. From this time until the end of World War II one man, J E Sears Jnr, held the Superintendency. Metrological work had begun at the NPL at the turn of the century, an obvious function for the type of organisation that the founders had in view; the stable temperature conditions of Bushy House basement provided an obvious site for the most precise work. The facilities had been augmented by the erection of a special-purpose building in 1908, to which had been added a substantial wing to handle the gauge testing work undertaken during the war years and a separate gauge workshop close to the Laboratory gates.

The Department was responsible in this period for the measurement of the physical quantities of length, mass and time, in both standards and industrial contexts, and of the direct derivatives of these such as area, volume, density, pressure and so on. By arrangement with the Board of Trade the Department undertook the statutory decennial comparisons (in 1922 and 1932) of the British Imperial Standards of the Yard and the Pound with their respective Parliamentary Copies. It had custody of the British National Copies of the International Metre and Kilogramme and these were intercompared at intervals with the BIPM at Sèvres. The standard of time, essentially based on astronomical observation, was the responsibility of the Astronomer Royal and the NPL used time signals from the Royal Observatory in the maintenance of time standards. Other essential duties of the department included finding suitable materials for the construction of secondary standards and developing techniques of measurement in all its various fields.

The staff did on occasion deplore the limited opportunity for 'pure' research, since their activities invariably involved only measurements of a relatively simple character. Yet the multiplicity of precautions required, and the great care which had to be expended on every step even of a simple process, called for a continuous high order of scientific application. The overall benefits which accrued to the engineering industry of this country are incalculable.

The NPL line standards of length were material bars of nickel, steel or invar, measured between lines scribed at right-angles to the length; in the case of end standards the length was defined as the distance between the parallel end faces. Ingenious comparators were developed to deal with both sorts in the Laboratory and on the shop floor.

Throughout this period experiments were being made to discover satisfactory conditions for using the wavelength of light as the ultimate standard of length. An outstanding experiment was completed in 1932 under carefully controlled temperature conditions, when the metre was determined in wavelengths of one of the red lines in the spectrum of cadmium using a series of Fabry–Perot type interferometers—$1, \frac{1}{3}, \frac{1}{9}$, and $\frac{1}{12}$ m long—in conjunction with a one metre end standard. During the period 1892–1940 nine wavelength determinations of the metre were carried out in various laboratories by optical interferometry, two of them at NPL. The mean of these results was later used as the experimental basis on which the metre was defined in terms of the orange radiation of krypton-86.

Length measurement test work involved the calibration of yard and metre scales and of tapes and wires used in geodetic surveys. To test the latter a corridor room with a 50 m tank and bench had been included in the 1908 building; over the period from 1911 to 1931 this bench was found to have extended by one centimetre. In 1921 two invar sag wires were built into the base so that its extension could be measured from the degree of sag. Here customer's tapes were calibrated to one part in 10^6 against NPL standards, which were in turn related to the primary length standards (figure 110).

In 1886 J H Poynting had a balance of advanced design constructed, and used it in an experiment to determine the mass of the earth. This balance was later passed to the Laboratory and came under the charge of the Metrology Department. It was used for building up secondary standards of mass until the early 1930s. In 1932 a new balance of NPL design came into service. It

57   The Poynting balance.

was installed in a closely controlled temperature environment in the basement of Bushy House where it operates to this day. For highest accuracy it is important that weights are interchanged on the balance pans without separating the knife edges from their bearing planes and this is done by directly steadying the beam after determining the equilibrium position. All manipulations are carried out by remote control from outside the balance enclosure.

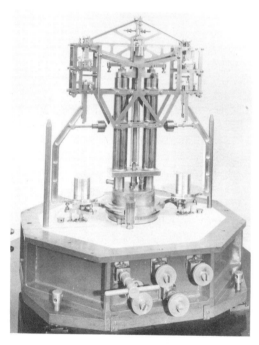

58   The precision balance, built in 1932, and used until recently.

The primary standards of mass were (and still are) of a platinum–iridium alloy, but this is too expensive for working standards and experiments were carried out to find alternative materials. These must be hard wearing, stable and uncorrodable, as well as non-magnetic. Stellite (a cobalt–chromium–tungsten alloy), nickel–chromium, Tobin bronze (a copper–zinc–tin alloy) and tungsten were all studied; ultimately nickel–chromium was preferred and recommended. In addition to the continuing programme of intercomparisons—national and international—the usual verification and testing of balances and weights and measurements of density for outside customers continued to provide an income throughout the decades.

During this period the work of NPL on time standards was limited to the subdivision of the interval between time signals received from astronomical observatories. Between 1912 and 1927 the subdivision was carried out by the Morrison (Galton) clock[8], which operated at constant pressure in an airtight case. After 1927 radio time signals from Greenwich (via Rugby), Paris (Eiffel Tower) and Hamburg (Nauen) were picked up on a receiver designed

59   Chronograph for comparing time signals.

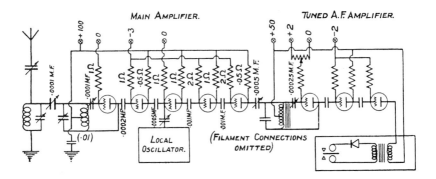

60   Selective receiving circuit for long and short wave time signals.

in the Wireless Division of the Electricity Department and recorded simultaneously with a telegraph signal from Greenwich received over Post Office lines; a Shortt clock, having two pendulums, a master and a slave working synchronously, carried out the subdividing function. The master had an exceptionally small coefficient of expansion and operated at a pressure of 3 cm of mercury. Thermostatic control of the ambient temperature was introduced in 1930. These various facilities, too, utilised the stable conditions of the Bushy House basement.

61   The Shortt clock in the basement of Bushy House. The clock remained in use until the mid 1950s when it was given to Liverpool City Museum.

An interesting introduction was that of the vibration clock, brought into service in the early 1930s. This utilised an invar bar maintained in longitudinal oscillation at its natural frequency by means of valve amplifiers. An AC output from the amplifier in exact synchronism with the bar was used to drive a small synchronous motor at 26 RPS, from which a worm reduction gear gave 1 RPS. It was impossible for this motor to run other than in step. Time measurement with an accuracy of 0.2 ms and free from some of the problems besetting pendulum clocks was claimed, but before this device had really got into its stride it was overtaken by quartz crystal controlled sources of even greater stability.

Watch testing, which had been done at Kew Observatory from 1884 to 1912, was continued at Teddington and eventually became part of the Metrology Department. Manufacturers, many of them Swiss, competed for success in Class A Tests, where entrants were placed in order of merit ('watch of the year') in a process which took 45 days to complete. Marine chronometers received an even more exhaustive treatment lasting 55 days.

In cooperation with the Electricity Department an experiment analogous to the Michelson–Morley experiment was made in 1936 to ascertain whether the effect of the Fitzgerald–Lorentz contraction on the frequency of longitudinal vibration of a rod had the consequence predicted by relativity theory. The beat frequency between two similar longitudinal quartz oscillations, one stationary, the other rotated in a horizontal plane, was measured, but no change was observed.

Area test work included instruments such as planimeters, areameters and leather measuring machines, while that for volume covered a wide range of volumetric glassware such as measuring flasks, burettes and pipettes. The volumetric glassware industry in this country only began to operate at all after the Continental cut-off of 1914, and it was fostered in its early years by the careful work of the Department. The number of vessels tested per annum rose from 400 in 1918 to 8000 in 1921 and thereafter fluctuated between 3000 and 7000 per annum.

A considerable range of pressure test work was processed—all manner of barometers for the meteorological service, surveying aneroids, altimeter aneroids and so on. Of particular interest were the aneroids taken to Mount Everest in 1922 and various certification measurements made on barographs employed in height record breaking flights (e.g. to 15 223 m in 1935).

Though experiments directed towards the design of a standard barometer had started before the War, only in 1921 was it decided to construct two of them. The first of these, the No 2 standard, was completed and installed in 1927. The glass limbs, so shaped as to place the two mercury surfaces on the same vertical axis, were immersed in a stirred water bath. A micrometer gauge, 30 in long, which measured the distance between the surfaces, could be removed and calibrated against length standards. The accuracy was estimated at ± 0.0005 in. The primary standard was completed in 1930 and came into service the following year. There were no glass tubes. The mercury column was contained in a stainless steel receptacle with glass windows for observation. Again the two mercury surfaces had a common vertical axis and the distance between them was compared directly with a line standard mounted alongside the barometer. The vacuum above the mercury surface was continuously maintained by vacuum pump. The accuracy was estimated at 0.0002 in.

The main working standard remained a Fortin type barometer transferred from Kew in 1912.

In 1938–9 an absolute value of 'g' was determined in the Department by means of a reversible pendulum. The result confirmed a similar measurement made in the USA and showed that the Potsdam reference value, taken as the international datum for gravity determinations, was too high. The value at Teddington was 981.1815 ± 0.0015 cm s^{-2}.

Important experimental and theoretical work was done on molecular cohesion and its influence on the wearing of surfaces. This was the kind of phenomenon to be explained: where two steel surfaces in relative motion came into contact — in the case of sliding motion with even light contact forces a single passage produced a track of rust but in the case of pure rolling motion there was no discernible effect. G A Tomlinson was able to develop molecular theories of solid friction and elastic hysteresis and a tentative theory of the solid state based on an empirical law of atomic repulsion, which was derived from a consideration of cohesional properties.

The Metrology Department had charge of the Blythswood ruling engine for diffraction gratings acquired by NPL in 1908. A screw thread of 20 turns per inch was driven by a 720 tooth gear wheel, so that an advance of one tooth advanced a nut on the screw by $1/14\,400$ in. A diamond tool attached to the nut scribed the line. This was the standard spacing; provision was made however for working at multiples and submultiples. The machine began regular operation in 1920 and continued throughout the inter-war years providing 200 or so first class gratings having between 2400 and 28 800 lines per inch.

A superficially convincing case can be made out that a calibration made at the Laboratory (e.g. for a slip guage of highest quality) needs error limits four orders of magnitude smaller than those required for components manufactured on the shop floor. Certainly the lead which has to be maintained does in some cases approach this.

The contributions of the Department to the engineering standards of this country have been substantial. Before 1914 such standards were almost non-existent. The very great effort devoted to the calibration of gauges in the war years transformed the industry. Then between the wars the Department continued to contribute ideas, instruments and high grade calibrations to every facet of engineering activity. The list is impressive—gauges, cylindrical gauges, plug and ring gauges, screw gauges, templates (e.g. for railway and tram rails), measuring machines, micrometers, surface plates and straight edges (general flatness and straightness measurement), gears and hobs, alignment and measurement of large structures. The standard leading screw lathe, transferred in 1912, was recontructed in 1934 to have a traverse of 5 ft (in place of 3 ft) and to deal with screws of all pitches (in place of 0.5 in pitch only). Its first job after reconstruction was to correct a 4 in screw threaded for 5 ft with a 0.25 in pitch Acme thread. The pitch was correct within 0.0005 in over the whole length at 68 °F.

Another important role played by the Department was in making precision measurements for other areas of NPL. The Electrical Standards

62   Gauge testing—a very important part of the Laboratory's function.

63   The standard leading screw lathe, after reconstruction in 1934.

Division of the Electricity Department in particular, in their work required accurate length measurements on the Lorenz machine, on the current balance, on the Schuster magnetometers sent to Abinger and on the calculable mutual inductance standard, while the tubular mercury resistance defining the International Ohm needed precise determination of bore diameter.

Last of all, and apparently unconnected with all the rest, comes the testing of taximeters. This work had started at Teddington in 1907 and was transferred to a special out-station in South London a year later. The Department continued to have responsibility for these tests in the inter-war years, carrying out type approval of new models and verifying some 10 000 meters per annum.

Aerodynamics Department: 1919–1939

Aerodynamics research was begun in the Engineering Department of NPL in 1909 and was continued in the Aerodynamics Department founded in 1917. Bairstow, the intended Superintendent, left at this time to take up an appointment in the Air Ministry and Stanton continued until R V Southwell took office in 1920. He in turn was supplanted in 1925 by E F Relf, who continued in the post until the end of World War II.

During the 1914–18 War activity in aerodynamics expanded dramatically and NPL made major contributions to the advances in theoretical and practical aspects of the stability of aeroplanes, airships, kite balloons and parachutes. Techniques had been developed for testing scale models of wings, ailerons, propellers and of complete models of aeroplanes in wind tunnels, and for interpreting the results in terms of the full size machine. Close cooperation was maintained at all times with the Royal Aircraft Establishment at Farnborough, with joint supervision of research programmes by the Aeronautical Research Committee of the Air Ministry.

By 1920 the following wind tunnels were in action on the site: the 'Duplex' of 7 ft × 14 ft cross-section, three of 7 ft × 7 ft cross-section having different HP and maximum speeds, two identical 4 ft × 4 ft tunnels and a 1 ft square tunnel—and these were sufficient for the experimental needs of the 1920s.

Meanwhile, in the Engineering Department, Stanton built the first effective supersonic tunnel in the world in 1921 and measured the drag of shells 2.3 mm in diameter. By 1931 his technique for designing wall shapes to give uniform steady flow had advanced sufficiently for him to achieve reliable tests on aerofoils and shells at up to 3.25 times the speed of sound in a 3 in diameter tunnel.

64 The duplex tunnel. This room was later converted to a staff canteen.

There were, however, limitations to the use of tunnels working at atmospheric pressure, since the flow patterns round two bodies of identical shape but different size will only be identical if the Reynolds number is the same for both. This condition can be more nearly achieved if the model tests are carried out in a medium having a higher kinematic viscosity, i.e. by using air at a higher pressure. A tunnel of this type was built in the USA in 1923 and considered sufficiently promising to encourage a similar construction at Teddington.

This had a working jet 6 ft in diameter, housed in a steel shell of 17 ft internal diameter and 50 ft long. The shell was 2.5 in thick and had a factor of safety of five when operated at 25 atmospheres. The four huge rings and hemispherical end-pieces, from which it was constructed, were transported by road from Sheffield and assembled on the site. An air screw driven by a 400 HP motor gave an air speed of 90 ft s^{-1}. Ingenious methods were developed for making the usual wind tunnel balance arrangements. The work was completed early in 1931 and the machine (the CAT) was in service by the end of the year.

The Aerodynamics Department's first high speed tunnel, completed in 1934, operated from high pressure air available when the CAT was being decompressed. This was capable of an air speed of 600 MPH.

Circulation in all the earlier tunnels was produced by an air screw (in the Duplex tunnel by twin air screws), which drew the air through the working section and discharged it to the room again—open return tunnels. In 1933–

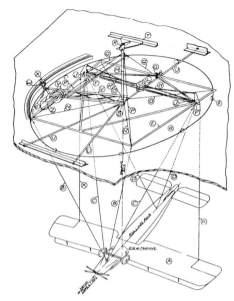

65   Balance to measure rolling and yawing moments on an aeroplane
model in a wind tunnel.

34 two open jet tunnels of elliptical section, with axes 7 ft × 9 ft, were added
to the facilities. Here the air was circulated by air screws through closed
return ducts above and below the working section. This served to minimise
the dissipation of the energy of the moving airstreams and air speeds up to
140 mph could be obtained.

The study, both theoretical and practical, of fluid flow around objects of
relevant shape occupied a significant proportion of the Department's effort.
In addition to the wind tunnel tests, further experiments on the tracing of
streamlines were carried out in an electrolytic water tank, using a model
made of conducting material and observing its effect on the electric field in
the tank. Important results of this work were published in 1929—systematic
application of the knowledge of streamline flow could greatly reduce aircraft
drag. The outcome was a clean-up of the designs of aeroplanes; the
decreased drag, in conjunction with the increased engine power available,
meant that speeds increased rapidly. The resulting problems of landing
were solved by the use of flaps or other projecting plates on aircraft wings—
another subject calling for extensive theoretical and wind tunnel investigation. Later retractable undercarriages were also tested.

The testing of complete models formed an important part of the work of
the Department. The rapid growth of the aircraft industry in the early 1920s
made it impossible to test all types, so it was decided to select one machine
and test it exhaustively. A 1/5 scale model of the famous Bristol Fighter was
subjected to a long series of tests between 1922 and 1924 (making it the most

66   Bristol Fighter model in the wind tunnel, 1923. The balance is positioned above the ceiling.

tested aircraft of all time until the advent of the Boeing 707). This was the first wind tunnel experiment in which the model incorporated an air screw driven by a specially designed internal electric motor.

In 1927 the Air Ministry decided to attempt to win back the Schneider Trophy (awarded for an air speed record round a closed course) then held by Italy. The NPL was asked to test 1/4 scale models of the proposed racing seaplanes. Measurements were made of the drag of wings, floats, fuselage and struts and/or combinations of these; as a result significant reductions of drag effects were obtained. The Duplex tunnel ran all through the night before the final contest to resolve a control instability. The aircraft was modified only hours before the race. The Trophy was won and then retained in 1929 and 1931. These planes were the forerunners of the later famous Spitfires.

The mathematical treatment of the stability of aeroplanes in flight was one of the earliest tasks undertaken by the Department. The phenomenon of stalling (loss of lift followed by loss of control), and the use of wing-tip slots to combat it, were studied in the wind tunnels during the early 1920s.

The flight phenomenon known as spinning—rapid rotation of the aeroplane in the stalled condition—was little understood in the early days of flying and was thought to lead inevitably to a crash. However experiments eventually showed that recovery was possible with correct use of the controls. Subsequently some machines were found to develop different spin characteristics; the rate of rotation was higher and the standard recovery

67   The Schneider Trophy seaplane.

tactics were found to be unworkable—the so-called 'flat spin'. Wind tunnel studies of spinning turned out to present great difficulties and special apparatus had to be designed to simulate the conditions. It was found that the design and location of tail-plane and rudder played a significant role.

As monoplanes were introduced for passenger carrying there were a number of fatal crashes. In some cases buffeting of the tail-plane by turbulence from the wing fractured the tail-plane. In others vibration of the wing-tips, known as 'flutter', was sometimes so violent that the structure of the wing failed. Wide ranging studies of this phenomenon, based on models of a Junkers monoplane and a Puss Moth aircraft, were inaugurated. Whereas most wind tunnel models were made as solid and rigid as possible, those for flutter had to be flexible with the weights and stiffnesses of the various parts of the model in the proportions they had in the full size aircraft. Devices to limit the range of movement had to be installed to prevent break-up of the model. The results of all these tests defined much more closely the parameters for the future design of wings, tails and control functions.

Research on air screws, again both theoretical and experimental, was continuously carried out. In the early 1920s families were tested with systematically varied shapes, numbers of blades and blade angles. The interaction between the body of the aircraft and air screws of both pusher and tractor types was also studied. A kindred problem cropped up in the autogyro, a rotating wing aircraft introduced to this country in 1925. A 10 ft diameter model was tested in the Duplex tunnel and its main flight characteristics determined.

Until the crash of the R 101 in October 1930, the airship had successfully contended with the aeroplane as the future means of air passenger transport. Government work on airships had been carried out since before the 1914–18 War, both on wind tunnel models and on the machines themselves in flight. Shapes and outlines, stability and control, lift and drag—all received close study in this period. There was a considerable set-back in August 1921 when the R 38 broke in half and crashed into the River Humber; two members of the NPL Aerodynamics Department (Pannell and Duffield) lost their lives. The accident happened during acceptance trials for the US Navy when the airship was put through manoeuvres at low altitude which it had been designed to withstand only in the rarefied air of much higher altitudes. Theoretical and experimental work was conducted towards the design of the R 101 and assistance given also towards that of the privately built R 100. After the disaster to the R 101 at Beauvais, when the heavily overloaded airship lost buoyancy as the barometric pressure fell sharply in a severe storm, had its fabric torn by severe ground turbulence, dived into a hillside and was destroyed by fire, the Government banned all further airship development.

International intercomparisons of wind tunnels were carried out during the 1920s, when aerofoil characteristics of a set of models (two airship forms and one wing form) were determined here and in France, Italy, Japan, USA, Canada and later Germany. The results were found to vary consistently with the intensity of turbulence in each tunnel and thus demonstrated convincingly the importance of turbulence in aerodynamic measurement.

Simultaneous records of horizontal and vertical components of wind speed taken on various high structures—the NPL towers, the Cardington meteorological tower and the Blackpool Tower—enabled the effects of gusts on stresses in aeroplane structures to be evaluated and at the same time provided valuable data for meteorologists in their studies of the influence of vertical gusts on weather phenomena.

Other measurements for which the Department became especially competent were in the field of air movement other than flying. Investigations were made on windmills, parachutes, aeroplane carrier ships, kite balloons; the wind resistance of planes, spheres, cylinders and spheroids was measured. During 1929 a model of the Rock of Gibraltar was used to determine the distribution of wind currents in its vicinity, information of considerable value to pilots flying in the neighbourhood; the results were found to agree closely with full scale observations. Tests were also made on the wind resistance of models of racing cars and of models, six coaches long, of LMSR and LNER trains.

The other departments of NPL collaborated frequently in aerodynamic problems—particularly noteworthy were the contributions of the Engineering Department on elasticity and fatigue (particularly in thin sheets), on engine problems and on heat transmission and friction over surfaces in an air current, and of the Metallurgy Department on materials for aircraft construction, light alloys, fabrics, dopes etc. Seaplane tests were carried out from time to time in the William Froude National Tank (WF Laboratory).

The tremendous contribution made by the Aerodynamics Department to the theoretical aspects of the subject must not be overlooked, though its complexity puts it outside the scope of this book. The Department was also responsible for the establishment of a host of techniques, measurement methods and instruments in this new and rapidly advancing science. The method of measuring air speed, for example, was based on a standard Pitot-static tube, which was designed and calibrated before World War I on the first of the whirling arms. Subsequently carefully made copies were distributed to other countries. Recalibration in 1926 could detect no change in the standard, though at this time certain more robust sub-standards were created in order to preserve the original.

68   The whirling arm, used until World War II.

As the shadows darkened in the later 1930s the work of the Department was concentrated increasingly on the needs of the rearmament programme. Some research lines disappeared, not to resurface until after 1945, others continued in secret and the results were seen in the skies rather than in the literature.

Ship Research: 1919–1939

The William Froude National Tank was constructed on the Laboratory site between 1909 and 1911, thanks to the generosity of Sir Alfred Yarrow who gave £20 000 towards the cost. G S Baker served as Superintendent from the foundation until retiring in 1941. During the 1914–18 War considerable contributions had been made to all aspects of naval warfare—the laying of mines and defences against them, torpedoes, submarine nets, fast craft for submarine chasing, seaplane floats and so on.

The tank was 550 ft long and 30 ft wide with a centre depth of 12.5 ft; the model under test was towed by an electrically driven carriage spanning the tank, which ran on carefully levelled rails enabling a uniform speed to be maintained over a greater part of the length. The apparatus for determining the resistance of the water to the motion of the ship model, or for making other required measurements, was installed on the carriage. Facilities for wavemaking were added in 1920 (2–6 ft high, 600 ft long or 2–12 ft high, 120 ft long with an average scale of 1/25).

The models, made of paraffin wax, were first moulded approximately to the form required and then shaped with the aid of a special cutting machine, to reproduce the lines of the ship as designed. The use of wax enabled the model to be rapidly and accurately made, and allowed the form to be altered subsequently to test the effect of modifications to the hull.

The programme of research and of testing came under the control of a special Advisory Committee with members elected by prominent shipping organisations and including some members of NPL's Executive Committee.

Increasing demands for test work during the 1920s led the Government in 1929 to offer funds for the construction of a second tank. This was completed in 1932 and is 678 ft long, 20 ft wide and 9 ft deep, with a similar arrangement of towing carriage. The two tanks are at right-angles along the sides of a re-entrant in the boundary between the Laboratory site and Bushy Park. The common facilities for model preparation, workshops, offices etc were placed at the junction of the two.

Another facility, provided this time by the generosity of Sir James Lithgow, was a propeller testing tunnel, installed and operational by 1937. This comprised a hooped pipe, 15 ft in diameter standing vertically, the cross-section of the pipe being 2.1 ft² in the experimental section at the top and 9.6 ft² at the bottom. A propeller circulated the water at speeds up to 30 rps; the tunnel could accommodate test propellers up to 9 in diameter under reduced pressure down to 5 % atmosphere.

The cost of overcoming resistance is one of the largest items in the balance sheet of any vessel. These tank experiments provided the best guide to the most economical form of hull and propeller and thus large savings in fuel consumption and general running expenses. Up to 1920 a total of 335 model tests had been carried out and a further 800 were completed during the inter-war years. Before the second tank was constructed the Laboratory staff often had to resort to shift work in order to get through the programme. The result of these tests was to achieve economies in the horse power of ship designs which amounted in some cases to 20–30 %. In the record number of 88 designs tested in 1936, four were improved by over 10 % and 48 more by 3 % (and this after a quarter of a century of this type of measurement on

69   No 2 Tank under construction.

behalf of the industry!). By 1936 it was estimated that an overall reduction of 10 % had taken place in the resistance to motion of a good ship form and this amounted to a saving in coal bills for British shipping of £4.5M per annum.

Experiments on models in the tanks were supplemented, whenever possible, by observations on actual ships. Members of the staff of the Laboratory made many voyages to obtain data relating to the motion of ships in rough weather and to study the conditions affecting the steering and manoeuvring power of ships, for comparison always with conclusions derived from work in the tanks. Such comparisons were vital in the general interpretation of results obtained from models.

Extensive studies were made in the tanks of the seaworthiness of ships— the influence of waves on resistance, propulsion and pitching. Also investigated was the manoeuvring of ships in both deep and shallow water, leading to important discoveries in the subject of rudder design.

The Department concerned itself continuously with optimising the designs of propellers. A series, one foot in diameter, incorporating variations in blade outline or pitch, blade section shape, number of blades, rake and pitch ratio, was tested behind a 24 ft hull and the optimum conditions determined. Variations of propeller behaviour with immersion were studied. Comprehensive tests were carried out on twin screw propellers, on

70 No 2 Tank. The workshops and offices can be seen on the extreme left.

the operation of propellers in backing a vessel, and on vibration and cavitation.

Between 1928 and 1932 the wind resistance of marine superstructures was investigated first by towing an inverted model in the tanks and later by obtaining comparative figures on the Laboratory's wind tower. A model of the *Mauretania* was floated on a tank 60 ft above the ground; good agreement was obtained with the inverted test in the main tank. The results enabled the wind resistance of some ships to be reduced by as much as 30 % by redesign of the superstructure. The effects of wind on manoeuvrability were also studied.

Programmes were devoted to the design of special-purpose vessels. Work begun in 1929 on coastal vessels produced a design having many advantages over previous forms. Barge forms were studied and the final design showed a speed gain of 33 % while using 3 % less power. The position and height of the paddles used on paddle steamers was reported upon. On behalf of the Air Ministry, and in collaboration with the Aerodynamics Department, work was done in the tanks on seaplane floats (for the Schneider Trophy planes and others) and on flying-boat hulls, at the time when these machines looked likely to dominate the long distance air passenger transport market.

71   The wind testing tower with a model of SS Mauretania on top. The
roof of No 1 Tank is in the foreground.

All this experimental work was backed, of course, by theoretical studies
which placed the William Froude Laboratory in the forefront of similar
organisations throughout the world. By the late 1930s the needs of war
meant a concentration of effort into appropriate channels and a clamp-down
on any information likely to be of assistance to a potential enemy.

Engineering Department: 1919–1939

The Engineering Department dates back to the foundation of the
Laboratory. The first special-purpose building on the site was erected for
their use in 1901, and this was extended northwards successively in 1907,
1910 and 1920 as the Department grew in size. A building for creep testing
was added in 1938. From the start T E Stanton held the Superintendency
and he continued in post until his retirement in 1931, when he was
succeeded by H J Gough. The Aerodynamics Department, originally a part
of the Engineering Department, separated off in 1917 but, because of the
almost immediate departure of Bairstow, Stanton continued to superintend

until 1920. Road research, started in 1911, remained in abeyance during the war years, but was then revived and finally, in 1933, became the Road Research Station at Harmondsworth, where it came directly under the charge of the DSIR.

The testing equipment of the Department had been built up before and during the War to include testing machines and apparatus for determination of strength, elasticity, ductility, hardness, abrasion resistance, fatigue resistance and impact resistance of engineering materials, apparatus for aero-engine testing, apparatus for calibration of air and water flowmeters, apparatus to test the efficiency of steam pipe covers and apparatus for the calibration of pressure gauges. The build-up of facilities continued throughout the inter-war decades.

The closer Government control now exercised by the DSIR meant a large increase in research work owing to demands for investigations by Government Research Committees and Research Associations. Lengthy programmes of work were carried out for DSIR Committees dealing with lubrication, gas cylinders, springs, high temperature metal properties, and buildings for the Aeronautical Research Committee, the Air Ministry, the Ministry of Transport, the Institution of Mechanical Engineers, the British Standards Institution, the Electrical Research Association and the British Non-Ferrous Metals Association; also to a lesser degree for the Home Office, the Forest Products Research Board, the Board of Trade, New Scotland Yard, the Mechanical Warfare Board and HM Office of Works.

Some of the earliest researches of the Department related to the strength of materials and these were carried forward with the aid of an ever increasing selection of test machinery. Of particular importance were the investigations of the effects of repeated and alternating stresses—tension, compression, shear, torsion, bending, etc, i.e. the causes of failure of metals and other materials on account of fatigue. Earlier work had provided information of practical value in engineering design; now researches were devoted to relating fatigue phenomena to the atomic lattice structure by making measurements on metal single crystals, the changes in which could be studied by x-rays, microscopy and other techniques. Experiments were carried out also to demonstrate the role of corrosion in the apparent results of fatigue testing. Metallic aggregates were also studied. Special machines were designed for applying any desired combination of bending and torsion to a specimen.

High temperature studies provided a continuous programme of work which grew in importance throughout the decades. As early as 1923 measurements of tensile strength, torsion, fatigue, impact and hardness were offered at temperatures up to 700 °C. As engineering designs called for increasingly higher working temperatures and stresses, the behaviour of materials under these more extreme conditions was studied in cooperation with NPL's Department of Metallurgy and Metallurgical Chemistry, not

72   Engineering main bay with various test rigs set up.

only for better utilisation of existing materials but also to develop new alloys which would meet the new demands. 'Creep', or the flow of metals under load at high temperatures, was studied under closely controlled conditions in special furnaces.

A lengthy investigation was held into the mechanical properties of standard spring steels, including tests on complete laminated springs fitted to lorries. In a 30 cwt lorry driven at 18 mph a stress range of 19–42 tons per square inch was found to be imposed 25 times an hour. A machine was built to apply endurance tests to springs in the laboratory. As a result improvements took place in design and performance, since it was revealed that fatigue failure depended largely on surface conditions and not on bulk shortcomings of the material.

Failure of other mechanical engineering items were also studied—wrought iron chains and lifting gear, rails, bolts and studs, crane hooks, etc, which were referred to the Department and the causes found and reported upon. An investigation of the failure of wrought iron chains at low temperatures was made in conjunction with the Metallurgy Department. No intrinsic brittleness was found in the temperature range in question (down to $-78\,^{\circ}$C), but surface defects were found to produce notched-bar brittleness leading to the observed failure.

73   Chain testing machine with 20 ton hammer.

Other investigations dealt with the methods of notched-bar impact testing, including determinations of the stress–strain–time relations measured electronically during the test. The Department's work became the basis of the British Standard Specification and contributed to eventual international agreement on test methods. A study of hardness test methods

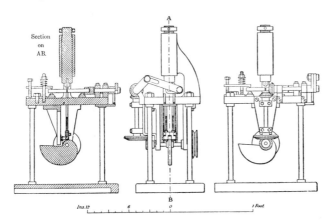

74   Repeated impact testing machine for bending notched bar specimens.

led to the adoption of the Brinell test by the British Standards Institution and the development of a diamond indentation hardness test used to measure thin films with very low loading. Special machines were also designed to study resistance to wear.

The effect of wind pressure on structures had been one of the earliest studies demanded of the Department and this work continued steadily throughout the period. Some of the early experiments were made with models in a wind tunnel, but later tests were made on full size structures in the open. Tower Bridge, with a span of 225 ft and a height of 141 ft, was a subject for many years; later similar work was done on the 1340 ft span of the Severn Railway Bridge at Sharpness. With gusts up to 55 mph, the maximum effect of a gust was only occasionally in phase at any pair of points (even only 260 ft apart), i.e. the wind front was always made up of eddies. Attention was also given to the measurement of wind pressure on large roofs—of a factory in Manchester and, at a later date, of an aircraft hangar.

In the early 1920s the Department was requested to assist in improving the ventilation in the Debating Chamber of the House of Commons. Experiments were carried out at NPL on a 1/8 scale model, after the validity of the comparison between this and full scale had been determined. Recommendations were then made which were put into effect on the site. The direction of air flow in the Chamber was demonstrated by observation of smoke produced by a special firework.

75   Ventilation tests in the House of Commons Debating Chamber.

So diverse is the range of the problems tackled by the Department in these years that they have to be treated piecemeal hereafter, with almost no room left for comment. They include—the transmission of heat from surfaces to fluids flowing over them, which has important applications to the cooling of motor car and aeroplane engines, the study of the allied subjects of fluid friction and the friction between surfaces and fluids, research on the detonation or explosion of gaseous and liquid fuel mixtures and experiments on the flow of oils and other liquids in pipes.

Floors up to 16 ft × 6 ft and columns up to 20 ft long made of concrete or reinforced concrete were tested with loads of up to 50 tons in a special machine, offered to NPL in 1914 and designed jointly by NPL and Sir John Cowan, who donated it. Other tests carried out on concrete included percolation tests and repeated loading tests (77 loadings per minute for a year).

The efficiency of engines and of toothed gear and worm wheels was often determined. A spur gear testing machine was presented to the Laboratory in 1921, enabling measurements to be made under various conditions of load, speed, centre distance and lubrication; these studies were extended by the production of special gears having known deliberate errors. Another machine, due to Daimler–Lanchester, was used for tests on worm wheels.

76   Testing lubricating oils in the Lanchester Worm Gear Machine, 1920.

From time to time the Department was called upon to make measurements of vibration and movement of buildings. The problems included the vibration of the (then) New Scotland Yard building when District Line trains passed below it, and work continued on the relative movements of parts of the Tower of London, where the Salt Tower was found to move 1 mm per year towards the River, while the Quay wall moved 0.5 mm per year in the opposite direction.

Studies were also undertaken of the motion of streamline forms (in part by experiments on very small models in a high velocity air current, up to 3.5 times the speed of sound), lubrication, requiring further specially designed machines, the strength of cylinders used for the storage and transport of compressed and liquefiable gases, pipe flanges for use at high pressures and temperatures, the application of electric welding to steel building structures, driving belts, crankshafts for aeroplane engines, keys and keyways, leading to a revision of the British Standard Specification, the forces on cutting tools during the machining of metals and optimum working speeds for various materials, brake lining efficiency, rust prevention in stored steel parts, the air resistance of passenger trains, the strength and elasticity of overhead transmission lines, roller bearings for tramcars (experiments in

77   Floor and column testing machine.

Wigan and later London), production and testing of standard reference jets for carburettors, shatter tests on safety glass, wear of tractor track links, and many, many more.

The routine test work, amounting to 1000 to 1500 items per annum, also covered a wide range—strength of materials especially fatigue, impact, wear and hardness, tests of the efficiency of engines and gears, testing of agricultural tractors and implements, of steam pipe coverings, pressure gauges, lubricants, bearing materials, fans, etc. Cast iron girders 40 ft long from the British Museum (cast in 1834) were tested to destruction in a special set-up.

The road research facilities (until 1933) covered the endurance and wear of concrete and other road surfaces, carried out partly with the Laboratory test facilities, to which was added an asphalt mixing plant in 1922, and partly on experimental road sections in the field. The effect of vehicle impact, both on roads and on vehicles, was the subject of a further study. The mechanism of skidding was explored with the aid of a motor cycle and special sidecar, the wheel of which had multiple movement and braking facilities. A model four wheel vehicle, of wheelbase variable up to 12 in and with the wheels independently braked, was also employed. This was one of the first NPL activities to move out to an independent existence; it was the forerunner of the present-day Transport and Road Research Station at Crowthorne.

Metallurgy Department: 1919–1939

The Department of Metallurgy and Metallurgical Chemistry was established in 1906 from what had been a section of the Physics Department. The first Superintendent was Dr W Rosenhain and he held office until retiring in 1931; he was replaced by Dr C H Desch, who continued until World War II. The Department was housed in a new building donated by Sir J Wernher in 1910, a rolling mill was added in 1913 and a second storey to the Wernher Building in 1922. Finally a new workshop was added in 1932. Close liaison was always maintained with the Engineering Department and many joint studies were undertaken into the failure of metal components in various engineering fields.

The primary work of the Department was the investigation of the physical and mechanical properties of metals and alloys and of their constitution and structure. The work had many aspects. It included systematic examinations of over 50 systems of alloys, in which the proportions of the different constituent metals were varied over a wide range and the properties of the resulting materials were carefully studied with a view to determining in what manner the several constituents affect them and to selecting for further investigation those alloys, or groups of alloys, in the series which might be most valuable for a variety of practical purposes. The work included also the careful investigation of the effects, in the production of such alloys for practical use, of different heat and mechanical treatments, and of the various processes which must be employed in the application of the material for constructional purposes. The experimental methods adopted ranged from microscopical and x-ray examination of the structure of the metal or alloy to mechanical, thermal and electrical tests of the resulting product; here assistance was often given by other departments of NPL. Related studies included types of furnace and refractories for furnace lining and for non-contaminating specimen containment.

For most of the period the Department was actively engaged in the study and development of aluminium and magnesium alloys. The introduction of light alloys of aluminium for aircraft construction during the 1914–18 War had been largely due to the work of the Laboratory. This line of research was continued during the 1920s and led eventually to the discovery of two important new series of alloys. The first, containing magnesium with small amounts of aluminium, silver and other metals, had greatly increased strength at ordinary temperatures; alloys in the second series, containing cerium and small proportions of other metals, retained their strength at high temperatures better than many light alloys previously in use.

An important contribution to this work came from the discovery of methods to eliminate dissolved gases (notably hydrogen) from metal melts. The melt could be cooled slowly, expelling dissolved gas, and then remelted quickly; dissolved gas could be removed by bubbling nitrogen through the melt; another method involved the use of volatile chlorides.

Considerable effort was devoted to the preparation of metals, including some which in those days were less well known, in a high state of purity, the products obtained serving for the determination of the physical properties of the pure metals and for the study of alloy systems free from impurities. In particular the production of pure iron (99.985 % iron) in ingots weighing about five pounds was reduced to a routine operation. The iron was prepared initially by electrolysis of ferrous chloride; then cleaned, dried and melted in an alumina crucible *in vacuo* or in an atmosphere of hydrogen; finally prolonged exposure of the melt to a stream of pure dry hydrogen was followed by fusion under vacuum. Chromium was produced by the electrolysis of chromic acid, manganese by the alumino–thermic method in an induction furnace, being collected as a vapour and then condensed. Very pure silicon was produced by a chemical method for use in the alloy studies. Other metals prepared in a high state of purity included magnesium (in much demand for the light alloys work), cadmium (which, alloyed with copper, produced a material highly suited for overhead electrical conductors) and beryllium, which until the 1920s had never been produced in quantity. In spite of its lightness beryllium made little contribution at this stage to light alloy studies, but alloys with heavier metals showed remarkable age-hardening properties.

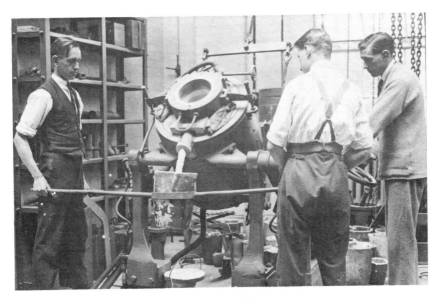

78   Tapping a crucible, 1920s.

Throughout this period the Department carried out a series of penetrating studies of this phenomenon of age-hardening of alloys and made significant contributions to both theoretical and practical aspects of what proved to be a highly controversial subject.

A programme of study of alloys of iron (with oxygen, phosphorus, silicon, chromium and manganese) ran for many years under a committee of the Institute of Mechanical Engineers. This involved a wide ranging assessment of refractory materials, suitable for the containment of melts without contamination, which in turn provided a basis for many future industrial processes. Trials were carried out to discover the best heating methods and the most suitable designs of furnace. High frequency induction heating offered many attractions. An American design, working at 25 kcps (25 kHz) derived from a mercury spark gap was replaced in 1927 by a valve generator designed at NPL operating at 500 kcps–1 Mcps. Considerable precautions had to be taken to confine the radiation inside the furnace.

Another important alloy system was that of nickel–chromium, which produced materials with outstanding high temperature properties—the ancestors of the Nimonic alloys used in jet engines.

From the start it had been realised that research on constructional materials could not be effectively conducted by laboratory experiment alone. Accordingly equipment was acquired for production and working of metals on a semi-industrial scale. The various processes of casting, forging, rolling etc could be carried out under conditions admitting of precise control

of the factors affecting the ultimate product and especially of the temperature and general heat treatment. The facilities included a foundry, in which
were installed furnaces of various types including the high frequency
induction models, a rolling mill, driven by a 60 HP electric motor, and
mechanical hammers for forging.

79   The rolling mill, 1919.

For many years a study of dental alloys was carried out, especially of those
amalgams used for filling teeth. Techniques had to be developed for the
alloying of mercury with other metals and for examination of mercury alloys
at reduced temperatures.

An important sideline to the specific researches was the continuous
development of techniques of metallurgical research. Methods were evolved
for plotting heating and cooling curves and a chronograph designed for the
plotting of inverse rate curves (the time for a given temperature change
versus temperature). The actual heating or cooling of the specimen was in
the meantime carried out by moving through a uniform temperature
gradient in a special furnace. Instruments were also designed to plot
resistivity, expansion and magnetic susceptibility against temperature
and time. The application of x-rays to metal studies was also actively
pursued.

Special investigations were frequently undertaken on behalf of industry to elucidate, and if possible find remedies for, difficulties occurring in engineering manufacturing practice. This was the main area of collaboration with the Engineering Department. Among the components reported upon were: boiler plates and particularly the cracking of these between rivets; connecting rods and other engine parts such as gudgeon pins, crankshafts and pistons; chains and hooks, which were found to fail as a result of surface hardening; springs and their failure under fatigue conditions; boiler tubes; turbine blading; permeability of wood to gases; and so on. Gas cylinders which had failed in service were examined and the cause of failure determined. This work, done for the Home Office, has continued to the present day.

Alloys suitable for coinage were reported upon for the Royal Mint in 1928; in the late 1930s an interesting series of studies of ancient metals was undertaken on behalf of the British Association, when objects from Troy, Cyprus, Palestine and elsewhere were examined spectrographically and under the microscope. Dr Desch, the then Superintendent, had strong archaeological interests.

A chemical laboratory attached to the Department carried out systematic analyses of metals and alloys and produced a series of standardised samples of steel for various applications. This was the principal analytical chemical laboratory in the whole of NPL and therefore provided a service to other departments. In the early 1920s major studies were made on behalf of the Aerodynamics Department of substances and processes relevant to airships and aeroplanes—the doping of fabrics, the permeability of doped fabrics, their deterioration in sunlight and so forth.

In addition to the chemical facilities the Department offered unique collaboration facilities to other departments of the Laboratory, demonstrating the powerful tool created by assembling diverse scientific disciplines within the walls of one establishment. In collaboration with the Electricity Department a new resistance alloy, called Ohmal, having properties similar to those of manganin, was developed and manufactured for the winding of standard resistors. Collaboration with the Physics Department led to advances in protective sheaths for high temperature thermocouples which benefited the sciences of both temperature measurement and metallurgy. Materials for the construction of standards of mass and length were researched and prepared on behalf of the Metrology Department.

World War II: 1939–1945

With its long connection with Services departments and with many branches of industry, and with diverse facilities in a range of disciplines, the

NPL entered World War II in an excellent position to aid the war effort. Control continued to be vested in the General Board and its Executive Committee, but in 1943 a revision of the terms of reference increased the numbers on the former and included on it for the first time representatives of the British Standards Institute and the Institute of Metals. In 1945 the Tank Advisory Committee was reconstituted as the Froude Ship Research Sub-Committee of the Executive Committee.

Dr C G Darwin, who took office in 1938, was Director throughout the war, though during a lengthy absence in Washington as Director of the Central Scientific Office of the British Supply Council, Sir Edward Appleton, Secretary of the DSIR, acted in his place. Early in the War NPL Departments were renamed Divisions, while the portions of departments formerly called Divisions were now called Sections.

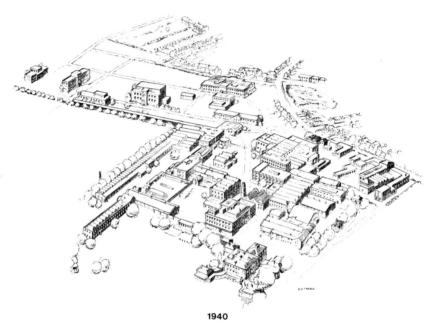

1940

80   The site 1940, by R. D. Treble.

Organisational changes involved the creation in 1940 of a separate Light Division, comprising the Photometry Section of the Electricity Division and the Optics Section of the Physics Division; T Smith was the first Superintendent. In 1945 a Mathematics Division was set up with J R Womersley as Superintendent. There were Superintendency changes in most divisions; E F Relf left the Aerodynamics Division in 1945 and his place was taken by A Fage; E H Rayner retired from the Electricity Division in 1940 and was replaced by R S J Spilsbury; S L Smith left the Engineering Division in 1944 and was succeeded by G A Hankins; C Sykes replaced C H Desch, who left the Metallurgy Division in 1940 and he in turn gave way to N P Allen in 1944; W G C Kaye of the Physics Division died in 1941 and his place was taken by W F Higgins, the Secretary of the Laboratory, who combined both offices until 1944, when E S Hiscocks took over as Secretary; control of the Ship Division passed from G S Baker to J L P Kent in 1941; the Radio Division stayed throughout with R L Smith-Rose and the Metrology Division with J E Sears Jnr.

Between 1939 and 1945 new building was confined entirely to extensions for the Aerodynamics Division, whose work was of unique importance in the war situation. Their high speed tunnel, adjacent to the compressed air tunnel, was completed in 1939. Then in 1940 followed a series of buildings at the far end of the Parks Estate in the north-west corner of the site—whirling arm (a hexagonal structure); low turbulence tunnel; 13 ft × 9 ft tunnel; twin 9 ft × 7 ft tunnels; and a water tunnel.

Preparations for war had included the digging of trenches in the grounds between the buildings and here and there a number of deeper shelters. Sadly the only bomb to land on the site and explode scored a direct hit on one of these in November 1940 and 5 townspeople from Teddington sheltering there overnight lost their lives. A large bomb which fell alongside No 2 Tank failed to explode but subsiding slowly into the clay subsoil (34 ft deep and 14 ft sideways) provided considerable problems to the Bomb Disposal men, which were not solved until April 1941.

81　Digging shelters and trenches, 1938.

In the Aerodynamics Division it was decided, alongside all the practical problems requiring rapid solutions, to continue with fundamental aerodynamical research; this was amply justified by a series of results which had immediate applications. Practical advances were made in the research on low drag aerofoils leading to a marked improvement in aircraft performance. The only high speed tunnels in the country in the early days of the War were a one foot circular and a 20 in × 8 in rectangular tunnel, and these were continuously used for study of high speed phenomena. Later the one foot tunnel was modified to enable tests to be carried out at supersonic speeds. Schlieren and direct shadow photographs of flow past aerofoils at supersonic speeds were the first taken in this country. New problems of stability and control, and of flutter, which arose as the speed of aircraft increased, were overcome and the results quickly applied in the air.

82   Removing an unexploded bomb from below the ship tank.

Prototype aircraft tested in model form in the Duplex wind tunnel included the Horsa and Hamilcar gliders, the Miles Monitor, Spiteful and Spitfire VI. A great deal of time was devoted to reducing the hazards of flying to aircraft carriers. Work was also carried out on designs for parachutes and barrage balloons; the compressed air tunnel was used to investigate the drag and stability characteristics of projectiles, depth charges and mines; measurements were made on rockets; the wind resistance of Bailey bridges was determined; and aid was given in the development of a system (FIDO) for the dispersal of fog from runways.

83 A Schlieren photograph showing the shock wave around a circular
cross-section vehicle.

In addition to continuing a high level of calibration work the Electricity
Division carried out a number of special military projects. The protection of
ships against magnetic mines and torpedoes was studied in collaboration
with the Admiralty; the detection of buried bombs and mines was explored
and apparatus built for fitting to a tank, which enabled it to travel at 5 mph
and still detect anti-tank devices in its path. Considerable effort went into
the protection of barrage balloons and their crews against lightning.
Currents of hundreds, even thousands, of amperes were found to flow in
cases of direct strike; complete protection was impossible but lightning
conductors on the balloons reduced the risk, while precautions could be
taken on the ground to safeguard the crews almost completely.

An electrical resistance measuring device was developed to provide a
rapid non-destructive test for armour-piercing shot; 180 samples of a
photoelectric gauge designed in the Division for the inspection of small arms
ammunition were produced commercially. Spark gap modulators were
designed for a radar transmitter; the voltage characteristics of radio
frequency cables were measured; a range of magnetic measurements
contributed to several areas of war effort; NPL acted as the national
standards laboratory for radio measurements; a moisture meter and a meter
for measuring small time intervals were developed in the Division and
manufactured commercially.

The Engineering Division continued with its broad categories of work,
namely, the properties of engineering materials, and the principles of fluid
dynamics and their application to gas and liquid flow and to lubrication. In
the recently completed Creep Building 43 creep testing machines were in

continuous use throughout the war. High temperature alloys for gas turbine blades were exhaustively studied for creep and fatigue—existing materials, others newly developed in the UK and the USA, and others captured from the Germans. Other investigations were made of aluminium alloys for aircraft engine pistons and carbon steels used in steam heaters and pipes.

A programme of stress analysis of aircraft and other structures included a wide ranging series of subjects—materials of a fibrous type, sandwich structures, as used in the Mosquito aircraft, plastics and in particular fibre reinforced materials.

The work on gas cylinders was extended to balloon barrage hydrogen cylinders, to containers for liquefied gases and to the design of a new and lighter tanker wagon for road transport of ammonia. The failure of helical springs used in small arms artillery was investigated and their behaviour in weapons such as the Bren and the Piat evaluated. Some of the earliest strain gauges made in this country were the work of the Division, which supplied them to many outside research projects.

A 50 ton standard load machine was set up and the load blocks calibrated against NPL mass standards. Mounted in a temperature controlled enclosure, this was soon being used for test work on behalf of national and allied scientific effort.

An 11 in supersonic wind tunnel was completed in 1942, providing wind speeds up to 2.5 times the speed of sound. Problems concerned with ballistics, guided projectiles, rockets and the possibility of supersonic flight were thereafter studied.

The lubrication of bearings for the gas turbines used in jet aircraft and many general problems in fluid mechanics were also successfully tackled. Other special war projects included work on the Pluto pipeline; the proposed floating airfield to be made of ice (Habakkuk), anti-tank mines, net defences against torpedoes, flame throwers and apparatus for dealing with unexploded bombs—a diverse range helping every branch of the Services.

The Optics Section of the Light Division confined itself entirely to war work; a very large volume of testing was handled in addition to many special investigations. Contributing to the design of optical instruments, studies were made of light transmission and its measurement, scatter, airtightness, contrast between faint objects and graticule markings and precision of sighting with various forms of graticule. Photographic apparatus was reported upon on behalf of all the Services. In colorimetry, investigations were made of the colour temperature scale, new glass optical filters, glass bloomed with cryolite, haemoglobinometry and many other items.

The Photometry Section of the Light Division also handled a range of work similarly divided between testing and research. The projects in the latter category were numerous and only a few can be listed—luminescence and luminescent materials, the brightness of the night sky, light transmission through the atmosphere, photometry of searchlight illumination, the effects of glare on vision, visibility and threshold intensity of various sources, obscuration of moonlight by a smoke screen, lights as a dazzle source, sky scanning with binoculars, glaze effects of gun flashes, gunlayers' telescopes, incendiary marker bombs, photoelectric sun compass and so on.

The Metallurgy Division also made extensive contributions to the war needs of the nation. Particular problems which received attention were the examination of steel plates perforated by bomb fragments, the failure of alloy steel gas cylinders, the utilisation of duralumin scrap, the porosity of castings, armour-piercing shot and shell caps (which took up a high proportion of the effort), heavy naval shells, magnetic powder core materials for high frequency inductance coils, tank track shoes, industrial welding, cutting tools, gun barrel broaches, and moisture-proof packing.

Some items in the pre-war research programme were deemed of immediate importance and work on them continued. The Division pursued studies of magnesium alloys, the behaviour of materials at high temperatures, the gas content of metals and the use of x-rays and electron diffraction in metallurgical work. An electron microscope was set up in 1940, the only one of its type available in this country at that time, and a diversity of problems was solved with its aid. New refractories were developed and the usual range of investigatory test work, concerned with the failure of metals in practice, was undertaken. Tests were made on welds, springs, gun parts, tools and high speed cutting steels, gauges and gauge steels, rivets and mandrels, metal from burnt-out buildings, agricultural equipment, steel cartridge cases, smoke bomb bodies etc.

During the war years the Metrology Division concentrated, as might have been expected, on measurements involving the basic parameters of length (the ruling of scales and a vast range of test work), mass (non-magnetic material for weights and another range of test work) and time (watch testing and the provision of standard time signals; the comparison of radio signals and clocks at the Laboratory was improved to ± 0.0002 seconds per day).

As in World War I their contribution to the armament industry by precision testing of gauges was quite outstanding. Preparations began in 1936 when adequate stocks of gauges were planned to meet future needs. Between then and 1945 2 050 000 were tested; 50 staff did nothing else throughout the war years, while the overall number engaged in all work rose from 117 in 1937 to 267 in 1943. Pneumatic gauging methods developed at NPL enabled four or even six dimensions to be checked simultaneously. In one year 4.6M shells were gauged at 900 per hour, saving 16 000 operator-hours in the process.

A new test chamber for barometers, in which direct comparisons between test and standard could be made, enabled 1000 to be calibrated per annum. 800 other instruments were tested per year; tests were carried out on large machine tools and, between 1943 and 1945, 20 leading screws corrected and calibrated on the standard lathe. An assortment of mechanical measuring equipment was designed and prototypes made; particularly newsworthy was a set of 12 block gauges which could be used in combination to produce any angle in steps of 3 seconds of arc between 3 seconds of arc and 81° and, in conjunction with a square block, any angle up to 360°. Research was continued into the manufacture and testing of gears; surface finishes were evaluated; the screw threads on the British service rifle rationalised; and discussions carried forward with allied countries on international engineering standardisation.

The Physics Division met a wide range of problems with its particular expertise. The Heat Section studied alternative materials for cold storage insulation; the transport and storage of meat in the tropics; the heat treatment of stored grain to prevent pest infestation; the design and operation of a large chamber for testing vehicles and equipment under tropical conditions; heat transfer in temporary buildings used in the tropics; improving temperature conditions inside tanks for desert use; and the thermal conductivities of substitute insulating materials and of sprayed metal coatings. Measurements of temperature were made on jet turbine blades, on air at high altitudes, on gun barrels, in the pasteurisation of milk, and on flame projectors. Test work, particularly on clinical thermometers, never flagged.

The Radiology Section made its chief contribution in the fields of x-ray radiography, dosimetry and protection and in radium measurement. X-ray radiographic techniques were adapted for the study of plastic armour (granite chippings in non-inflammable bitumen), of bomb and shell fragments, of the structure of jet turbine blades and of miniature metal rectifiers, while 3500 complex aircraft castings were tested for flaws by a multi-directional method. Dosimeters, previously of Continental origin, had to be constructed and calibrated in this country. A simple dosage test, determined from the blackening of photographic film, was introduced for all x-ray workers (now in compulsory use as a safety measure), while their equipment and protective devices were extensively tested and made safe. During the war years about 175 g of radium were measured at the Laboratory, mainly for medical services both civil and military; some was used in uranium fission experiments, some for luminising the dials of aircraft instruments. Sensitive equipment was developed for the detection of lost radium samples on bombed sites.

The Acoustics Section calibrated instruments for the Services. The sound insulation of aircraft cabins was studied, the noise of tanks and its reproduction on sound films, the reduction of noise from aero-engine test houses. Building acoustics provided an important study throughout. After the destruction of the House of Commons in 1941, the acoustic characteristics of the House of Lords, now occupied by the Commons, and of the King's Robing Room, now functioning as a home for the Lords, were measured and the chambers modified for their new roles. The Section's advice was sought in 1944 in the preparation of plans for a new House of Commons. Investigations were made of the acoustic problems presented by probable post-war building techniques—the drumming of rain on roofs, the sound insulation between rooms and so on.

At the beginning of the War the possibility of dividing up the Radio Division among the radio departments of the various Services was considered, but finally rejected by DSIR. It was felt that the basic investigations of the last decade should be continued with the strong probability of contributing to all branches of the war effort in this field. In the event the decision was amply justified. Studies of the propagation of radio waves at all frequencies were continued. The mysteries of the ionosphere continued to be plumbed and the problems it contributed to propagation. Ionosphere observation stations were established world wide.

Direction finding techniques were widely applied to the location of hostile sources of transmission and to the tracking of balloon borne transmitters for meteorological or military purposes. These were used to measure wind velocities, pressure, temperature and humidity at high altitudes. Long range radio sounding was carried out at distances up to 1000 miles. A network of wind velocity stations was soon established and contributed valuable meteorological data. A technique was developed for obtaining meteorological data from far afield by the simultaneous recording of lightning flashes at stations sufficiently far apart to provide a long baseline, a service which was soon operating continuously. Direction finding techniques were also employed to monitor the height of a balloon barrage minefield, set up for the air defence of London in 1940, also the height and distance of special balloons used to drop propaganda literature over occupied Europe and for trailing cables across enemy power lines.

At the same time the Division did not lose sight of the Laboratory's traditional standards role and techniques were developed for measuring electrical quantities—current, voltage, power, field strength up to 10 GHz, and frequency to 50 GHz.

The Ship Division was perhaps even more deeply involved in war work than any other. The tanks were in continuous use contributing data to many of the new techniques of warfare. Work was done on mine-sweeps, moored signal buoys, oil booms to confine burning oil, limpet mines and a new enclosed design of lifeboat to sail through burning oil.

A large concrete pontoon 200 ft long with a 60 ft superstructure and weighing 3000 tons had to be launched sideways-on into the River Conway after building. Models were used in the tank to develop techniques for this and to study the towing properties after launch. Parts of the Mulberry Harbour, used in the invasion of Normandy in 1944, were designed as a result of laboratory tests—wavebreakers, flotation and towing of concrete pontoons and of floating bridges, fenders—and mooring experiments on harbour items. Tests were also made for the Army on pontoon bridges, on flotation of tanks across waterways, and on the design and propulsion of assault amphibians.

An unusual proposal, thoroughly investigated with tank models, was the construction from a huge block of ice of a mobile sea-drome (a suggested requirement was 2000 ft long, 130 ft beam and 150 ft draft with a displacement of 2.25×10^6 tons and propulsive power to maintain position against a tidal drift of three knots). This was found impossible to achieve and attention was turned to a construction of logs with a flight deck 1500 ft long, 250 ft wide and 82 ft above keel. Though this seemed practicable the changing fortunes of war meant that a full scale version was never actually produced. A model of yet another floating landing field was also tested, but this was found to have the upper surface constantly awash.

Tests were carried out on numerous ship models (a record 190 in 1944)—merchant aircraft carriers, small submarines, target towing launch, hopper barge, puffers and tugs—the list is a long one.

A spectacular contribution, afterwards featured in the film *The Dam Busters*, was the study of the bouncing bombs, designed by Barnes Wallis and later dropped on the Mohne and Eder Dams in Germany in one of the best known incidents of the air war.

Notes

1   HMSO (1928) *Units and Standards of Measurement employed at the NPL* (HMSO 1 shilling).

2   The Editorial Board under the chairmanship of A E Bailey had three NPL members out of four, while 50 % of the contributors came from the Laboratory.

3   658 000 were tested in 1923, 563 000 in 1926 (when the all time total was estimated to have reached 7 000 000), 620 000 in 1929, 480 000 in 1932 and 454 000 in 1935.

4   Thereafter the figures slumped rapidly; nevertheless an average of 1500 telescopes were tested per annum throughout the 1920s, while sextant numbers fluctuated between 300 and 700. In the slump of the early 1930s the figures dropped still further, but they rose again later in the decade in the build-up to World War II.

5   These are now housed in the NPL museum.

6   On alternate Tuesdays, with power detectable over a range of 100 miles. The frequencies, in the range 320–60 kHz, were set up by beating with the multivibrator.

7   This building is now used as the garage.

8   The Morrison clock is now in NPL Museum.

Part IV

The Post-War Period

Post-War NPL: 1945–1980

In 1950 the Laboratory celebrated its Jubilee with a reception at the Royal Society and this was followed in 1951 by a week of Open Days when current work was displayed to large numbers of visitors. Behind was half a century of scientific endeavour of which it had every reason to be proud.

For much of its history the NPL had revealed the appropriateness of the title of what was for many years its parent government department. While always maintaining its national standards role, it fluctuated over fairly long periods between outgoing appearances which were sometimes 'scientific' and sometimes 'industrial'. Immediately following the War, to help the country on to its feet once again, the role of aid to industry predominated; by the mid 1950s the atmosphere had become highly academic—a huge organisation for research, with some of the traditional functions receiving support which was less than enthusiastic. Ten years later when the control passed to the new Labour brain-child, the Ministry of Technology, the pendulum had swung right back to emphasise once again the industrial role.

The relation between NPL test work and that of industrial organisations was questioned once again in 1954, when it appeared that the Laboratory could perform one particular type of work at a considerably cheaper rate. The Executive Committee confirmed the Laboratory's policy of 'undertaking test work only where it can be regarded as in the national interest and where comparable facilities are not provided by consultants etc elsewhere'. Where NPL was responsible for the maintenance of standards, it would continue to calibrate appropriate secondary standards and instruments.

The five day week, already enjoyed by industrial and academic counterparts for at least the last ten years, did not arrive for NPL scientists until July 1956.

Between the end of the War and 1958 the pattern of Laboratory organisation remained substantially recognisable as that of the pre-war decades, the Divisions of Aerodynamics, Ship, Metallurgy, Light and the new Mathematics Division continuing relatively unchanged. Engineering was the first of the original divisions to disappear, when in 1952 it formed the nucleus of the new Mechanical Engineering Research Laboratory of the DSIR at East Kilbride (later called the National Engineering Laboratory). The hydraulics research work had already split off in 1947 to become the Hydraulics Research Organisation of the DSIR at Wallingford. A small section of the work was left behind in the Physics Division and in a unit working on high temperature metal properties which, after being independent for a time, eventually became part of the Metallurgy Division.

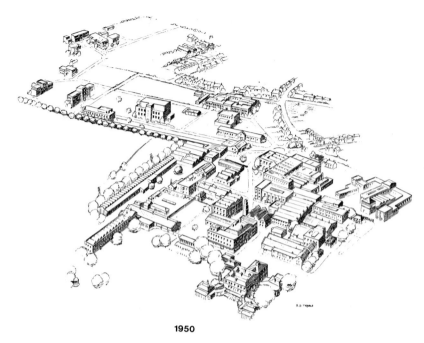

1950

84   The site 1950, by R D Treble.

The Radio Division was transferred during 1952 to the Radio Research Organisation of the DSIR, which occupied new premises erected on the Division's out-station site at Slough. However an electronics section, founded some years earlier for the development of computer circuitry, remained behind to form, with sections transferred from the Electricity Division and later from the Metrology Division, the nucleus of a new electronics group. This was called the Control Mechanisms and Electronics, and later the Autonomics Division.

A Test House was set up in 1949 to deal with routine test work, staffed mostly from the Divisions of Metrology, Light and Physics, and this maintained an independent existence until 1958, when big organisational changes resulted in its reverting to the Applied Physics Division.

The changes of 1958 were far reaching. A new research division, Basic Physics, was founded with the primary objective of studying the relations between the bulk and the micro properties of new materials, and particularly of plastics. A new staff of research fellows was recruited and joined with a number of sections from the old Physics Division; the latter now became the Applied Physics Division. To make way for the change (since it seems to have been impossible just to create an additional division), the Electricity

Division was split up—standards work to the Standards Division, the rest to the Applied Physics Division (and from there soon afterwards the high voltage work departed to the laboratories of the CEGB at Leatherhead). Since all these were organisational or administrative changes they made little impact at the laboratory bench and were relatively unnoticed by those concerned all their time with working science. Research was rampant and standards work moribund.

Sir Charles Darwin, appointed in 1938, continued as Director until 1950; he was succeeded by E C Bullard, Professor of Physics at Toronto University, an earth scientist and a great extrovert, and he in turn in 1955 by G B B M Sutherland, an infrared spectroscopist. Both continued at NPL to make important contributions in their respective areas of expertise. Whereas Bullard was in and out of laboratories at all times, much less was seen of Sutherland, but this may well be accounted for by the ever increasing load of directorial administration work, which soon necessitated the appointment of Deputy Directors. During Sutherland's Directorship, the deputy post was held in succession by E Lee, G G MacFarlane and J V Dunworth.

With the continuing expansion of scientific research, the broadening of its base within the Laboratory and the opportunities which were cropping up

85 Four Directors of NPL together in 1961. From left to right: C G Darwin (4th), E C Bullard (5th), G B B M Sutherland (6th) and W L Bragg (3rd).

elsewhere, the turnover rate for Superintendents of divisions increased[1].

There was little new building in the immediate post-war period. Teddington Hall (with statuary above the door and a particularly grotesque Victorian fireplace in one of the main rooms) at the north end of the Parks Estate was acquired in 1945. The Chemical Research Laboratory accommodation was extended in 1952 by the construction of a special-purpose building for radioactive chemical work. The Aerodynamics Division spread ever wider over the north side of the Parks Estate with a new high speed tunnel building in 1953, compressor house 1955, workshop 1957, hypersonic shock tube building 1958, helium tunnel 1960 and turbulence tunnel 1960. The Metallurgy Division also grew at this time with a new laboratory building in 1954 and a mechanical working laboratory in 1962.

But the most spectacular arrival in this era was a huge new tank for the Ship Division. Too large to be accommodated on the Teddington site, this was erected at Feltham close to London Airport. The main towing tank is 1300 ft long, 48 ft wide and 25 ft deep, with a versatile wavemaker; there is a subsidiary 100 ft × 100 ft × 8 ft deep, also with wavemaker, for manoeuvring tests on radio-controlled models. The workshops are equipped to produce models in wood or in wax up to 40 ft long and 7 ft in breadth, also propellers up to 24 in diameter. The impressive building housing these facilities was opened by HRH the Duke of Edinburgh in 1959. A water tunnel for propeller and static body testing was completed in 1965. It has its working section at ground level, but the lower limb, 14 ft in diameter, is 180 ft under ground—thus serving to redissolve in the water any air set free by cavitation.

The early 1960s, the heyday of research science, saw an impressive new building programme worth (then) some £2M. A mechanical working laboratory was added to the facilities of the Metallurgy Division in 1962, followed by large new buildings for the Basic Physics Division (Mott building) and for the Autonomics Division (Babbage building). The former was a distinct advance in laboratory building design—a lay-out of offices and laboratories which could be readily adapted to the needs of any discipline, with all the services available in ducts but not brought into laboratories until needed, mobile benches, wall and ceiling fixing for apparatus, and so on. Special facilities included a clean room, variable temperature room, chemistry laboratory and a bank of controlled temperature rooms[2].

The building housing the duplex tunnel, no longer used, was gutted and redesigned as a Laboratory Centre with staff restaurant on the ground floor and a well equipped lecture theatre (seating 400) and committee rooms on a gallery. This enabled the Laboratory to host symposia and colloquia on a scale much larger than theretofore, which it increasingly did during the 1960s and 1970s. This new feature of the Laboratory, named Glazebrook Hall, was opened by Sir Richard's eldest daughter in February 1961. Another ex-Director to be thus honoured was Sir Joseph Petavel, whose

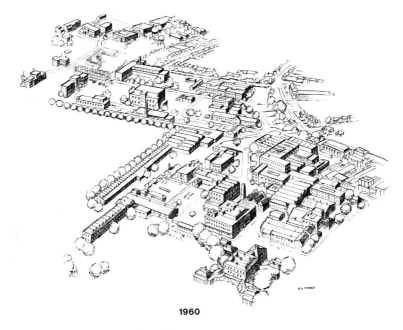

1960

86   The site 1960, by R D Treble.

name was given to a large building erected for the use of sections of various divisions on the Parks Estate site and completed in 1970.

The huge hall of the high voltage building, vacated in 1961 when the work transferred to CEGB, was adapted in the following years to house a 2 MV Van de Graaff generator used by the Radiation Section of the Applied Physics Division in their work on neutron standards. The most recent new building on the site contributes to the same area of work (now in the Division of Radiation Science and Acoustics). This was finished in 1975 and houses an electron linear accelerator used for precision radiation measurement (dosimetry) over a wide range of energies and intensities.

After the early 1960s the complexities of the organisation of the Laboratory become too difficult to follow (see Appendix 3) and anyway are, by and large, not significant when considering the science which continued to flow from the establishment. Particularly after the Labour Government closed down the DSIR in 1965 and assigned NPL to the new Ministry of Technology[3], schemes for improving the service given to the nation were constantly being hawked from above. The laudable efforts of the internal authorities to implement all these continued through the years. Cost–benefit studies were carried out in circumstances where the results were almost meaningless. All Divisions struggled to recover part of their costs by doing repayment work for outside bodies, involving factors of confidentiality.

Justifiably, open-ended research was severely cut back and in its place all research projects had to have a 'customer', who had to be persuaded of the viability and value of each project and agree to make available the funds to carry it out. The 'customers' were the so-called Requirements Boards set up by the presiding Ministry and staffed by experts in the appropriate fields. Their meetings required regular preparation of cases by Laboratory scientists in time which could ill be spared from practical work, yet all in all they seemed to work reasonably well.

The emphasis on academic research of the late 1950s brought a new atmosphere to some sections of the Laboratory, which came to ressemble University research departments rather than having the traditional NPL image. But this did not last for long. A complex pattern of reorganisation of divisions ensued, the details of which are summarised in Appendix 3. Some of the changes mirrored the uncertainties in departmental attitudes to government science in this period, referred to above; others served to match changes in national scientific needs. Materials science and radiation science became major topics, electrical science was restored to the programme with a considerably wider remit, while mathematics and metrology also saw changes.

87   Aerial view of the site 1970.

During 1970 Aerodynamics finally left the Laboratory on amalgamation with the Royal Aircraft Establishment at Farnborough, with which very close links had always been maintained. Left behind was a so-called Environmental Unit dealing with industrial (non-flying) aerodynamics and acoustics, which later (1971) became the nucleus of a new Maritime Science Division. The Ship Division, which had incorporated the work of the Government's Hovercraft Unit in 1967, continued under the NPL banner until 1976, when it joined with the Maritime Science Division to form an independent Government body, the National Maritime Institute. The ship tank and wind tunnel facilities on the NPL sites now fall under the charge of the Institute.

Presiding, apparently imperturbably, over this multiplicity of changes was the seventh Director, J V Dunworth. In a period of considerable enforced change the NPL would seem to owe him a great deal for coping with these disturbing outside influences in such a way that the scientist in his laboratory remained comparatively unaffected. The scientific output of the Laboratory continued at a high level in both quantity and quality. After his retirement in 1976 an interregnum saw temporary control exercised by I Maddock (Chief Scientist of the Department of Industry) and by D Davies, who succeeded him. Then during 1977 Paul Dean was appointed eighth Director, the first permanent holder of the office to have risen from the ranks of the Laboratory.

The period 1965 to date has seen a multiplicity of Superintendents, acting Superintendents and Officers-in-Charge of various divisions and groupings[4].

88   J V Dunworth, seventh Director of NPL.

89   P Dean, eighth Director of NPL.

Space forbids any lengthy discussion of the complexities of the staff structure. The post-war reorganisation of the Scientific Civil Service set up three grades—Scientific, Experimental and Assistant; in each case there was a guaranteed career grade, which all but a very few should reach, while there was some prospect of further advancement. The recruitment of the late 1940s produced some ten years later a bulge at the top of the Experimental Officer grade (the career grade in that class) from which the prospects of promotion were extremely limited. By the 1970s these three grades were combined into one Scientific grade, ostensibly with equal opportunities of promotion for all. Complex reports on staff ability were, and still are, produced annually, each rank reported upon by those above and reporting in turn on those below; often these took the form of 'alternative answer' papers.

Over the years there have been a number of attempts to preserve some of the historical apparatus associated with the NPL story; indeed choice items have found their way into the Science Museum at South Kensington. A local collection, set up in the 1930s in the entrance hall of Bushy House, appears to have been dispersed at the outbreak of war and has disappeared without trace. During the 1950s and 1960s some care was taken over documentary records and research was carried out into the history of Bushy House and the early days of NPL. Finally in the 1970s Dunworth revived the idea of an apparatus collection, giving the task first to Barrell and then to Bailey. At this stage (1974) the writer became involved in the design and layout of the Laboratory's Museum, which now occupies two large rooms in Bushy House. An up-to-date study of the history of Bushy House was prepared and published, while in 1977 a three month exhibition was mounted in Orleans House Art Gallery at Twickenham.

An important series of NPL publications began in 1951 with the first number of '*Notes in Applied Science*' entitled *Gauging and Measuring Screw Threads*. These were published by HMSO. By 1964, 34 different texts had appeared covering many branches of NPL expertise. A numbered series of Symposium Proceedings began in October 1953 and reached No 16 in June 1963; thereafter publication of similar material continued in miscellaneous formats.

A number of volumes of mathematical tables were published arising out of the work of the Mathematics Division and its successors.

Up to 1945 the general background to the measurement work was described in the booklet *Units and Standards employed at the National Physical Laboratory* (reprinted from the 1928 *Annual Report*), and in a series of Test Pamphlets giving particulars of the tests and fees. These were updated in a series of publications which appeared from 1951 onwards. In the early 1970s, in the heyday of repayment work, these became more glossy and exotic, setting out details not only of the traditional test facilities but also of the many special investigations which could be undertaken, based on the tremendous range of equipments and techniques available, either by NPL staff or by outside scientists working under NPL supervision.

A successful house journal, *NPL News*, began in May 1950 and appeared monthly without a break until June 1978. It struck a balance between technical and domestic material and has proved very useful as a historical source. Subsequently the *News* appeared quarterly, supplemented by a monthly *Bulletin* dealing with purely domestic matters. For many years the production has been carried out on the site by photolithography.

There have been numerous specialised books, some slender, some massive. A series of booklets gives particulars of the tests carried out in various parts of the Laboratory. An overall view in general terms was taken in the soft-cover book — *NPL Jubilee Book of the National Physical Laboratory* by John Langdon-Davies, which appeared in 1951. There is a comprehensive treatment of the relation between NPL and Government throughout the years in a PhD thesis, as yet unpublished, by Russell Moseley — *Science, Government and Industrial Research: the Origins and Development of the National Physical Laboratory 1900–1975* (University of Sussex 1975).

Electronics, Computers and Mathematics: 1945–1980

Early in 1948 the Superintendent of the Radio Division was appointed Director of Radio Research, DSIR. Arrangements were made for the work of the Division to be transferred to new buildings soon to be erected on the site of the out-station at Datchet near Slough. The move was completed during 1952, thus bringing to an end the NPL role in the radio field. The Radio Research Station, which in the ensuing years developed a programme encompassing space science (with rockets, balloons and satellites), radio astronomy and telescopes and atmospheric, stratospheric, tropospheric and ionospheric studies, was later called the Appleton Laboratory. It finally merged with the Rutherford Laboratory in the austere days of 1979.

Up to 1952 the radio work went on at Teddington on much the same lines as before and during the War. Propagation phenomena in the troposphere and the ionosphere were studied, along with the utilisation of radio techniques for meteorological purposes, for storm location and for radio noise determination. The NPL effort in these fields formed part of an international network, with results exchanged round the world. Vertical incidence observations on the ionosphere were taken continuously on a fully automatic recorder. A relation was derived between solar noise and sudden radio disturbances. New cathode ray directional recording equipment for atmospherics was installed at four meteorological stations and used for storm location.

An Electronics Section was detached from the Radio Division in 1948 to be responsible for those items of the Divisional programme not being transferred, namely the development of electronic computers and the industrial and research applications of electronics.

Work began in 1946 to develop a stored-program digital computer named ACE (Automatic Computing Engine). System design and programming were developed in the Mathematics Division, electronic design and construction in the Electronics Section. In 1948 the teams were merged and the work concentrated on a pilot model, known later as 'Pilot ACE'[5] which began to work in May 1950, one of the first computers in the world and one of the fastest at the time.

Pilot ACE was taken into service by the Mathematics Division in 1952, the installation providing one of the world's first widely-used computer bureaux. Its work included flutter calculations for the Canberra aircraft, calculations arising from the Comet disasters, the first simulation of road traffic control and the verification of Bullard's theory of geomagnetism.

Since 1948 there had been close cooperation with the English Electric Co. and this firm went ahead with the construction of an engineered version (DEUCE), which was a great commercial success and launched part of the British computer industry.

During this period the Electronics Section also worked on the large scale mechanisation of clerical operations with electronic computers, as well as offering an electronic service of advice and components to all other Divisions of the Laboratory.

In addition to the programmes of research in the specifically electronics part of the Laboratory, electronics of course played a major role in a great

90   The Pilot Model of ACE.

many of the scientific programmes in the post-war period. Each Division utilised the services of its own electronics experts to deal with its own particular problems, some (and one could cite examples in every field) involving more electronics than science. For the first two decades the thermionic valve held sway, only to be made almost completely obsolete by semiconductor devices, the integrated circuit and, of late years, the microprocessor.

At the end of 1953 it was decided to set up a new Division of Control Mechanisms and Electronics. This absorbed the Electronics Section engaged in the above activities and the Control Mechanisms Section (founded in 1946) of the Metrology Division, which was working on automatic controls and servo systems. Their chief contribution to date had been an analogue computer used to study the dynamic response of physical systems used for automatic control.

The full scale model, brought up to date, of the ACE Computer (three times faster than the early pilot model, since it could add 30 000 14-figure numbers per second) was completed in 1958 and handed to the Mathematics Division. The storage drums ran at 12 000 rpm and recorded digits at 300 000 bits per second on the surface. The cost of design and development of ACE was £250 000, or about one year's rental of the only commercially available (American) machine. It was soon utilised for solving partial differential equations, as encountered in the design of aircraft, ships, electronic apparatus, atomic reactors and so on.

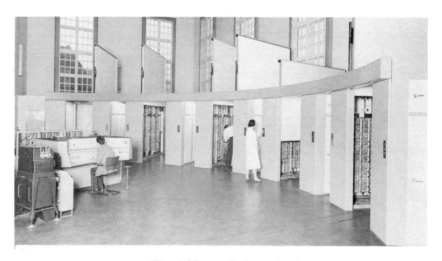

91   The ACE installation at NPL.

In 1960 the name of the Division was changed to Autonomics and the terms of reference expressed much more generally—'to carry out automatically, tedious and fatiguing mental tasks which must be done to an ever increasing extent in many walks of life'. The Division aimed to produce both improved and entirely new equipment for high speed computing, adaptive control and automatic character recognition and to develop more sophisticated techniques for machine translation and library information retrieval.

The possibilities of using superconductors in the form of very thin films as computing elements were assessed in one section of the Division and considerable advances made. By this time the transistor had taken over from the thermionic valve as the switching element in computers and the whole subject was setting out on the long trail of miniaturisation. The computer industry was expanding rapidly and having demonstrated the possibilities with ACE, there was no further call for the NPL to design computers.

The work on adaptive control systems extended the programme originally initiated by the Control Mechanisms Section. These systems were designed to deal with control situations where the controlled process is subject to random disturbances, the characteristics of which alter with time. A conventional controller cannot handle such a problem. A technique of trial and error is used; transitory changes are made in set points in the process to be controlled and cross correlations made between these changes and their effects on performance. These techniques were first applied in NPL to the adaptive control of a distillation column.

A control system continually learning from past experience gives some insight into the neuro–physical problem of detecting the physical basis of memory in humans. A small team used this and other experiments, therefore, to make psychological studies of the learning process.

A technique for automatic recognition of printed and handwritten characters independent of position and orientation was developed, starting first with Arabic numerals and subsequently moving on to problems of greater complexity. Apparatus working on these principles was taken up eventually and produced commercially.

Within the same group St Dunstan's scientists collaborated in reading aids for blind people, endeavouring to substitute information on alternative sensory channels. These various activities called for the unusual cooperation of psychologists and engineers and these groups working alongside one another led to studies of visual perception.

One of the earliest demands on the talents of the Division was for the production of machine translation from Russian into English. An automatic dictionary was compiled on magnetic tape and made operative in the ACE Computer; it included short phrases as well as single words. After dictionary reference, texts were analysed syntactically and Russian word patterns transformed to English word patterns. As can be seen from the figure (*over*) the method has limitations, nevertheless it quickly received practical application.

Mechanised methods of indexing and retrieval of information were studied and computer programs developed to handle this vast problem which, on account of the continuing steep increase in published material was getting beyond the unaided capabilities of human operators.

In 1967 the Division was renamed Computer Science, with terms of reference tied perhaps a little more closely to the applications of computers than hitherto. The technical management of the national Advanced Computer Technology Project, which coordinated computer research among the various firms manufacturing computers, peripherals etc became the responsibility of the Division. The internal research programme continued very much as before.

The work on pattern recognition was extended to hand-written numbers. Equipment was designed and produced for the validation of signatures while they were actually being written, providing a useful security aid in government and business establishments. Yet another example of pattern recognition which came under investigation was the use of speech to enter data into computer systems ('talking to a computer'). The methods developed could even be used in a noisy environment, and were later applied to aircraft. This work was the first to recognise words from any speaker and in context, in running speech.

Work on natural language processing continued with the Palantype transcription project, where the output of a Palantype shorthand machine

ИССЛЕДОВАНИЕ ГРАНИЧНЫХ СЛОЕВ МЕЖДУ ДОМЕНАМИ
В НЕКОТОРЫХ ФЕРРИТАХ СО СТРУКТУРОЙ ШПИНЕЛИ

А. И. Дрокин, В. Н. Синегубов

С помощью методики, использующей полярный эффект Керра, проведено исследование ширины доменных границ, их полярности и распределения в них намагниченности. Изучено влияние термообработки на ширину доменных границ в монокристаллах ферритов состава MnFe₂O₃ с избытком марганца (25% гаусманита), Co₀.₈₄Fe₀.₁₂³⁺ Fe₀.₉₆O₄ и Ni₀.₈₄Fe₀.₁₆³⁺²⁺Fe₂O₄. В железомарганцевых и железоникелевых ферритах ширина границ соответствуют нескольким микронам, в железокобальтовых ферритах она на порядок меньше. Приведены графики распределения намагниченности в границах 180- и 71-градусных соседств. Установлено, что в железокобальтовых и железоникелевых ферритах, чувствительных к термообработкам, ширина границ уменьшается в результате длительного отжига, при этом константа анизотропии возрастает по абсолютной величине, а параметр решётки, хотя и незначительно, уменьшаются. Это явление находит себе объяснение в рамках теории Нееля.

Investigation of boundary　layers between domains in some ferrites with
　　　　　　　　　　　　　　threshold

structure shrine

A. I. Drokin, V. J. Sinegubov

By means of method, utilizing polar effect of Kerra, is conducted investigation
　　　　　　　　　　　　　　　　　　　　　　　　　　　installed
　　　　　　　　　　　　　　　　　*　　　　　　　　　　passed

of width of domain boundaries, their polarity and distribution into them of
　　　　　　　　　　　　　　　　　　　　　　　　　　　　　　in

intensity of magnetization.

Is studied influence of thermo-processing onto width of domain boundaries in
　　　　　　　　　　　　　　　　　　for

mono-crystals of ferrites of compound $Mn Fe_2 O_3$ with surplus of manganese(25
　　　　　　　　　　　　　　　　　　structure

% gausmanit), $Co_{0.84} Fe_{0.12}^{2+} Fe_{0.96} O_4$ and $Ni_{0.84} Fe_{0.44}^{2+} Fe_2 O_4.$

In ferro-marganic and ferro-nickel ferrites width of boundaries corresponds to

several microns, in ferro-cobalt ferrites it onto order　　　　less.
　　　　　　　　　　　　　　　　　　　　for　arrangement

92　Russian translation by computer.

was converted into intelligible English by means of a computer which used a specially created Palantype-to-English dictionary.

Studies were also directed towards the use of computers by untrained people. Computers were applied in hospitals for the taking of medical histories, in business and industry for specialised job training, in architecture as an aid to graphic design and in the general field of personality and aptitude testing.

A system of storage and retrieval of information, called 'Scrapbook', was developed and installed at NPL. A central computer stores all the information which can be called up and displayed at VDUs all over the site, where it can be questioned, revised or added to as needed. By interconnection with other networks, including the public telephone network, information in Scrapbook can readily be shared with collaborators in other organisations in the UK and abroad. This technology has been successfully transferred to industry and Scrapbook systems are sold commercially.

Probably the most important single development in the Division was a new technique for data communication, known as 'packet switching', which was developed to link computers and users on a large scale. This led to the interconnection of computers in networks on a national and an international scale. 'Packet switching' is now in use world-wide.

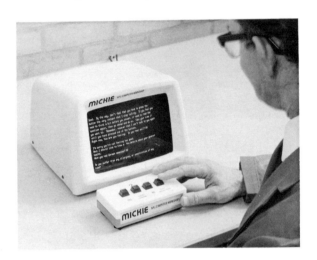

93   'Mickie', the medical interviewing computer.

```
--------------- CUT HERE ---------------

SERIES NO  0

MALE
LESS THAN 25
             FEELS WELL

GENERAL MEDICAL HISTORY
             RUBELLA
             ALLERGIC
             HEART DISEASE
             JAUNDICE
             BLOOD TEST

PRESENT CONDITION
             SMOKER
             >20 CIGARETTES/DAY
             COUGHS
             HEADACHES
             HEARING DETERIORATED
             SORE-THROAT
             COLD RESULTED
MORE SYMPTOMS TO BE INVESTIGATED

--------------- CUT HERE ---------------
```

94   Print-out from 'Mickie'.

With the ever growing importance of microprocessors, a research project was initiated with an industrial partner to explore the possibilities of linking microprocessors together to form cheap, but extremely powerful, microprocessor systems.

The Mathematics Division was established in 1945 to give advice wherever possible in government and in industry on mathematical matters and computational services. Initially there were three sections dealing respectively with computational work and function tabulation, statistical science, and study of new computer methods and machines. Apart from fulfilling these functions on an ever increasing scale, the early years saw the Division acquire a differential analyser (for the solution of differential equations) and joint work with the Electronics Section in developing the pilot model of the ACE computer.

The ACE pilot model became operational in 1950, fed by punched cards from a Hollerith machine and punching out the results similarly. This was followed in 1955 by the commercially engineered DEUCE computer and later (1958) by the full scale ACE. A new differential analyser (with 120 miles of interconnecting cables) having 20 integrators, against eight in the earlier machine, linked by electrical servo mechanisms, was designed and built to replace the earlier one. The construction was partly carried out at Minden in Germany, part of the Government policy to assist the recovery of German industry. By now the Division was handling a large number of problems on behalf of other divisions of NPL as well as developing new techniques for computer programming.

By the end of the 1950s commercial high speed computers were becoming available and the emphasis shifted to the other running programmes—research on numerical analysis, computing methods, construction of mathematical tables (many of which were published) and the use of high speed computers in applied mathematics.

In the researches in numerical analysis the whole field of linear algebra and the solution of polynomial equations was explored. Considerable effort was devoted to the numerical solution of differential equations and the numerical evaluation of integrals, always with emphasis on automatic computation. Methods were developed for computer solution of various partial differential equations and also integral equations. A powerful technique of error analysis was evolved, which was to have a far reaching effect on the future development of mathematical software. Curve and surface fitting and numerical optimisation were also explored.

Contributions in applied mathematics were made to heat conduction and diffusion, stresses in concrete cooling towers and various aerodynamic problems. A group working on theoretical physics applied high speed computer methods to the vibration of disordered two-component lattices, to a study of polymer molecules and to molecular self-consistent field calculations.

Alongside all the research a computer group continued to provide a service for the whole of the Laboratory. An English Electric Leo KDF9 computer installation, acquired in June 1964, became the centre of the service. The purchase of similar equipment by a number of other research organisations promised the setting up of extensive collaborative facilities. (By now the speed of computers was such that a solution of 100 simultaneous equations, correct to, and demonstrated correct to, 23 decimal places could be derived in 13 s.) Meanwhile the ACE was still working 17 hours a day.

In 1967 an independent Central Computer Unit was set up which inherited from the Mathematics Division the task of providing the general computing service to the Laboratory. Following this the name was changed to the Division of Numerical and Applied Mathematics, without any considerable additional change in terms of reference or programme. As before the Division continued to handle a wide range of mathematical work, expanding all the while its expertise in those areas already developed of linear algebra, optimisation, differential and integral equations, curve fitting, and so forth. The Applied Mathematics and Theoretical Physics groups extended considerably their activities in these fields; staff from these groups were later transferred (1971) to other divisions in the Laboratory to provide theoretical support in mixed experimental–analytical teams engaged in materials, measurement and maritime work. At the same time the responsibilities of the Central Computer Unit were transferred to a newly-formed Computing Branch of the Division, which was itself renamed the Division of Numerical Analysis and Computing.

A further reorganisation occurred in 1978 when a merger with the Division of Computer Science took place, giving the present Division of Numerical Analysis and Computer Science. The previous Computing Branch then became a separate Computing Services Unit dealing with all the services provided for NPL divisions and others. It was claimed that these various activities occupied 15 % of the total scientific effort at NPL.

Work continued on numerical methods directed to improving the effectiveness and efficiency of computer usage and to developing new and more complex applications of computers and information technology. By now almost all the research in this field was devoted to software[6].

Work continued on information systems arising from the pioneering development of 'packet switching' in the Division, and on the human–machine interface with particular reference to assessment of the user's view of interactive systems. Research began in 1978 into the use of cryptography to provide secure transmission and storage of data. The programme in numerical analysis continued to concern the use of computers for technical calculations and to build an ever larger algorithms library. There was international collaboration on developing standards in programming languages. Computer processor and language compiler performance were also studied.

Metrology—Standards and Quanta: 1945–1980

In the years immediately following the Second World War the pattern of work in the Metrology Division remained essentially unchanged—the provision and maintenance of accurate standards of length, mass and time and of some of the direct derivatives of these such as volume and density, and in due course force and pressure. Research continued to be directed to improving the accuracy of measurement of standards and the development of new techniques and equipment for this purpose. The programme of intercomparisons, both national and international, also went forward. Postponed from 1942, the decennial comparison of the Parliamentary copies of the yard and the pound with their respective Imperial Standards took place in 1947, using a new length comparator constructed in 1939 and a special balance, also of pre-war design and manufacture.

In 1952 the speed of electromagnetic radiation was determined by a free-space microwave interferometer operating at 24 GHz. The value reduced to vacuum condition, believed correct to one part in 300 000, was some 17 km s^{-1} higher than the previously accepted value, but in good agreement with current measurements elsewhere. An improved determination a few years later became the internationally agreed figure for more than a decade.

The nature of the organisation changed from time to time, but the pattern always remained comprehensible. The Division continued to be called Metrology until 1958, when it was renamed the Standards Division and added to its responsibilities the electrical standards work from the defunct Electricity Division. In 1949 the routine metrological tasks had been hived off to a Test House, which after a period of independence came under the charge of the Applied Physics Division from 1958 to 1965 and then reverted to the Standards Division. A new organisation to handle routine test work, the Metrology Centre, was set up in 1967 and this finally, in 1972, became part of the new Division of Mechanical and Optical Metrology. In 1958 the Standards Division acquired thermometry standards; in 1967 they relinquished electrical standards. The name was changed at this time to Quantum Metrology in cognisance of the fact that material standards were progressively giving way to atomic (or quantum) definitions of basic physical quantities.

For many years the Division had participated in the international researches which culminated in 1960 in the CGPM decision to recommend the orange radiation of krypton-86 as the new atomic length standard (1 m = 1 650 763.73 wavelengths) in place of the material standards used theretofore. Krypton-86 lamps operated under defined conditions reproduce the wavelength to better than one part in 100 000 000. Secondary

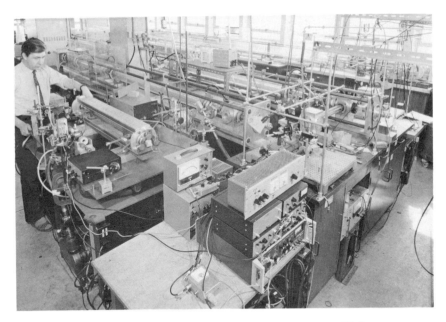

95   An array of lasers used to measure the speed of light.

standards were also produced based on further lines in the spectrum of
krypton-86 and others from mercury-198 and cadmium-114, and these are
accepted internationally for use in interferometry.

This novel standard is readily realisable everywhere and provides a means
of comparing lengths without the tedious and time consuming transfer of
the material standards round the interested countries. Complex comparators for direct measurement of length bars in terms of light waves were
designed and set up.

Another source later adapted for use in length measurement was the
helium–neon gas laser operating at around 633 nm which, stabilised using
saturated absorption in iodine vapour, gives a reproducibility of 3 parts in
10^{11}. The wavelength in terms of the krypton-86 standard is 632.9914 nm.
This radiation was used in the day-to-day realisation of length standards.
Later in the UK the 3390 nm wavelength of the helium–neon gas laser,
stabilised to an absorption line of methane, was adopted giving an even
better performance.

Alongside this standards work came the development of a surveying
instrument, the Mekometer, which uses light polarisation modulated at
about 500 MHz. It has a sensitivity over distances up to 3 km of ± 0.1 mm
with an accuracy of 3 mm per km. It soon found many practical applications
in baseline measurement, civil engineering structure movement, etc in many
countries. Recent developments include the Georan, a two-wavelength

96   Using the Mekometer.

Mekometer, which works over a greater range, and the Geoponder, the first optical transponder developed for geodetic research. It has thus become the basis of a new generation of surveying instruments.

In 1966 the Division collaborated with the Department of Geodesy and Geophysics at Cambridge in developing an interferometric system, working over a distance of 100 m, to measure small strains in the Earth's crust. Strains of the order of 3×10^{-9} could be detected. The equipment was primarily intended for the study of the deep structure of the Earth, but it could also be used to detect movement at geological faults.

Meanwhile the material standards of mass and the means employed at NPL for comparing them, with accuracies approaching one part in 10^9, remained as previously described, since the needs of industry in this field had been comfortably anticipated. Engineering standards of force were acquired to measure force in terms of the primary mass standards. The range of forces (tension or compression) is now from 450 N to 500 kN and this can be extended to 5 MN by a hydraulic amplification system. Forces up to 30 MN in compression only are also available. Calibrations are carried out of proving rings used to verify materials testing machines, and of electric strain gauge load cells which are used in a range of industrial applications.

The standard of time and the comparison of time signals had always been

97   Weighing the Concorde aircraft.

the responsibility of the Metrology Division, which it continued to handle, as well a large amount of watch testing (e.g. 200 for the London Olympic Games in 1948). Meanwhile the related standards of frequency had been almost exclusively dealt with in the Electricity Division and thus came under the Standards Division in 1958. An atomic frequency standard was realised in the mid 1950s with the construction of the first long beam apparatus based on a transition in the caesium-133 atom. Successive developments of this have remained the fundamental standard up to the present day[7]. Meanwhile the working standards were, first of all, a set of Essen ring quartz oscillators, and later a set of commercial atomic frequency standards. The standards are disseminated by radio transmissions from Rugby. The second is defined as 9 192 631 770 periods of the radiation and is nowadays realised at NPL to a few parts in 10^{13}.

In addition to the standards and calibration work the Division made a continuous and highly important series of contributions to engineering metrology in industry. These involved not only the development of calibration apparatus and methods for use in the Laboratory, but also the adaptation of these same ideas to the design of apparatus for use on the shop floor. Special instruments were produced for the measurement of length, angle and area, for diameter and bore diameter and straightness, for the diameter of fine wires and small balls, for levelling and long distance alignment, for screw threads, screw gauges and ring gauges, for gear wheels, for thickness of sheet, and so on. Machine tools and special-purpose machinery of all kinds were tested and advice given on their design. The pitches of lead screws were measured; the standard lead screw lathe was used to correct lead screws up to 3 m long. Early in the 1950s the Division studied the use of granite as a material for surface plates; in a six-month-long test the wear on the granite was not measurable, less than 1.25 µm, while a cast iron plate subjected to the same conditions wore at the centre by up to 10 µm.

The Division also continued the precision measurement of engineering parameters for other divisions of NPL, such as height measurement on standard barometers, dimensions of electrical coils for the current balance and the standard mutual inductor, length measurements on the standard microwave attenuator and on the calculable capacitor, the contours of propellers etc.

98   Calibrating barometers in the early 1950s.

A more precise knowledge of the value of the acceleration of free fall (i.e. the acceleration 'due to gravity') was demanded in various applications and the problem was attacked simultaneously by a number of scientific nations. During the early 1960s a new determination was made at NPL by a symmetrical free motion method, in which a glass ball was timed in upward and downward passages in a vacuum across two horizontal planes separated by a vertical distance of about a metre. The planes were defined by a pair of slits, the ball serving to focus light from one slit on to the other. Distances were measured interferometrically and timed using the NPL standard frequency service. The new value was $9.811\,817\,7\,\mathrm{m\,s^{-2}}$ (standard deviation $1.3\,\mathrm{\mu m\,s^{-2}}$), $14\,\mathrm{\mu m\,s^{-2}}$ lower than the 1939 reversible pendulum figure. Other values determined elsewhere showed a total spread for all results of only $31\,\mathrm{\mu m\,s^{-2}}$. Since before the War one of the Division's Laboratories had been designated the 'British Fundamental Gravity Station' and the results of these various measurements were recorded on a wall plaque.

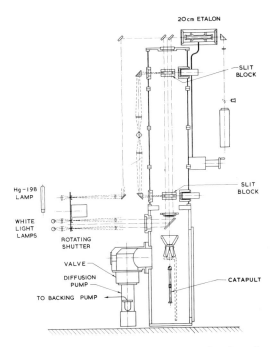

99 Apparatus for the absolute determination of *g*.

The measurement of some physical constants (such as the steam point) called for increased accuracy of pressure measurement and it therefore became necessary to determine the density of mercury to about one part in 10^6. Two methods were adopted—the first finding the apparent weight in mercury of a 90 mm cube of tungsten carbide of accurately known dimensions, the second deriving from the mass of mercury filling a hollow cube of silica of accurately known dimensions.

Another field to attract researchers in the mid 1960s was that of spectroscopy in the ultraviolet, to aid the interpretation of data gathered from rocket and satellite observations of the sun and the stars. A scanning photoelectric Michelson interferometer, operating in a vacuum, was used for wavelength measurement.

While the high precision calibration work on standards continued to be done in the Division, after 1948 the Test House dealt with the more routine aspects of the work[8]. By 1958, when it became the responsibility of the Applied Physics Division, the facility was handling 50 000 items a year, plus half a million clinical thermometers, and earning a considerable sum in test fees.

A further attempt to segregate the test work took place in 1967, when the Metrology Centre was set up 'to coordinate Laboratory calibration and advisory services for industry' and to act as a focus for collaboration in mechanical metrology with the British Calibration Service and the British Standards Institution. The Test House organisation formed the major part of it, plus other sundry small groups, such as vision, colour and spectrophotometry from the Light Division. The Centre now controlled most of the straightforward calibration work, being responsible for mass, length, force, hardness, colorimetry, photometry, barometry, watch rating, temperature and viscometry. A special feature of this new set-up was an Advisory Secretariat to deal with all technical information problems coming into the Laboratory.

Soon afterwards taximeter testing and some straightforward liquid-in-glass thermometer testing were transferred to the BSI, while the Admiralty was persuaded to undertake the testing of its optical instruments, for many years done for them by NPL. In 1972 the Centre became part of the Division of Mechanical and Optical Metrology.

These efforts to relieve scientific staff of routine work each served for a period to facilitate the development of the next generation of measurement apparatus and to stimulate recruitment to metrology. In particular, Quantum Metrology was set up initially with only a low work load of calibration.

After 1965 temperature measurement became the responsibility of the Standards Division. In 1948 the International Temperature scale was updated by international agreement to take account of work done since 1927. Basically the changes were small, reflecting more accurate knowledge of the fixed points in absolute terms and improvements in the interpolating means. The scale ran from the BP of liquid oxygen ($-182.97\,^{\circ}$C) to the FP of gold ($1063.0\,^{\circ}$C) with further fixed points between (the FP of silver was redefined) and extrapolation at the upper end by radiation methods based on Planck's Law in place of Wien's Law. The value of the constant C_2 in Planck's equation was redefined and the word 'Celsius' substituted for 'Centigrade'.

Work now continued to improve the reproducibility and extend the range. For example, international intercomparisons included measuring

0°C and 100°C in ten laboratories in eight countries using the same three resistance thermometers (one American, one English and one Russian). The 0–100 °C interval was reproduced identically to within 0.001 °C. Three countries agreed within a range of 0.0015 °C for the FP of zinc.

This culminated in the International Practical Temperature Scale of 1968, which renamed the unit of temperature the kelvin. It extended from a fixed point at 13.81 K (the triple point of equilbrium hydrogen) to a fixed point at 1337.58 K (the FP of gold) and could be extrapolated to beyond 3000 K by radiation methods based on Planck's Law. The important fixed point is the triple point of water (the temperature at which ice, liquid water and water vapour exist together in equilibrium). This is defined as 273.16 K exactly and is realized to $\pm$ 0.1 mK in a triple point cell designed and made at NPL. The temperature 0 °C on the Celsius scale is defined as being 273.16 K exactly.

In the pre-satellite era there was some international competition for altitude records for powered aircraft. In the early days of flying the NPL used to standardise the air borne barographs for the Royal Aero Club. A Bleriot aircraft with a Gnome engine reached 8000 ft (2438 m) in November 1911. Later the height attained was determined by collaborative effort between NPL temperature and pressure measuring facilities, the Aerodynamics Division and RAE, Farnborough. One such record was that of the de Havilland Vampire which reached 18133 m on 23 March 1948.

The change of name from Standards to Quantum Metrology in 1967 emphasised the new role of atomic devices in standards work. By now the old standards of time (based on astronomical observation) and of length (based on two lines on a unique bar) had been replaced by definitions based on atomic constants. It therefore seemed appropriate to establish more units in atomic terms and to measure a range of atomic constants to a higher order of precision than theretofore. This became the long term basis of the work of the Division.

Important advances took place in the measurement of frequency in parts of the electromagnetic spectrum previously inaccessible due to lack of sources and detectors. Various laser systems were discovered and their frequencies stabilised in the sub-millimetre wavelength range (from 1 mm to the visible). Now, with newly developed detectors, it became possible to multiply and modulate quartz crystal controlled frequencies from microwave sources and use them to measure the frequencies of these various lasers to the same degree of precision. In a joint programme with the Division of Electrical Science simultaneous determinations of wavelength gave a new figure for the speed of light, correct probably to 3 parts in 10^9.[9]

This opened up the intriguing possibility of replacing the atomic standards of length and time by a single standard of frequency, taking the speed of light as a conventional constant from which length could be derived from a measurement of frequency or of time.

A more accurate knowledge of certain physical constants (see below) was considered vital for the Division's programme, since traditional units and standards can be related through them by quantum principles to measurements of frequency. The NPL now has a primary responsibility in the UK for these determinations. Furthermore, discrepancies between measurements of fundamental constants can also lead to new insights into physics.

The gyromagnetic ratio of the proton (γ'_p), is one such since it provides for the dissemination of the Tesla by a frequency method. In addition, measuring it by two methods yielded a value independent of the maintained electrical units. There was a possibility, which was in fact never realised, that the value of the gyromagnetic ratio of the proton thus determined could be used to maintain the unit of electric current, by measuring the precession frequency of protons in the field at the centre of a solenoid.

100   Apparatus for measuring the gyromagnetic ratio of the proton.

In 1969 the NPL became the first of a number of metrological laboratories to measure $2e/h$ by the Josephson Effect. Later the experiment was inverted and used as a quantum method for realising the volt[10].

The Division also worked on the evaluation of the magnetic moment of the proton (μ_p/μ_h), the fine structure constant ($\mu_0 e^2 c/2h$), the Faraday ($N_A e$), Avagadro's Constant (N_A), Stefan's Constant (σ) and the gas constant (R). A value for Boltzmann's constant (k) can be derived from N_A and R an order of magnitude more accurate than hitherto known. Yet another atomic constant under investigation in recent years was the Rydberg.

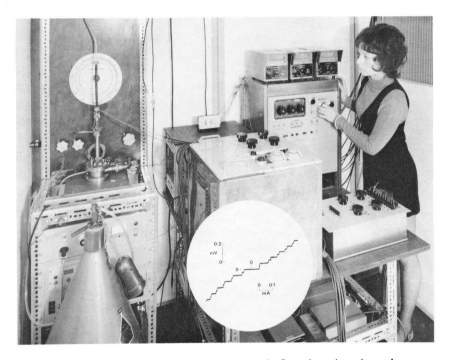

101   The quantum voltage standard compares the Josephson junction voltage with a standard cell voltage.

When Quantum Metrology was set up the attack on temperature measurement took place on a much broader front than hitherto. Research probed to the limits of a range of measurement extending from 0.02 K to 20 000 K. A variety of techniques was employed in addition to the classical gas thermometer. The range 90 K to 373 K was explored by measuring the dielectric constant of argon by a capacitance method. The gas constant (R) was determined by measuring the velocity of sound in a gas at the temperature of the triple point of water. Photoelectric pyrometers were developed to establish thermodynamic temperatures on the basis of Planck's Law in the range 1337 K to 4000 K; at the low temperature end several different approaches were made successfully to establish the scale down towards absolute zero. Radiation methods of comparing sources at fixed

102   Apparatus for measuring Rydberg's constant.

temperatures enabled the fixed points above 273.16 K to be determined without recourse to the gas thermometer. Fourier transform spectroscopy was utilised for measuring values of radiant energy and variations of emissivity over a span of wavelengths.

Temperatures in the range 600 K to 4000 K were measured by an infrared emission–absorption method. A wall-stabilised arc was developed as a standard source up to 10 000 K.

As a result of one of the periodic reappraisals of the work being done in the infrared and sub-millimetre wave length ranges in the Division of Electrical Science, it was decided to embark on a programme of measurement of atmospheric pollution. This arose originally from investigations of the effects on the stratosphere of freons from aerosols and of supersonic aircraft and the fear that they might destroy the protective ozone layer therein. Later the programme was transferred to the Division of Quantum Metrology with a broader base of studying pollutants at all levels in the earth's envelope by remote sensing methods. Measurements at high levels were carried out by balloon and aircraft borne equipment. Lower down, techniques of direct laser absorption in the near and mid infrared and of differential absorption lidar were used. The Division of Electrical Science produced the reference spectra on which this exploratory work was based.

103   Balloon borne apparatus for atmospheric pollution measurement.

Electricity and Electromagnetics: 1945–1980

For the Electricity Division the important event of the immediate post-war period was the adoption by international agreement of the Absolute System of Electrical Units. These had been established at the Laboratory for many years, and related to working International Units by the Ayrton–Jones current balance (for the ampere), the Lorenz machine (for the ohm), the Campbell bridge equipment (also for the ohm) and the latter in conjunction with a calculable standard mutual inductor and various AC bridges (for capacitance and inductance).

The Division continued to maintain a wide range of primary and secondary standards—standard cells and resistors, standard inductors and capacitors for telephone and radio frequencies, standards of phase angle, attenuation, and so on, backed by high precision measurement apparatus. Methods of measurement and details of construction of physical standards were continuously improved. The working standards of the testing stations of the British Electricity Authority were periodically checked and type approval was given for new designs of electricity meter. (This work was given up in 1972.) A development of this period was the measurement of high power at audio frequencies, as required in work with induction furnaces and for testing instruments and equipment used in aircraft. Ferrites, the new low loss, high frequency core materials, were investigated in conjunction with the Metallurgy Division.

The High Voltage Laboratory continued to function as the main laboratory of this type in the country. High voltage insulation tests were made on solids, liquids and gases and combinations of these, up to 1 MV at power frequencies and at surge voltages at first of 2 MV, a figure raised in the early 1950s to 3.2 MV by a newly installed generator. An absolute voltmeter for power frequency measurements up to a 400 kV peak was developed; studies of techniques for measuring surge voltages included the design and construction of cathode ray oscillographs incorporating sealed tubes, the recording of light intensity with photomultipliers and linear amplifiers, and the development of a robust and sensitive null detector for bridge circuits.

A range of special investigations of industrial problems and of test and calibration work for outside organisations continued steadily. An experimental high voltage transmission line, similar to those used for the national grid, was erected adjacent to the high voltage building and often used in the work.

104   The high voltage laboratory immediately after World War II.
This work passed to the GEC in 1961.

As a change from purely electrical matters the Division collaborated in 1955 with Torry Research Station in improving the kippering process, which employed an electrostatic precipitation technique.

The separate existence of the Electricity Division terminated in 1958, when it was divided to make way for the new Basic Physics Division. The standards work went to the Standards Division, the rest to the Applied Physics Division, from which the high voltage work passed on in 1961 to the CEGB Research Laboratories at Leatherhead. At this period the traditional NPL test and standards work reached a low ebb, the 'new' outlook emphasising for a time the role of research in fields of science more nearly 'pure'. However the change made little difference in the laboratories where the traditions of accuracy and dedicated service continued to be maintained, as well as the essential close liaison between the standards and test functions.

This state of affairs lasted a decade during which (in 1965) the control of NPL passed to the Ministry of Technology. In 1967 a new Division of Electrical Science was created with a remit covering the standards and test work of the old Division (though not the high voltage studies), and in addition a commitment to standards throughout the electromagnetic spectrum and, in the course of time, to complete control of time and frequency standards. It incorporated the Advanced Instrumentation Unit from the Molecular Science Division, which concerned itself with generation and measurement in the little exploited sub-millimetre (far infrared) wavelength region between 100 μm and 1 mm.

The test and standards work at DC and low frequency continued on traditional lines, but the demands for increased accuracy and the advent of new techniques and methods and particularly the widespread introduction of electronics increased the tempo of change. Measurements at low frequency demanded the use of a transfer instrument giving the same readings for both AC and DC. For many years electrostatic voltmeters were used for this purpose, but now thermal converters, both single and multi-junction, took over the role. Power continued to be measured by a standard quadrant electrometer; this was used to calibrate secondary standard dynamometer wattmeters used by electricity authorities to calibrate watt–hour meters (very important customer protection in a major consumer industry).

A later development in this field was a sampling digital wattmeter which is more accurate and has a frequency range wider than electrostatic or electrodynamic instruments. It can also carry out spectral analysis. At the heart of the design there is digital multiplier circuitry.

The inductive voltage divider, developed in the old Division during the 1950s, made an important contribution to standards and precision measurement work in many fields, replacing the DC potentiometer in many cases and bringing a new accuracy to low frequency AC measurements. In spite of the transfer to CEGB of the high voltage facilities pioneered at the NPL, there was a growing demand for test work at ever higher voltages and a DC measuring facility had eventually to be provided working to 300 kV.

An important advance in electrical standards work was the advent of the Thompson–Lampard calculable capacitor, the capacitance of which can be determined by a single length measurement. The uncertainty is a factor of 10 less than that of the calculable mutual inductor (which needs a great number of measurements), leading to a corresponding improvement in our knowledge of the absolute value of the ohm. It is interesting to note that the calculations required the accurately known value of the speed of light, which was being measured concurrently.

105   The Thompson-Lampard calculable capacitor.

Some redeterminations of the ampere, using the Ayrton–Jones current balance, were made in the post-war period, but the last of these, carried out in the 1970s after careful redesign of some parts of the apparatus, did not substantially decrease the uncertainty of the measurement. Alternative methods have been tried, such as one involving the gyromagnetic ratio of the proton. However the most promising of them, based on the movement of a coil carrying current in the field of a large permanent magnet, is still undergoing lengthy proving trials.

The volt, determined in absolute terms by measurement of the absolute ohm and the absolute ampere, was maintained for many years by assigning a value to the EMF of Weston cells constructed by a specified technique, regularly intercompared between various national laboratories through the BIPM. During the 1970s a new method of relating voltage standards was evolved, eliminating the tedious process of transferring cells from country to country. This was based on the Josephson effect—accurately defined and stable voltage steps which appear in the voltage–current characteristic of a superconducting tunnel diode irradiated with RF energy. The Josephson constant, the relation between the voltage step and the radio frequency, has been set by international agreement at 483 594 GHz V^{-1}. Equipment based on these principles, which can readily be set up anywhere, is now used as the transfer standard.

The average values of working standards based on banks of standard cells had been laboriously determined for many years as part of the ongoing standards exercise. Computer-controlled test gear revolutionised this sort of measurement. Large numbers of items could be intercompared, each with every other one, in a very much shorter time and the results and averages recorded automatically. Highly stable temperature environments could now be provided for apparatus which remained permanently undisturbed.

Meanwhile magnetic measurements continued on traditional lines, with the provision however in 1971 of an equipment for standardising digital magnetic tapes.

When the Division was reformed in 1967, NPL and RRE (Malvern) both fell within the ambit of the Ministry of Technology, and it was decided to set up a microwave standards group at the latter establishment to contribute to the programme of RF and microwave standards. The combined effort was placed under the control of NPL and in the ensuing years notable contributions were made to measurement methods and standards for attenuation, power, impedance and noise, for both waveguide and coaxial line, in a frequency range extending from a few MHz to 90 GHz. Of particular note was the application of automatic network analysers to standards type measurements and the consequent development of wide range impedance standards for use with them. Later there were complications when the control of RRE passed to the Ministry of Defence, but in fact the collaboration at scientific level continued to go forward smoothly. Intercomparisons of standards with other national laboratories have also been carried out.

The NPL group also made notable advances in the measurement of permittivity and loss angle of dielectrics in an even more extended frequency range, producing data valuable for the design of communication networks (particularly low-loss cables) etc. Such measurements can be correlated with values measured at even shorter wavelengths using the techniques developed by the sub-millimetre group of the Division.

The NPL was also concerned in the late 1970s with setting up standards and calibration facilities for free-field parameters. These were needed for the calibration of microwave radiation hazard monitors and for antenna gain and RF interference measurement. An open-ended anechoic chamber initially covering the frequency range 2.45 to 12.4 GHz formed the major feature of the installation. This frequency range was later extended to 10 MHz to 18 GHz.

An important event in the story of time took place in 1967, when the definition of the second was changed from one based on astronomical observation to one based on atomic constants (namely the duration of 9 192 631 770 periods of the radiation corresponding to the hyperfine transition in the ground state of the atom of caesium-133). The corresponding time scale, International Atomic Time (TAI) based on this definition, was introduced in 1971. Thenceforward the task of the Division was to realise the unit, to construct a time scale based on the integration of the unit and to ensure dissemination of both unit and scale nationally and internationally.

The realisation is accomplished by the long beam caesium standard—three successive designs of which have been operated in NPL since 1955[11].

106   Anechoic chamber for power flux density measurements.

107   The third long beam primary caesium standard in the mid 1970s.

The second is determined with an uncertainty of a few parts in 10^{13} (i.e. one second in 300 000 years). The precision of these time measurements is such that irregularities in the rotation rate of the earth can easily be detected and man is able, for example, to navigate to the moon within close limits or to pinpoint a location on the earth's surface within feet.

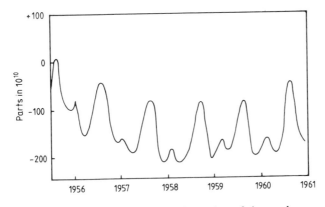

108   Variations in the rate of rotation of the earth.

The atomic time scale is maintained by a group of commercial caesium clocks calibrated in terms of the primary standard. It is compared with International Atomic Time maintained by the Bureau International de l'Heure (BIH) in Paris by daily monitoring of time signals from various countries. The national dissemination is achieved by radio transmission from Rugby of a subsidiary standard maintained in synchronism with those at Teddington. The carrier frequencies have the precision of the atomic standard.

The sub-millimetre wave group of the Division has been almost entirely concerned with a range of wavelengths of which little was known until work began at NPL in the 1960s. A powerful laser, based on HCN and working at 891 GHz (337 μm), was discovered and developed as a source, first of pulses and later of continuous wave radiation. Subsequently a range of discharge pumped and optically pumped lasers was developed enabling spectroscopic and other types of measurement to be carried out between 1 mm and 20 μm. A tuneable solid state spin-flip Raman laser was also produced operating near 10 μm. Radiation from broad band sources was also employed in this range with Fourier transform spectroscopy.

The results have bridged the gap in many fields of measurement between the highest radio frequencies and the longer wavelength infrared radiation previously tackled largely by optical methods. The optical properties of low loss materials used in telecommunications and astronomy were examined and the extended spectra of many potential atmospheric pollutant gases studied to the great benefit of the NPL's programmes on atmospheric and stratospheric pollution. Sub-millimetre equipment was flown in an early experimental Concorde aircraft.

The development of the point-contact Josephson junction for use as a detector and frequency multiplier was a great asset to this work. In particular it enabled the frequency measurement techniques of micro-waves—multiplying, heterodyning and so forth—to be extended into the sub-millimetre range to determine the frequencies of the HCN laser and later of others up to the stabilised helium–neon laser (88 THz). These techniques were used in a joint project with the Quantum Metrology Division for a new determination of the speed of light (qv).

In spite of the high scientific interest, techniques employing the sub-millimetre waveband have so far turned out to have little industrial application. However they are playing an important role in thermonuclear fusion research, which will provide, it is hoped, the clean power generation of the future. The problem of containment of the very high temperature plasma involved, which is not yet solved, can be evaluated by measurements of losses in this wavelength range and, in particular, by studying electron temperature and its spatial distribution. The research is being actively pursued in collaboration with many leading countries.

A small group in the Division has also contributed in the fields of laser energy and laser beam profile measurement, laser safety standards and fibre optics standards.

The NPL Museum, set up in Bushy House in 1977–8, is particularly rich in relics of the electrical standards programmes. These include the Lorenz machine, the Ayrton–Jones current balance, two generations of calculable inductor, the silver voltameter and mercury column resistance standard (which established the old International Units), the Board of Trade standards of current and voltage, a galvanometer enclosure with a six metre mirror scale, the Galton clock, the mark II long beam caesium standard, one of the earliest sub-millimetre lasers and a comprehensive collection of galvanometers and other electrical instruments.

Light and Optical Applications: 1945–1980

The Light Division, founded in 1940, defined its sphere of activity as 'falling between wavelengths of 0.2 to 50 µm, with special concern for the visual region between 0.4 and 0.8 µm'. In the immediate post-war period the pattern of programmes was expanded and, while old problems (including for example the illumination of buildings by daylight and artificial light) continued to be researched and advised upon, work was also begun covering a much wider field.

A General Optics Section designed lens systems and measured and calculated the properties of the elements of optical systems. It advised upon, and tested a range of optical instruments—telescopes, binoculars, sextants, theodolites, clinometers, photographic lenses, polarimeters, saccharimeters and quartz control plates, colorimeters, meteorological radiometers and industrial radiometric instruments. After 1948 routine aspects of test work were progressively transferred to Test House, e.g. sextants, life test of lamps etc. In 1955 a new 15 ft diameter integrating sphere photometer was installed there for luminous flux testing.

There was a long standing programme of refractive index measurement and recording refractometers were built for the wavelength range 300–2500 nm (later extended to 14 µm). Special instruments were designed for the measurement of optical flatness and of the radii of curvature of spherical surfaces. Photoelectric polarimeters were designed, the first of which is still in use at NPL for the calibration of quartz control plates. Subsequently a prototype instrument (saccharimeter) using a Faraday cell as modulator was designed and built for the sugar industry[12]. This was followed by a

109   Set-up for the calibration of sextants.

sophisticated spectrophotometer, also made commercially, which was used for studying molecular structure.

A Radiometry and Standards Section concerned itself mainly with the non-visual aspects of radiation, employing a range of detectors for its measurement work in these parts of the spectrum—photocells, thermopiles, bolometers etc. Photocell spectral responses were determined and filters developed to produce any desired spectral characteristics. Standards of total radiation intensity were maintained and radiometers calibrated. A technique was developed for coating glass with a thin metallic film, conducting to electricity yet transparent to light, which was used for screen heaters on diesel locomotives and aircraft.

The same section was responsible for the primary standard of light and the secondary lamp standards and their intercomparison with those of other national laboratories, also for establishing and maintaining standards of colour temperature.

A Photometry and Colorimetry Section supervised the photometric work of Test House, as well as carrying out measurements of candlepower distribution, luminous flux from fittings and special light sources of all kinds, checking of photometric apparatus and testing of luminescent materials.

110   The large integrating sphere photometer in use. Light from the
test lamp inside the sphere is compared with the light from the standard
lamp seen on the photometric bench on the right.

The selective absorpotion and emission of radiation which, in the visible
region of the spectrum, results in colour was a further concern of the section.
Colour measurements were made using the International Commission on
Illumination system of 1931, which was the basis of British Standard
Specifications for road and railway signals, navigation lights, airport runway
lights etc. Colour standards for control of clinical tests of the haemoglobin
content of blood were developed and put into service.

An extensive programme of research on vision, investigating those
properties of the eye which bear on the measurement of light or colour, was
actively pursued.

Research had been carried out on diffraction gratings, first of all for use in
spectroscopy, but these had been produced in collaboration with the
Metrology Division, where the Blythswood ruling engine continued in
operation until 1957. In 1948 however the Light Division inaugurated
a programme based on a new method of production suggested by Sir
T Merton. The grating, having up to 15 000 grooves per inch, was generated
on a cylinder by means of a lathe; its periodic error was eliminated by a
'flexible nut' and it was then transferred to a flat surface by a replica process.
All these stages involved intensive development. The gratings so produced
were used in two commercial models of spectrometer.

In due course the production of 'moiré fringes' by crossed gratings established their use in precise measurement of length and angle, which led to improvements in the control of industrial machine tools. Later photographic moiré gratings having 1000 lines per inch were produced from a master.

Early in the 1960s work began on optical masers (lasers) which appeared to have tremendous potential for the advancement of the whole range of the work of the Division. The first ruby laser in this country was brought into operation during 1961. An early task was the removal of the limitations on the operation of solid state lasers. Short pulses of very high power were soon available and experiments were carried out on dielectric breakdown, high speed interferometry and the spectroscopic study of the hot dense plasma produced when the laser beam was focused onto a solid target *in vacuo*. Work was also done using gas lasers for the adjustment of optical resonators and other interferometric applications.

Research went on into the technique of waveform reconstruction (known as holography) where laser light diffracted from a solid object is combined with direct light to form interference fringes which are photographed. The photograph (a hologram) contains information about the object from which a three dimensional image of the object can be reconstructed. By making this image coincide with the original object, interference fringes are formed which are a measure of any changes to the object since the hologram was made. This technique was found to have many engineering applications.

Contemporaneously the Radiometry Section extended its work into the performance of radiation detectors under high pulse illumination, while modulation of light with microwaves using so-called electro-optical crystals (beautifully grown within the section) was also investigated.

Meanwhile the Colorimetry and Photometry Section was attempting to improve the basic accuracy of colour measurements by a factor of ten, to bring them into line with the high differential sensitivity of the human eye. Techniques of time-ratio photometry, determination of absolute spectral luminance factor and design of a double monochromator contributed to this end. The vision research produced a practical solution to the problem of specifying the colour rendering properties of light sources.

In December 1966 the Optics and Optical Maser Sections of the Light Division combined with a group concerned with large scale metrology from the Standards Division (soon to become the Division of Quantum Metrology) to form a new Division of Optical Metrology. The Light Division ceased to exist, the remaining sections transferring to the Standards Division (research aspects) and Metrology Centre (routine and test aspects). The terms of reference were simply 'to promote the use of optical methods of measurement in all appropriate fields', by means of

111   Measuring a geodetic tape using a laser interferometer. The room and tape bench were purpose-built in 1908.

research directed towards new optical principles and development of new optical instruments based on them, in conjunction with a study of materials and constructional aspects of instrumentation.

The production of improved diffraction gratings became an important activity of the new grouping. A ruling engine having an accuracy of 3×10^{-6} mm was constructed to meet the demands for these, now finding an ever widening role in process control in industries such as oil, chemical and steel working. By 1972 it also became possible to produce so-called 'blazed' interference gratings, having a groove profile which was sawtooth (as in mechanically ruled gratings) rather than sinusoidal (as in earlier interference gratings). A machine for producing extremely accurate radial gratings has also been designed and built in the Division (32 400 lines giving 40 arc seconds per fringe). This too was passed over to industry.

Optical projection devices, widely used in engineering applications, were studied with a view to higher accuracy and certainty of measurement. One such problem was the correct positioning of components (such as turbo-alternator bearings or the electrodes of a linear accelerator) with respect to a straight line. Typical optical systems were tested on a special bench, 162 m long, using an evacuated light path. Methods of discriminating against diffraction, a major source of error in large scale measurements, were also studied.

A series of quarter-wave plates using optical thin films was developed in the Division to widen the range of measurement of the versatile spectro-polarimeter. The films were also applied as polarising beam splitters in polarising interferometers and in alignment and orientation measurements. A Fizeau interferometer was developed for flatness measurement and a monochromator for determining the efficiency of diffraction gratings used at x-ray wavelengths.

A further reorganisation in 1972 combined the Division of Optical Metrology with the Metrology Centre to form the Division of Mechanical and Optical Metrology, thus joining together a great deal of the Laboratory's test work effort. The terms of reference were 'to engage in research into mechanical and optical standards and measurements and provide standards for use nationally', at the same time providing new or improved instruments of high accuracy, and of lower accuracy for hostile environments. Thus the trend towards optical methods in most aspects of mechanical measurement was duly recognised.

Recently introduced and rapidly developing techniques opened up the field of metrology in many directions. The laser was progressively applied in

112 Producing interference gratings by a laser beam technique.

holographic interferometry and was widely used in engineering measurement. Ruby and neodynium glass lasers were developed enabling high speed records of events to be made at 25 µs intervals. modern photoelectric methods used in conjuction with phase-modulated interferometers made possible mechanical measurements with a precision of a few picometres, and also, for example, the rapid measurement of electron density in plasma research. Fourier transform methods were applied to the investigation of diffraction effects in optical engineering metrology.

Measurements of length and diameter of engineering components need to be carried out with a high degree of accuracy to ensure interchangeability in complex mechanisms such as automobile engines. The Division continued to calibrate working standards to the necessary high accuracy with new and improved equipment employing laser sources. Linear scales and metrological gratings were calibrated in a helium–neon laser interferometer using a fringe counting technique—measurements and calculations being entirely automatic. Similar methods were employed for length bar standards and surveying tapes.

In the field of force measurement the Division concentrated on the development of high accuracy proving devices for calibrating secondary standard load measuring and materials testing machines, and on robust and inexpensive instruments for industrial uses, such as the weighing of aircraft, measurement of thrusts of jet and rocket engines and in structure testing. Demands for the measurement of very large tensile loads increased, particularly in the shipbuilding industry, where the loads needed for the testing of anchor chains for large tankers exceeded the capacity of existing measurement methods. In the civil engineering industry, too, for the testing of piles for multi-storey buildings, compression loads up to 10 MN (1000 tonf) have to be measured. Force calibration equipment working up to 30 MN in compression was installed to handle these problems.

The application and refinement of holographic techniques continued, soon making possible an interferometric measurement of rapidly moving objects or processes, such as shock waves, with further applications in solid state and plasma physics. Sensitive methods were developed for studying the gradual change in shape, or the vibration, of an irregular engineering component, or for comparing it against a holographically recorded master shape. Other new applications for coherent light included the laser speckle interferometer for determining patterns of vibration and surface strain. For large structures, like buildings or pressure vessels, deformation was measured by applying a grid pattern to the surface and photographing this in white light with a camera giving 300 lines mm^{-1} resolution. The negatives were analysed to produce moiré fringe maps giving displacements in detail.

Research into ruling engine designs with sophisticated interferometric control led on to applications in high precision machine control. Accurate, large scale methods of measuring deflection and alignment continued to be developed; these included an automatic laser plumb to detect tilt in high buildings and apparatus to monitor the sag in supertankers during launch.

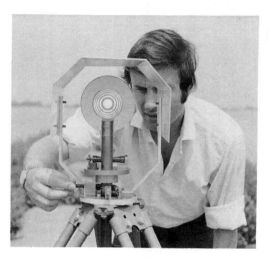

113   High accuracy laser based alignment and deflection measurements, using a 3-point alignment technique.

The preparation of optical surfaces and of optical thin films was studied and novel methods evolved for their evaluation. Computer facilities enabled the interferogram to be plotted which would result if a particular perfect optical component were placed in a Twyman–Green interferometer. The computer generated interferogram was then used in a modified interferometer for comparison with a manufactured specimen of the optical component. Null testing of aspheric surfaces and complete optical systems was thus made possible.

Surface quality is of paramount importance in components—mirrors, grating blanks etc—used for x-ray work. Research was undertaken into machining, lapping and polishing of such surfaces, the quality of which was evaluated by optical and electron microscopy, stylus measurements and x-ray optical methods. Theoretical studies were directed to improving the quality of x-ray gratings and instruments. In due course there grew up a new industry of x-ray optical technology, in which the UK had a substantial lead, and NPL became involved in a number of European and American x-ray telescope projects and in the design of an x-ray microscope.

The creation of standards in vacuum and pressure metrology constituted an important field for research. Both static and dynamic methods of establishing low (i.e. 'high vacuum') and accurately known pressures were investigated and applied to the calibration of ionisation gauges, mass spectrometers and other vacuum devices. Molecular beam techniques were employed to study gas–surface interactions.

A new range of pressure balance standards was created in which pressure was measured in terms of known forces, derived from calibrated weights, applied to the precisely measured cross-sectional area of a piston/cylinder combination. In the modern aerospace industry accurate pressure measurements are needed in order to calibrate altimeters and air speed indicators. To meet these requirements a new barometer was devised employing laser interferometry to measure the height of the mercury column. Careful elimination, or estimation, of systematic errors reduced the measurement uncertainty to 2 or 3 parts in 10^6.

Towards the end of the 1960s the colorimetry scientists at NPL, spurred on by the very high sensitivity of the human eye to shades of colour, tackled the problem of producing standard colour materials for checking industrial colorimeters. Collaboration with the British Ceramic Research Association and the Royal Society of Dyers and Colourists produced a series of ceramic tiles with fired-on colours of great stability and reproducibility. Twelve colours were chosen after exhaustive tests of optical properties to form a standard range for calibration purposes. 1978 saw an interesting application when the National Gallery began using these in a programme of monitoring colour changes in old masters, as an aid to research into conservation and into the nature of pigments and varnishes.

The main object of the radiometric work was to provide standards and calibrations for measuring spectral power distributions of sources and spectral sensitivity of detectors. However, the NPL also participated in an international effort to bring about a unification of photometry and radiometry by redefining the basic photometric unit in terms of radiant power at a specified wavelength. An absolute radiometer developed at the Laboratory contributed to this work. Radiometric work was also carried out in the infrared, concerned with meteorological studies and with advice on the European satellite project for measuring the radiant balance of the earth. Standards for ultraviolet measurements from the visible down to 165 nm were established using synchrotron radiation.

Engineering, Physics and Radiation Science: 1945–1980

The Engineering Division, one of the first to be formed and active in so many diverse fields during the War years, did not survive long in peace time on the Teddington site. The Mechanical Engineering Research Board, which carried the responsibility for most of the programme, decided to set up a new Mechanical Engineering Research Laboratory (it became the National Engineering Laboratory in 1959) at East Kilbride near Glasgow, and most of the Division was transferred there in 1952.

As in most other parts of NPL, work in the years immediately following the War continued very much as in previous decades—assessment of materials and study of their behaviour in service, particularly under conditions of repeated or fluctuating fatigue stresses. The deleterious effects of stress concentration produced by screw threads, fillets of small radius, keyways, oil holes, unmachined and poorly finished surfaces etc were studied. Work was done on the Unified Thread forms adopted by the UK, the USA and Canada. Tests of creep were continued with some 90 machines operational in 1950. In the same year the Division tested wires for bed mattresses, did loading tests on spring mattresses, tested safety glass, surgical needles, steel chains etc—a wide range of activities.

Photoelastic methods of strain analysis were introduced based on freezing the stress into transparent materials, which were then sliced up to discover the stress at any point within the solid. Strain gauge methods were also developed to study dynamic strains in service.

A model of the Debating Chamber in the new House of Commons (roughly a four metre cube) was built to study heating and ventilating problems. Work also began on the use of tidal models to study water flow, navigation and silting problems in river estuaries. Here again a correlation had to be established between the model results and the full scale landform. Models of the Forth, Wyre, Eden and Shatt el Arab estuaries were investigated, as well as certain other problems in the hydraulics field, such as the Severn Barrage. In 1948 this work became the basis of the DSIR Hydraulics Research Organisation, which occupied new buildings at Wallingford in 1951.

The calibration of test machines by means of proving rings calibrated on the 50 ton dead weight machine was continued. A dead weight hardness machine for standardising blocks for routine checking of industrial hardness testing machines was also introduced.

The departure of the main body for Scotland left behind the High Temperature Metal Properties (Creep) Section which later became part of the Metallurgy Division and a section dealing with miscellaneous problems which joined the Physics Division. The strength of aircraft structures, photoelasticity, torsion meter development for ship trials and some varied test work on items such as asbestos fibre pipe flange jointing, railway couplings and drawhooks, chains, welded plates and so on—stayed with the latter at Teddington.

This section continued with the measurement of the secular movement of buildings—the Tower of London (long standing) and Rochester Bridge (started in 1951). On a lighter note, tests were made for the Natural History Museum to determine the force exerted by a hawfinch in cracking cherry and olive stones with its beak.

And so the NPL lost almost all of its Engineering Division, part of the original *raison d'être* for its formation, but of course by now the tremendous advances in the scale of scientific effort meant that there was still more than enough to occupy NPL in many alternative fields.

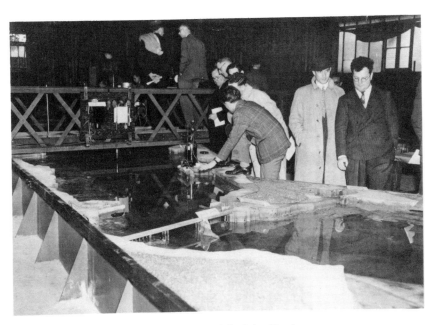

114   Tidal model of the Forth.

Dividing the Laboratory's work in 1900 into Physics and Engineering gave adequate coverage of science and technology in general to accord with the national needs. We have seen how, as time went on, the expansion and diversification of the work led to the founding of new divisions, and indeed to the founding of new laboratories. Thus the old subject division of physics into heat, light, sound, magnetism and electricity, so long hallowed by school curricula and the needs of examinations, delineated the principal divisions of the Physics Department in the first decade of the century. This lasted to 1917 when magnetism and electricity broke away; light followed in 1940, leaving the post-war Physics Division embracing heat (with a separate section for temperature measurement) and sound (acoustics). There was a large section working on radiology and between 1948 and 1952 small sections were acquired for ultrasonics, high pressure standards and engineering (left behind by the Engineering Division). The organisational changes through which these subjects passed are reviewed in Appendix 3.

After 1945 the Heat Section continued its work of research and testing on the thermal properties of materials over a range of temperatures—mostly conductivities[13] and specific heats. In 1949 a close study was made of the metal gallium, newly available in pure single crystal form from the Chemical Research Laboratory. It turned out to have a remarkable anisotropy in electrical and thermal conductivity and in expansion coefficient. By now the pages of *Kaye and Laby* were becoming well filled.

A Collins helium cryostat, installed in 1953, enabled experiments to be carried out down to $-271°C$. The apparatus could also supply liquid hydrogen if required. Precision techniques of bomb calorimetry were developed and used, in conjunction with the Chemical Research Laboratory, to measure heats of combustion of specially pure chemical substances of industrial importance.

An interesting development of the mid 1950s was the thermal comparator, a simple device for the measurement of thermal conductivity giving rapid results to within 10% over the range $0.002-40$ J cm cm^{-2} S$^{-1°}$ C^{-1}. Two phosphor–bronze balls, each fitted with a thermocouple, were mounted in a block of balsa wood—one to come into contact with the tested material, the other held just off contact. The temperature difference after 10 s, as indicated on a potentiometer, was a measure of the thermal conductivity. This provided a significant demonstration that useful scientific ideas in those days did not necessarily need to be complex.

After 1958 when this work was transferred to the Basic Physics Division it ran down fairly quickly, being hardly in accord with the ultra-pure science image then being fostered. Thermal conductivity testing of building materials was transferred to the DSIR's Building Research Station at Garston.

The Temperature Measurement Section soon found itself engaged in planning the revision of the International Temperature Scale, now long overdue. The routine testing of clinical and meteorological thermometers passed to Test House in 1948, but the calibration of all other thermometer types—precision liquid in glass thermometers, industrial thermocouple pyrometers, precision thermocouples, resistance thermometers, optical pyrometers and tungsten strip lamps—stayed with the Division until 1960, by which time Test House was a part of the Applied Physics Division.

Industrial temperature measurement was carried out in open hearth furnaces in steel works, on calender rolls and so on; improved designs of disappearing filament optical pyrometer were produced and radiation instruments developed based on infrared picture tubes and lead sulphide photoconductive cells. The research and test work functions passed to the Standards Division in 1958.

The Acoustics and Sound Measurement Section originally dealt with problems in architectural acoustics, the measurement of noise, the development and maintenance of primary standards of sound pressure and the testing of instruments. The sound transmission of building structures and materials was measured in the laboratory and on site, and advice given to architects and designers; this work however was phased out during the 1960s. Measurements of noise were made in the field using a mobile acoustics laboratory, which travelled the country working on items as diverse as aircraft in flight, aero engine test beds, ships' hulls, factory noise and so on. This vehicle, constructed in 1948, was the first of its kind in the country; it was superseded by a more elaborate vehicle in 1962[14].

In 1952 part of the Section was diverted to work on high pressure standards, but the remainder continued to flourish and expand (threefold) amid all the comings and goings of the Physics Division. The calibration of microphones, which served as reference standards for most acoustics workers in the country, was continued. The properties of the human ear were investigated. The dependence of loudness on frequency and sound pressure level was determined over the whole audible range, giving data fundamental to understanding the hearing process and to satisfactory measurement of hearing loss. Particular attention was given to the establishment of a scale of loudness and of instrumental means of measuring it. The

115   The acoustics test chamber, 1950s.

Section researched audiometric standards, the subjective measurement of noise (needed for legislative control of noise from motor vehicles), sonic boom, and began its involvement with the effects of occupational exposure to loud sounds which continues to the present time.

The transition to the Aerodynamics Division in 1966 had no major effect on the programme. Studies of aircraft noise propagation continued using aircraft such as the Vulcan and the Comet, measurements being taken in conjunction with kine-theodolite tracking. Investigations of non-linear transmission were started.

Sound pressure standards were established over the frequency range 0.01 Hz to 100 kHz for use in the calibration of microphones and sound level meters. Derived standards were also developed and maintained for hearing—minimum audible sound pressure for air conduction and minimum audible skull surface acceleration for bone conduction. The direct measurement of these quantities is not practicable in everyday use, so equivalent values were obtained using artificial ears and mastoids, designed to simulate the respective acoustical and mechanical properties.

The relation between subjective loudness and physical characteristics (intensity, spectrum, temporal variation and direction of arrival) was

116   The reverberation chamber. Sheets of plywood provide sound diffusion.

probed. Psychological consideration, as well as auditory perception, play a part in determining reaction to noise from different sources; a series of subjective tests was carried out therefore in collaboration with the Medical Research Council, the Royal Aircraft Establishment and Motor Industry Research Association.

The demise of the Aerodynamics Division left the Acoustics Section to pass, by way of the Environmental Unit, to the Division of Maritime Science. Improvement work was carried out on the study of traffic noise in an urban environment and the effect of road configuration, barriers and buildings on the spread of noise. Scale models were used to predict sound propagation in real-life situations, the scale effect taken into account by a corresponding scaling up of test frequencies. Predictions were verified by computer simulation of noise distributions and by field measurements at various sites.

The group continued to work on audiological research and standardisation and on the effects of noise on man. Throughout the 1960s studies were carried out in industry, with the aid of mobile acoustic and audiometric laboratories, to correlate noise levels and length of exposure with the state of hearing of noise-exposed workers. These investigations led to a prediction formula and to new noise measuring instrumentation. Methods of preventing occupational hearing loss were studied and also the acceptability or otherwise of a range of noise patterns, so that they might be compared and evaluated.

When the National Maritime Institute took over the Division of Maritime Science in 1974, the Section was retitled the Acoustics Unit and operated independently. Its circular tour of administrative affiliations was completed in 1977 when the Unit was reattached to the Division of Radiation Science, which also derived from the old Physics Division, to form the Division of Radiation Science and Acoustics.

In 1948 an expert in ultrasonics was transferred from TRE, Malvern ostensibly because this work was more appropriate to industry than to defence. Elastic constants of metal specimens were measured via the frequencies of excited resonances, flaw detection methods were developed, powerful ultrasonics sources were built and their industrial uses promoted. In fact the work was not particularly appropriate to NPL, making little impact on industry and none whatsoever on standards. Two members of the group, however, combining expertise in electronics and temperature measurement achieved limited success in developing a fundamental method of temperature measurement based on the Johnson noise generated in an electrical resistor.

This ultrasonics effort was transferred to the Basic Physics Division in 1958 and sank unnoticed into oblivion on the retirement of the group leader. However, some ultrasonics applications arising from a different source, the mechanical engineering group, did continue to be developed. Then many years later (late 1970s) a demand came for the measurement of ultrasonic power levels, by now used in hospitals for diagnostic and treatment purposes, giving rise to an entirely new programme in the Division of Radiation Science and Acoustics.

The mechanical engineering group, left behind by the Engineering Division in 1948 and consisting of scientists who did not for various reasons wish to transfer to Scotland, retained a handful of small programmes reflecting the expertise of their group leader. One such programme was concerned with the use of ultrasonics in the measurement of elastic constants, others included vibration, photoelasticity and secular movements of Rochester Bridge, as well as some test work, such as railway couplings, mine cage suspension chains and lifeboat quick-release gear hooks. Starting in the Physics Division these, too, in due course came under the Basic Physics Division and, after the retirement of the group leader, the staff was dispersed among more urgent projects. An exception was the ultrasonics work which continued on into the Division of Materials Applications, where it played an important role in the testing and characterisation of polymers.

The High Pressure Section was created out of part of the Acoustics Section of the Physics Division at the instigation of Bullard, who, as an expert on the earth sciences, had a personal interest in high pressures in the interior of the earth. Standards for the measurement of high static pressures were developed and fixed points determined on a pressure scale extending to 5000–6000 atmospheres. A study was made of the $P-V-T$ properties of certain gas mixtures in order to relate them to those of the components and thus derive information of value to chemical engineers.

   The work transferred to the Basic Physics Division in 1958, where it continued for a time. Plans were made to take over a 50–60 ft mercury column standard from Imperial College (shades of the one in Bushy House in the early days of the Laboratory!) and provision was made for it, with a spiral staircase for observation, in the new Basic Physics building. However, it was not to be. The standards and measurement work became part of the Standards Division (qv) leaving behind only the most spectacular effects of high pressures—their influence on the structure of solids and on chemical reactions.

The Test House was the responsibility of the Applied Physics Division from 1958 to 1965. The organisation continued to deal with vast numbers of items and to issue the much sought-after NPL Certificates or Reports, which aimed to 'state the truth, unequivocally and without mistake'. Very high standards were maintained. In 1963, in line with the government policy of transferring well established and fully routine tests to other competent organisations, clinical thermometers became the responsibility of the British Standards Institution. Later inhaler testing, hydrometers and volumetric glassware were in their turn transferred to the same organisation's Test Centre at Hemel Hempstead.

1965 saw the foundation of the British Calibration Service (BCS), a central government body, which approves and monitors continuously high class industrial and academic calibration laboratories, both electrical and mechanical, ensuring that their work is of appropriate quality and is based on standards traceable to the national standards realised at NPL. These laboratories then carry out calibration work and issue certificates covering all but the highest grade technical requirements. The expansion of this system in the ensuing years reduced the test work load on NPL, which was then able to concentrate on work of the very highest precision. In due course the BCS came completely under the control of NPL and worked from Teddington, being the responsibility first (1977) of the Superintendent of the Division of Electrical Science, later (1980) of the Superintendent of the Division of Mechanical and Optical Metrology.

After World War II the Radiology Section of the Physics Division continued the accurate measurement of the intensity of x-rays and gamma rays and to advise on protection problems; the latter was a rapidly expanding field and in 1952 an independent organisation, the Radiological Protection Service (RPS), was set up, headed by scientists from NPL, to deal with these problems.

At NPL a standard ionisation chamber, evaluating x-ray intensity in terms of the international unit, was the basis of tests on dosimeters. Geiger counters were used for low intensities and a special film service was provided (before the setting up of the RPS) for assessing the weekly dose received by workers exposed to radiation. X-ray dose in the laboratory was measured over a wide range from the easily absorbed 'Grenz' rays to 2 MeV radiation.

The Section was in charge of the British copy of the International Radium Standard and radium sources were calibrated by comparison with it. Radium containers were tested and new radioactive isotopes standardised. Facilities included a 2 MeV x-ray tube excited by a Van de Graaff type generator and a precision mass spectrometer designed and built in the Section.

New equipment was installed for the measurement of neutron standards (to assist in the future control of atomic reactors and of experiments in modern physics) and for the measurement of radioactive carbon (to assist the archaeologist and geologist in dating samples). In the early 1960s a 3 MeV proton accelerator was installed in the large building recently vacated when the High Voltage Section moved to CEGB, providing a source of neutrons with a wide range of energies for studies in neutron dosimetry.

Just previously there had been a proposal to acquire a nuclear reactor at a cost of £150 000, but this was shelved in favour of the proton accelerator and finally dropped altogether.

The radiation work gradually expanded within the Applied Physics Division, being divided by 1966 into three groups—dosimetry, neutron physics and absolute counting.

Exposure standards were maintained by free-air and cavity chambers and calibrations offered for x-rays generated over the range 7 kV to 2 MV for therapeutic levels and from 7 kV to 50 kV for protection levels. The neutron physics group aimed to provide standards of neutron dose and neutron flux using the 3 MeV van de Graaff accelerator to produce the necessary intense beams. The absolute counting group aimed to provide standards of the more important radio-isotopes by careful studies of their decay schemes. The work also involved the development of new counting systems and new detectors of radiation. Alongside this, work continued on dating samples up to 40 000 years old by the measurement of ^{14}C activity. Samples studied, amounting to some 25 a year, included *scrobicularia plana* for the Geological Survey, Scots Pine for the Meteorological Office, charcoal from central Queensland—a diverse range.

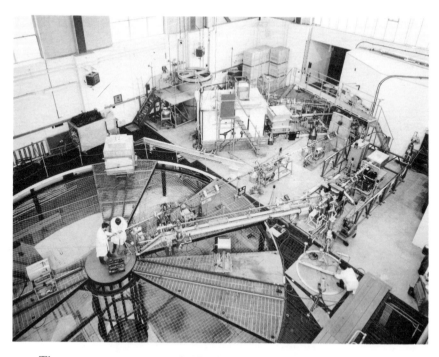

117   The neutron measurement facility in the former high voltage laboratory (cf figure 104).

On the final demise of the Applied Physics Division in 1967, the radiology work expanded to form the new Division of Radiation Science, with terms of reference—'to provide a national focus for the precise measurement of radioactivity and ionising radiations'. This was to be done by achieving a 'proper understanding of the fundamental interactions of radiation with matter on both the macroscopic and atomic levels', i.e. not only in the bulk, but in nuclei, atoms and molecules. Standards of measurement were to be provided in these fields and continually refined by research work and by intercomparisons both national and international.

A wide range of machine and isotope radiation sources was progressively installed backed up by high precision nucleonic measuring equipment and modern data-handling and computing facilities.

The work of the Dosimetry Section extended the range of both exposure and dose rate and of radiation energy. Cobalt-60 and caesium-137 sources provided dose rates from $1 \, R \, h^{-1}$ to $10^6 \, R \, h^{-1}$. At first the most energetic photon and electron beam source was a 2 MeV van de Graaff generator, but later (1975) the energy range was extended to 20 MeV by a new linear accelerator facility, known as Linac. This was installed in a special building with thick concrete walls round the radiation areas to protect staff from radiation hazards, and a 'total loss' air-conditioning system to remove

118   Part of the Linac installation.

noxious gases. The machine operates over a range of 2–20 MeV at intensities ranging from 'protection' levels, through 'treatment' levels to 'processing' levels for both x-ray and electron beams.

The Section developed new instruments for transfer purposes—a therapy level secondary standard exposure meter and a protection level secondary standard dose rate meter. Research was begun on graphite microcalorimeters for use as direct standards of absorbed dose ($J kg^{-1}$) particularly for use with high energy photon and electron beams.

The possibility of accurately comparing absorbed doses by measuring the extent of a radiation induced chemical reaction was explored. Reference standards based on the ferrous sulphate dosimeter were issued to centres using high energy electron beams and then returned for assessment. The absolute calibration of chemical dosimeters demands the simultaneous measurement of energy absorbed and amount of product formed; a system combining these measurements was later developed in which the solution functioned as the calorimetric body.

Absorbed dose was also compared by radiation induced thermoluminescence; the influence of impurities on the performance of lithium fluoride as a dosimetry phosphor was studied by growing doped single crystals. Some attention was also devoted to lyoluminescence.

In the field of radiation protection international agreement defined the maximum permissible levels in terms of neutron flux density as a function of neutron energy. The Neutron Physics Section aimed therefore to establish standards of neutron flux density over a suitable energy range, so that determination of standard neutron reaction cross-sections formed a significant part of the research programme.

Several methods were used for flux density measurement, e.g. counting charged particles emitted simultaneously by the neutron producing reaction, or measuring the residual activity of the target in cases where this is transformed to a radioactive nuclide. Beams of intermediate energy neutrons were measured by integration techniques in which the beam is completely absorbed in a detector and then detected by a suitable reaction, e.g. the activation of manganese or vanadium in aqueous solution.

Facilities installed included a thermal neutron flux produced by bombardment of beryllium targets in a graphite moderator by a deuterium beam from the 3 MeV van de Graaff accelerator, used for precise measurement of thermal neutron cross-sections. A second beam is used for the calibration of neutron monitors.

The Radioactivity Measurement Section continued the work of the Absolute Counting Section on standards and decay schemes of radioactive isotopes. Refinement techniques included radiochemical analysis and mass separation. A high precision, iron free, magnetic beta ray spectrometer was installed to study beta ray, conversion electron, Auger and photoelectron spectra and thus provide accurate data on nuclear decay.

Fluid Flow: 1945–1980

At the end of the War the Aeronautical Research Council, planning the further development of aircraft and the future advancement of aeronautical science, recommended strongly that 'the Aerodynamics Division of NPL should continue to engage mainly on research of a fundamental character'. Expansion of accommodation at the north end of the Parks Estate soon began; in fact it seemed at one time as though the Division might expand all over the site. However, a line was eventually drawn delimiting their area.

At that time attention had turned to the aerodynamic problems of flight above the speed of sound. The 12 in circular tunnel was converted for supersonic operation and produced the first Schlieren and shadowgraph photographs to be obtained in Great Britain of flow past aerofoils at Mach numbers greater than unity. The advent of swept wings, too, provided further new aerodynamic problems for solution.

The remit of the Aerodynamics Division now embraced the problems which arise in the design and development of aeroplanes, helicopters and missiles, such as those associated with take-off and landing, with cruising at subsonic, transonic and supersonic speeds, with control and stability in flight and with the hypersonic flight of long range missiles, satellites and other space vehicles. The total facilities available included wind tunnels, shock tubes, shock tunnels and a whirling arm, which together made it possible to work at speeds ranging from a few feet per second to about 20 times the speed of sound.

Several of the high speed tunnels were of the induced flow type operating up to $M = 1.6$ from compressed air stored at 25 atmospheres. Higher speeds were obtained in direct discharge tunnels, where the compressed air is discharged directly through the tunnel to atmosphere or to a large vacuum sphere. The first of the latter arrived on the site from Germany in the aftermath of the War; later two others were erected alongside[16]. A rotary compressor in the tunnel provided yet another alternative. These methods could be operated up to seven times the speed of sound with a range of stagnation temperatures and pressures.

Problems of flight at hypersonic speeds (i.e. greater than five times the speed of sound) were tackled with a further range of test facilities. It is necessary at these high speeds to reproduce not only the velocity corresponding to full scale flight but also, as far as possible, the intense heating to which the body is subjected. The last was achieved by passing a strong shock wave through it. Flows at speeds up to ten times the speed of sound, with a gas stagnation temperature of 2000 K, were maintained for a few milliseconds, during which time sophisticated instruments measured forces, pressures, temperatures, densities and the state of ionisation of the gas. This work became the basis of a programme on high temperature gas physics; at these temperatures air is no longer a perfect gas, on which most aerodynamic theory is based, but processes of dissociation and ionisation are also involved. The section working on these problems was transferred to the Standards Division in 1966, where radiation and spectroscopy under these conditions continued to be studied in more general terms.

Speeds approaching those for artificial satellites (25 times the speed of sound) were reached, but without pre-heating, in a wind tunnel using helium stored initially at 150 atm as the test fluid, taking advantage of the low liquefaction temperature of this gas. The 'hotshot' tunnel achieved Mach numbers between 10 and 20 for a period of 30 ms by expanding nitrogen gas (which had been heated to a few thousand degrees by the discharge of a 50 000 Joule capacitor) through a conical nozzle into a chamber of 625 cm^3.

Hypersonic flight takes place at altitudes where the distance between the air molecules is comparable with the size of the body. Air flow is no longer that of a continuous fluid but results from the movement of many separate molecules. The change in flow structure and its effects on body forces and pressures were studied in a special low density tunnel.

A considerable programme, both theoretical and experimental, was devoted to the shapes of wing sections. Aircraft which benefited from the results of this work included the VC 10, Trident, BAC 111, HP 'Jetstream' and HS 'Harrier'. An important discovery was the elimination of strong drag producing shock waves and of shock induced boundary layer separation by designing the wing profile to produce a 'peaky' velocity distribution instead of the conventional shape.

Developments in higher speed aircraft brought problems in the low speed flight conditions encountered in take-off and landing. These were studied in the largest cross-section wind tunnels, all of which had a top speed of around 150 mph. Research relating to VTOL and STOL aircraft was also carried out in these tunnels.

The ten years following the War saw considerable extensions of the work into the field of non-aeronautical aerodynamics. In 1946 a bridge across the Severn Estuary was being planned and, because of the startling failure of the Tacoma Narrows Bridge in the USA in 1940 due to aeroelastic instability, the designers turned to the NPL flutter team for guidance. A detailed model was constructed and a method evolved for testing sectional models which became the basis of all future work in this field. Subsequently many aerodynamics problems of civil engineering structures were referred to the NPL team, which became the British centre for research and *ad hoc* investigations in this field. The science of industrial aerodynamics eventually embraced studies of environmental flows (i.e. those affecting the comfort or safety of people), the wind loading of structures too stiff to vibrate appreciably in a wind, the wind excited vibration of flexible structures and other general topics unconnected with travel by aircraft.

Environmental studies included the flow of smoke and contaminants from ships' funnels over the superstructure. Model tests in the tunnels determined suitable designs, the effectiveness of which was confirmed in 1961 by full scale observations on *SS Oriana* and *SS Canberra*. Five years later extensive tests (involving 17 different models) produced an optimum funnel design for the Cunarder *SS Queen Elizabeth II*. The dispersal of efflux from power stations (Bankside in London was one of the first to be examined) and hospital chimneys as affected by local buildings and topography was painstakingly determined. The flow of wind over the decks of oil platforms was studied to aid helicopter landing and general worker safety. Cuttings were designed and tree planting schemes developed to alleviate snow drifting on the M62 Motorway.

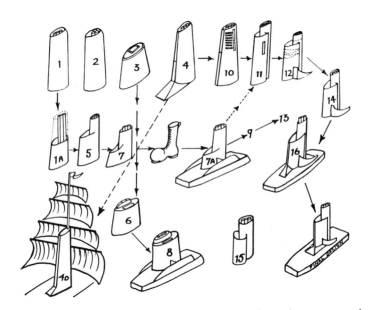

119 'Funnel Designer's Nightmare'—some configurations suggested for the QEII.

Loading on stiff structures involved work on the telescope at Jodrell Bank (and other radio telescopes and radar dishes), electricity pylons, the deflections of the Post Office Towers in London and Birmingham (where the sway must not deflect the microwave beam by more than a quarter of a degree), the wind loading on tall buildings, wind forces on ships and cooling tower design.

A great deal of civil engineering aerodynamics is concerned with various types of wind induced oscillations. In 1957 a helicoidal strake device was

120   Strakes fitted on industrial chimney stacks.

designed to prevent the oscillation of a circular chimney stack or structure
and this was followed by a perforated shroud for the same purpose. Later the
same shroud device was used to prevent oscillation of steel piles in flowing
water, first applied at Immingham in the Humber estuary.

The original Severn Bridge studies of the late 1940s were in fact first
applied to the Forth Bridge of 1964, the Severn Bridge having been delayed
by capital expenditure cuts. When the project was finally authorised fresh
investigations were made of the novel steel plated box structure, which was
adopted for the roadway deck. Other wind excited vibration studies
included television transmission masts, such as Crystal Palace and later
Emsley Moor, and numerous high buildings, notably the twin-block world
Trade Center in New York.

Windmill type electricity generators were examined for the Ministry of
Power, also the buckling failure of cooling tower shells.

In May 1970 the Minister of Technology decided to concentrate all
national aerodynamics work on aircraft at the Royal Aircraft Establishment,
leaving behind at Teddington, however, the industrial aerodynamics work
and most of the wind tunnel facilities. First termed the Environmental Unit,
this was later incorporated in the Division of Maritime Science. The
movement of equipment and personnel began in the October of that year,

bringing to a close some 60 years of research at NPL, which had contributed very substantially to the development of the aeroplane in this country.

Subsequent wind tunnel work included research, testing and advice on off-shore structures for North Sea oil drilling, a drilling ship with a massive superstructure and many other vessels. Design assistance was given for the Humber Bridge—on the towers and on the details of the closed box deck structure as first used on the Severn Bridge. Studies were made of the wind speed and behaviour in pedestrian areas close to tall buildings, smoke pollution from badly sited chimneys, the helicopter landing platform on the top of the Wolf Rock Lighthouse, the layout of the port facilities at Dover Harbour, and many more.

121　Model of Dover Harbour in a wind tunnel.

In July 1976 this work became part of the National Maritime Institute. At the time of the change two new tunnels were added to the facilities. A large area tunnel for natural wind studies was produced by major modification of the old 13 ft × 9 ft aeronautical tunnel to provide a range of wind speeds with correct vertical profile and turbulence properties. Large topographical models can be mounted on a turntable and vibration-free mountings are provided at the centre so that the dynamic response of structures can be studied. The second was a wind–wave facility—a wind tunnel section leads into an enclosed water tank, in which studies can be made of wind induced waves and the effects of wind and waves combined on model structures.

In the post-war period the unique tank facilities at Teddington continued to be in great demand among shipbuilders. While no longer on the wartime scale, the industry still functioned effectively and sought advice for the improvement of its products. In 1954, for example, 65 hull models and about the same number of propeller models were tested on behalf of industry and power savings (up to 10 % in some cases) achieved as a result. In addition 30 hull models were tested for research purposes. It was estimated that at this time 80 % of new British mercantile ship construction was based on designs tested by the Division. Among miscellaneous items, lightship designs and cable strains were tested for Trinity House and yachts for the Yacht Research Council.

Big changes were on the way, however, as the planning of a much larger towing tank was already in train. Finally opened at Feltham in 1959, this was twice the length, twice the width and twice the depth of the tanks at Teddington. (The length, 1300 feet, is such that the towing rails are not flat but follow the curvature of the earth in order to stay parallel to the water surface.) The facilities here, which also included a large sea-keeping tank where models are radio-controlled, a circulating water channel of advanced design (added in 1965) and two water tunnels, enabled a wide ranging programme to be undertaken.

The work now divided into seven main groups—resistance and propulsion of ships in calm water and waves, ship motions including manoeuvring and vibration, ship propulsion devices, high speed marine craft, design studies for new ships, hydrodynamics of surface and sub-surface bodies other than ships and instrumentation development.

Work on ship models continued to cut water resistance and save power—a considerable contribution to the design of very large vessels such as oil tankers. A bulbous bow design recommended for trawlers was much appreciated by one group of owners who, in 1960, wrote that in a recent gale their ship with its catch reached port many hours in advance of its competitors.

An investigation of bubble breakwaters, which suppress ocean waves by opposing a stream of water by a rising curtain of air bubbles, was carried out on behalf of the Military Engineering Experimental Establishment; also an examination of the towing characteristics of flexible oil barges.

The study of ship motions was directed towards developing ships with more kindly behaviour in waves, with improved manoeuvring qualities and which did not suffer from propeller excited vibrations. Sea state data were collected and analysed so that the necessary complex conditions could be reproduced in the tanks. The objectives of this work were the design of stabilising devices to control and reduce rolling and pitching and the improvement of steering and course keeping characteristics. Another phenomenon of vital interest was the potentially destructive 'slamming' which occurs when the hull of a vessel emerges from the sea in rough weather and then drops back. Yet another study on twin screw vessels demonstrated the improvement in control and manoeuvrability of inward turning screws compared with outward turning.

Some considerable attention was paid to rudder design and novel variants were produced exploiting aeronautical techniques of circulation control. An experimental 25 m cargo vessel, using a new rudder design based on work with models, could rotate about a vertical axis without gaining headway.

Work on propulsion was largely devoted to propeller design—extending the range over which conventional screw propellers would maintain high efficiency by taking steps to minimise cavitation. Unconventional propellers were also studied, including shrouded screws, and types where cavitation is encouraged rather than avoided. In practice there is a complex interaction between the propeller and the stern of the ship and the combination has to be treated as a system. Propulsion by water jets, used in some hydrofoils, was also studied.

122 Cavitation around a propeller.

Work was done on the hydrodynamics of high speed vessels of the hydrofoil and hovercraft types.

Safety at sea engaged the attention of the Division for many years. In 1946, for example, an investigation was carried out for the Admiralty in connection with the collision between the cruiser *HMS Curacao* and the Cunard–White Star *RMS Queen Mary*. The interaction of water forces upon the two ships when travelling at different speeds on converging courses was demonstrated by models in the tank (their movements being recorded by cine film) in front of members and expert witnesses from the Court of Enquiry.

Eventually most aspects of this subject became the responsibility of the Division of Maritime Science, but the Ship Division continued to deal with points affecting actual vessels.

That large following seas can lead to fatal rolling provided yet another complex problem. A damaged ship exposed to attack is a subject which cannot readily be treated by a theoretical approach. However, the Division was able to carry out a model study of the capsizing behaviour of a partially flooded ferry vessel leading to recommendations and international cooperation on stability standards for passenger ships. Also investigated was so-called 'squat', the increase in draught caused by Bernouilli effects when ships move in shallow water.

During 1967 the technical group of Hovercraft Developments Ltd at Hythe on Southampton Water was transferred to NPL and became the NPL Hovercraft Unit. The hydrodynamics problems continued to be undertaken by the Ship Division, with the Unit filling in the area between there and the practical craft. Apart from sea-going vessels the hover principle was also applied to the movement of large, heavy objects and to the design of a 'hoverbed' for treating patients with very bad burns.

123　An experimental hovercraft.

The Division of Maritime Science was founded at the request of the Government in 1971 to handle certain vital problems not previously within the ambit of NPL and not receiving attention at alternative sites. Major collisions in the English Channel created a demand for continuous carefully detailed monitoring of shipping in that seaway, a problem aggravated by the spectacular increase in size and number of really large ships (factors of 5 and 12 respectively in the previous decade) and their comparative lack of manoeuvrability. The rapid rise in the exploitation of the bed of the North Sea for oil and in techniques and equipment for its extraction brought a whole host of problems for the Division, which called for the coordination of the facilities taken over with the Industrial Aerodynamics Section and the tank facilities of the Ship Division, where some of this work had already started a year or two previously.

Surveys of shipping in the Straits of Dover were made by radar and other means, such as helicopter surveillance, to establish distribution, density and types of traffic and cargoes. This involved collaboration with many other organisations both in this country and abroad and produced information used in operational research studies to improve safety and efficiency of navigation. The manoeuvrability and handling of large ships in shallow and restricted waters, such as on the approaches to ports, were also studied.

Wind and wave tests were made in the laboratory on models of off-shore structures, while a 260 tonne research tower (11 m high × 3 m diameter, standing 8.5 m deep) was erected on the sea bed in Christchurch Bay, where sea conditions in relation to the size of the structure were similar to those of the North Sea. This incorporated facilities for measuring pressure and load at various depths, which long term effects of sea bed/structure interaction and marine growth could also be explored.

The new National Maritime Institute took over the Ship and Maritime Science Divisions of NPL with all the wind tunnel and ship tank facilities at both Teddington and Feltham and thus brought to a close some 65 years of scientific support by the NPL for those highly important areas of engineering.

Materials Science: 1945–1980

For more than two decades after 1945 the Metallurgy Division continued with its long standing programme of investigation into the constitution, structure and physical and mechanical properties of both ferrous and non-ferrous metals and alloys. The research was backed by an ever expanding service in chemistry, refractory development and metal working apparatus, in techniques and methods for examination and measurement and by studies in metallurgical thermodynamics. The accommodation was extended by a new two storey building in 1953, which housed the x-ray, ceramic and radioactive tracer sections.

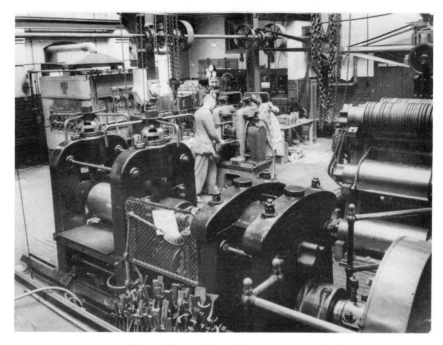

124   The rolling mill and heat treatment shop.

Studies continued of the creep properties of magnesium alloys containing cerium and small proportions of other metals, and these were later extended to the, then, little known titanium. This metal is very reactive and attacks all refractory materials at high temperatures, so that a special technique had to be developed to avoid contamination in its preparation. The metal was placed on a water-cooled copper hearth in a vacuum-tight system containing pure argon at low pressure; it was melted by an electric arc between the metal and a tungsten-tipped water-cooled copper electrode. This method was also used for other similarly reactive high melting point materials. One of the next to receive attention was niobium, which was found to be valuable as an additive element in high temperature alloys.

During the Superintendency of N P Allen there was a continuing strong emphasis on the work on iron and steel, though this has declined of recent years. Production of pure iron continued on a 25 + kg scale with profitable sales outside the Laboratory.

An important task of the period was the continued preparation of high purity samples of other metals, used for the determination of physical properties and for the preparation of contamination-free alloys. These included beryllium, chromium, cobalt, magnesium, manganese, silicon and vanadium. Techniques for purification included zone refining, where a

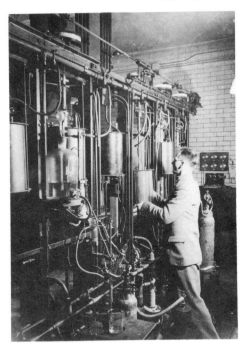

125 A creep unit being erected. The furnace is being lifted into place.

narrow molten zone caused to traverse a rod specimen carries impurities away to the ends. Many pure metals and alloys were obtained in the form of single crystals by this and other techniques, thus facilitating the measurement of properties and their relation to the crystal lattice. Later single crystals of other materials, such as alumina with regulated impurities (e.g. rubies) were also grown by various methods for research purposes.

The High Temperature Metal Properties Section, which came over from the Engineering Division, brought a comprehensive set of creep facilities for working with steady loads in the temperature range 20°C to 1250°C. Long term data, up to 100 000/h could be determined while cyclic fatigue conditions could be imposed at temperatures up to 900°C. There were facilities too for studying metal and alloy behaviour in steam plants at working pressures up to 1500 psi and temperatures up to 650°C. The machines were automatic and could detect creep strains of 10^{-8} per hour. Later some of this creep testing equipment was transferred to NEL and facilities at NPL were reorganised to enable a systematic study of the effects of minor impurities on the creep properties of pure iron and various high temperature alloys to be made.

The Division was called upon to test or report on items as diverse as an ancient sword found in the River Thames, a pair of mediaeval scissors, an

126   Experiments at high temperatures.

antique chisel, a nickel alloy for use in vacuum tubes, vanadium compounds in the ash deposits from heavy fuel oils which foul gas turbines, the deterioration of gas turbine blades fired with peat, and many more.

The new building programme of the early 1960s provided the Division with a Mechanical Working Laboratory opened in 1962. This added facilities for hot rolling four inch diameter 50 lb ingots, a 700 ton extrusion press, a swaging machine, a forging hammer (the original from the 1920s re-installed here), a precision mill for rolling strip and a wire drawing bench.

The x-ray and Metal Physics Section of the Division developed a soft x-ray spectrometer, which was used in conjunction with x-ray diffraction measurements to study the cohesive forces between the atoms of a metal. In the late 1950s a new electron microscope with a resolution of 10^{-6} mm enabled dislocations in metal under stress to be followed visually. Radioactive tracer techniques were employed to investigate the diffusion of atoms in a metal or of atoms of one metal in another. A field ion microscope built in the Division made possible observations of individual atoms in a limited range of metals. Techniques employing x-ray fluorescence from a micro-focus x-ray beam could detect the chemical composition of pre-cipitates in metals over a distance as small as a few microns.

The Chemistry Section, which had long supported the Divisional programme by conventional methods, enlarged its scope to take in neutron activation analysis, where impurities are detected from their radioactive isotopes produced by irradiation in an atomic reactor. Analysis of the various decay rates makes possible an analysis of the sample. The method could detect impurity levels in semiconductors such as silicon or germanium of 1 in 10^9 or 10^{10}, which can have marked effects on electrical properties. Mass spectrometry, giving a general picture of impurities in a sample in only one exposure, was also employed.

Later a Surface Chemistry Section, taken over from the National Chemical Laboratory, united many of these techniques in a study of the corrosion mechanism of surfaces.

Early in the 1960s the rise in interest in high field superconductivity alloys for the production of high strength magnetic fields led to the setting up of a team to investigate them. Single crystals of appropriate materials (often niobium alloys) were examined for superconducting properties and these were related to metallurgical factors.

In April 1958 a new Division, called Basic Physics, was set up to study, across the broadest possible field, 'the relation between the large scale physical properties of materials (mechanical, electrical and physical) and their detailed structure on an atomic or molecular level'. The aim was

> . . . to act as a centre for fundamental research in a number of branches of physics which are of potential importance to industry. In the past the Laboratory's contributions to the refinement of standards, the advancement of industrial techniques and the industrial application of research have tended to obscure its contribution to more fundamental work; the formation of this new Division will emphasise the research aspect and will serve as a source of scientific strength to the other divisions and through them to British Industry.

The swing from 'industrial' to 'scientific' seemed to be gathering momentum!

Certain Sections from the Physics Division—those concerned with Heat and Thermodynamics, Ultrasonics, Strength of Materials, High Pressure Physics and Low Temperature Studies, along with an infrared spectroscopy group from the Light Division, provided the basis.

However the outstanding feature of this new organisation was the recruitment of a number of young scientists, more-or-less straight from University, to engage on work entirely new to the Laboratory. The recently discovered technique of nuclear magnetic resonance, which could provide information about the detailed structure of the molecule, was made available in a huge spectrometer purchased from the USA. Work was also started on the allied technique of electron spin resonance, used for studying the nature of radicals produced by various forms of radiation (x-rays, gamma rays etc) and hence obtaining an insight into the modifications of substances produced by irradiation. Measurement of the general physical properties of polymeric materials was the aim of another group. The far infrared spectroscopy group worked mostly between 20 μm and 1 mm using interferometric methods. Atomic vibrations of crystals, the rotation of molecules in gases and the properties of electrons in superconductors were some of the subjects studied.

A considerable range of complex electronic circuitry had to be designed and made to support all these activities and whole equipments, such as the one to investigate, and utilise, the phenomenon known as spin echo, were constructed during this time.

Meanwhile work was also done in the field of high pressures, of the order of 100 000 atm, and physical properties measured of the materials thus produced. Some substances were found to undergo profound changes in properties—indium antimonide, for example, changed resistivity by a factor of 10^5 between 30 000 and 40 000 atm. This culminated in an experiment to make diamonds, (already carried out by scientists in the USA and South Africa) which in the event were just detectable by x-rays. In another group specific heats of fusion were determined over a wide range of temperatures.

Organisational changes in April 1965 combined the Basic Physics Division with the inorganic and organic chemistry group from the disbanded National Chemical Laboratory, to form a new Division of Molecular Science. A year later two groups from this Division were given independent status—an Advanced Instrumentation Unit, which included much of the infrared spectroscopy work, and an Inorganic Materials Unit, while low temperature physics[17] became part of the Standards Division.

The work on nuclear magnetic resonance and electron spin resonance and associated techniques continued to be extended and refined in the Division of Molecular Science, as did the studies of high polymers and the striving to uncover connections between their molecular structures and bulk electrical and mechanical properties. The availability of lasers as high intensity monochromatic light sources had generated an interest in non-linear polarisation of dielectrics and the possibilities of harmonic generation and frequency mixing at optical frequencies. A section was set up therefore to work on non-linear optics problems—to relate non-linearity at high intensities to other crystal and molecular properties. In this connection theoretical studies were made of crystal electrodynamics, while a section flourished for a time growing the single crystals needed for this and other programmes in the Laboratory.

Teams formerly with the National Chemical Laboratory were meanwhile studying electrochemistry, particularly with respect to organic synthesis, and high pressure chemistry, where reactions of organic and organometallic compounds were studied in the range 5000 to 45 000 atm.

The Division of Molecular Science was disbanded in 1970 and its programmes and personnel divided between the Divisions of Inorganic and Metallic Structure, Materials Applications and Electrical Science.

The Advanced Instrumentation Unit, after 18 months of independence, became a part of the new Division of Electrical Science. Work had continued on interferometric spectroscopy in the frequency range 10 μm to 1 cm, with an on-line computer to work out the spectra far more quickly than any previous technique, while the HCN laser, a high intensity monochromatic source at 891 GHz had been developed and widely utilised. This was the first high power source in this wavelength range, though a plasma–metal junction harmonic generator developed in the Standards Division a year or two earlier had produced detectable radiation at a similar frequency (the 29th harmonic of a 35 GHz source).

The life of the Inorganic Materials Unit was even shorter, since in less than 12 months it joined with parts of the Metallurgy Division to become the Division of Inorganic and Metallic Structure. Work had been done on silicate glasses with the object of producing new and improved materials, the structure being probed by a range of techniques, and a plasma furnace had been developed to study reactions of refractory materials in the temperature range 4000 to 12 000 K.

The closure of the National Chemical Laboratory in 1965 brought to an end a long and honourable service of chemical scientific support to industry dating back to the 1920s. The projects and personnel were dispersed, some to the Warren Spring Laboratory at Stevenage, some to the Divisions of Molecular Science and Metallurgy. The remainder became a new Division of Chemical Standards at NPL with a remit directed to 'the systematic measurement of physico–chemical, thermodynamic and spectroscopic properties of substances that are important in technology and science, or are likely to become so'.

The new Division took the advice of the chemical industry in formulating its programmes; accordingly, work was started on organic compounds containing oxygen or fluorine, on inorganic phosphorus compounds and on uranium compounds. The research, devoted mainly to chemical thermodynamics and molecular spectroscopy, was organised in seven sections—the purification of organic compounds (the Division pioneered the use of zone melting in this field—samples of pure chemicals were supplied to outside customers, building fairly quickly a comprehensive service in certified reference materials); heat capacity measurement (in a temperature range from 10 K up to 450 K, then 800 K and finally 1800 K—providing data for chemical engineers); measurement of heats of formation (using various special designs of bomb calorimeter); study of $P–V–T$ relations for gases and gas mixtures; molecular spectroscopy (from ultraviolet through to the far infrared, plus Raman types); nuclear magnetic resonance spectroscopy; and mass spectroscopy.

Later researches were extended to ceramics, to the measurement of thermal conductivities and viscosities of organic liquids, to metallurgical thermodynamics and to determining the molecular weights of polymers.

The variety of techniques applied to the last problem included membrane osmometry, light scattering photometry and ultra centrifugation. High pressure chemistry returned here after a spell with the Molecular Science Division to work on high pressure–high temperature standards in the region 1–4.5 GPa and 500–6000° C.

An Energy Unit, set up in the early 1970s at the time of the oil crisis, functioned for a number of years inside the framework of the Division, proffering advice and initiating external research programmes aimed at conservation and better utilisation of energy. This work later transferred to the Department of Industry HQ.

Throughout, the Analytical Chemistry and Glass-blowing sections provided a service for the whole Laboratory. The former, while remaining on the site and continuing to function as previously, became the responsibility of the Laboratory of the Government Chemist in 1977.

The Division of Chemical Standards was finally merged with that of Materials Applications during the economy drive of 1980–81 when a number of programmes were dropped altogether.

The Division of Inorganic and Metallic Structure was set up in 1967 combining parts of the Divisions of Molecular Science and Metallurgy. Its terms of reference were 'the study of the relationship between the microstructures and the properties of all inorganic materials', which were taken to include metals, glasses, composites, ceramics, powders, multiphase aggregates, artificially produced minerals, microcrystalline bodies and thin films.

Apparatus available included modern electron microscopes and field ion microscopes. A 1 MV electron microscope of advanced design was added in 1970, erected in a new annexe to the Metal Working Laboratory. Techniques for scanning electron microscopy and electron microprobe analysis were also developed.

High temperature studies were carried out using resistive or inductive heating up to 3000 K and thermal plasmas produced by electrical discharge in the range 2500 K to 10 000 K. Many high melting point substances were vaporised and fine powders produced by quenching, or were made to undergo chemical reactions to produce new materials. High temperature melts were also studied.

Work at high pressures was devoted to demonstrating the feasibility of constructing and operating laboratory equipment (capable of later development for industrial purposes) at pressures up to 25 000 atmospheres (2.5 GPa) and at elevated temperatures.

Glass ceramics provided another subject for study—refractory glasses with high strength at over 1000 K, low expansion materials with high thermal shock resistance and glasses to be used in conjunction with metals or with other ceramic types. Dental cements and chalcogenide switching

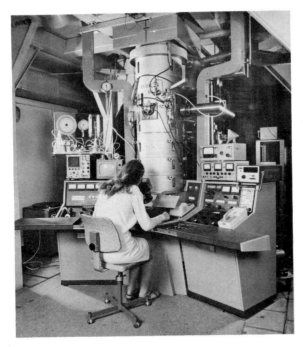

127   The one million volt electron microscope (a commercially built instrument).

glasses were also studied; the range of techniques employed included electron microscopy using ion-beam machining in specimen preparation, high temperature microscopy, x-ray diffraction, differential thermal analysis and the measurement of viscosity, creep, hot and cold strength, expansion coefficients and thermal shock resistance.

Work on composite materials included failure mechanisms under various loading conditions and fatigue behaviour. The factors determining fracture toughness were worked out and the toughness of some composites, e.g. reinforced plastics and cements, thereby improved. The mechanical properties of powder and fibre filled thermoplastics were also probed.

The Division included a section for the growing of single crystals—from melt, solution, gels and vapour. New high strength alloys were prepared by unidirectional freezing. Some effort was put into the preparation of long single crystal sapphire filaments, intended for use in a high strength composite. A sessile drop apparatus enabled the interaction of molten metals with refractories to be investigated.

An important series of studies concerned methods of measuring surface composition and topography. An Auger electron spectrometer, with a sensitivity of one tenth of an atomic monolayer, was used to study the composition of surface layers and transmission electron microscopy provided data on surface topography. Other complex investigations also went forward—e.g. of free energies of surfaces and grain boundaries over a range of temperatures, of grain boundary embrittlement etc.

Creep studies continued to promote the more accurate engineering use of metals. Three specific problems were noteworthy—the determination by examination of how much of the available life of a material has been used up, variable load testing to determine what recovery occurs at times of reduced load, and an assessment of the multiple-mechanical-thermal-treatment process as applied to stainless steel in nuclear reactors.

Advanced microscopy techniques were developed as an adjunct to the work—four 100 kV transmission electron microscopes were eventually available, while the 1 MV microscope extended the scope of the work to specimens six times as thick. The last could also penetrate to specimens working in environmental cells e.g. the hydration of cement, wet biological and medical specimens, chemical processes etc. A number of instruments were developed and utilised for the study of microstructure, some of them providing a service to the rest of the Laboratory. The use of the 1 MV electron microscope was discontinued in 1977.

In 1975 the Division ceased to exist and its programmes and personnel were divided between the Divisions of Chemical Standards and Materials Applications.

The Division of Materials Applications came into being at the same time as the Division of Inorganic and Metallic Structure, deriving its programme and personnel from the same sources. The terms of reference were to concern itself with 'the industrial applications of metallic and non-metallic materials', emphasising engineering properties—mechanical, thermal, electrical and optical and their relation with composition, processing parameters, microstructure and service conditions.

Studies concerned with optimising the composition and microstructure were carried out on steels used in steam turbine plant. Similar work on nickel–chromium alloys as used in gas turbines linked ductility with variations in composition. Grain structure was found to play an important role in strength at high temperatures. Mechanical properties and microstructure of hard-metals (metal bonded carbides of tungsten, titanium and tantalum) were examined to determine the structural factors that govern reproducibility of performance. Similar research was devoted to tool steels manufactured by the new processes of powder metallurgy and electro slag refining.

The physical and mechanical properties of numerous materials used in cryogenic engineering were determined in the range 1–300 K and an advisory service set up for the industry.

The oxidation of metals and alloys in service was investigated. Electron diffraction and microscopy were used to study the behaviour of iron–

chromium alloys in oxidising conditions and inhibitory treatments devised. This work was carried out at temperatures up to 650 K so as to cover the requirements of use in steam raising plant and hot water systems; conditions of protective film formation were studied. A flowing water loop enabled the combined effects of flow and temperature to be simulated. Work was also done on the oxidation of nickel–chromium alloys at high temperatures in atmospheres containing sodium sulphate. Subsequently a National Corrosion Service was started up on behalf of the Department of Industry. It offered advice and assistance, including design and materials selection, specification of preventive measures and remedial procedures, trouble shooting and failure analysis.

A programme on polymers concerned their characteristics as engineering materials and the understanding of the relation between properties and material structures at all levels. Polymers have special properties, unfamiliar in some cases to the classical engineer, which may be specially desirable or undesirable in a given application. The work involved an intimate theoretical/experimental mix. Theoretical models—of viscoelastic behaviour, anisotropy, inhomogeneity, non-linear mechanical behaviour and combinations of these—were developed and their applications analysed. Experimental techniques for polymer measurement included elastic moduli and mechanical damping (over a wide range of frequencies and temperatures using direct extensometry), ultrasonic pulse transmission, resonance and forced vibration methods. Structural studies to examine morphology, chain geometry, crystallinity and stress-induced orientations were carried out by optical and electron microscopy, infrared absorption and dichroism, x-ray diffractometry, differential scanning calorimetry, holography, ultrasonics etc. Particular attention was paid to the influence of commercial processing techniques on structure and properties.

Another section of the Division (later transferred to the Division of Electrical Science) studied the electromagnetic properties of non-metallic materials with applications in assorted fields such as communications, automatic control of factories, atmospheric pollution studies and light generation; all this with a strong emphasis on the infrared end of the spectrum. Novel instrumentation was developed and used to relate fundamental molecular aspects of materials to their electromagnetic properties.

Work continued on directionally solidified superalloys and eutectic alloys offering significant advantages over other high temperature materials for gas turbines. The solidification parameters leading to the required engineering properties were determined and optimised. Studies of dental materials and their bonding to teeth were also carried out.

The Auger electron spectroscopy equipment used for surface analysis was augmented by further models and facilities added for x-ray photoelectron spectrometry (XPS) and secondary ion mass spectrometry (SIMS).

A dramatic example of NPL service to the community occurred in August 1976, when the chiming mechanism of the Great Clock of the Palace of Westminster (Big Ben) disintegrated, after almost continuous operation since 1854. The shaft of the fly governor failed, the driving weights fell 50 m to ground level and so accelerated the chiming mechanism and the associated cast-iron gear trains that general break-up occurred. The NPL was called in, located the cause of failure and later designed a fail-safe device for the quarter-chiming mechanism to prevent similar disasters in the future.

NPL—Today and Tomorrow

Almost all that has been written above is in the past tense, yet many of the items in the later chapters are in fact on-going. The national standards laboratory for the UK, the NPL will continue to provide a national centre for relevant knowledge in the science of measurement and to act as a focal point for its dissemination to engineers and scientists in industry, government, commerce and academic research for many years to come. The objectives in the standards area will continue to be (much as they have always been):

(*a*) To develop and maintain techniques for the realisation of the units of measurement for physical quantities, and to promote the international agreement for such units.

(*b*) To disseminate measurement standards and related techniques of measurement by such means as the operation of the British Calibration Service, the direct calibration of instruments and the issue of reference materials.

(*c*) To provide an advisory service on the use of measurement standards and techniques to government departments and public and private organisations.

(*d*) To undertake the accurate measurement of physical and chemical constants.

(*e*) To measure the properties of materials, develop new and standardised methods for their measurement, define relevant characteristics of materials and relate the characteristics to behaviour, having regard to the effects of environment.

The NPL, as the national centre for measurement standards and techniques, is in daily contact with representatives of industry, government departments and commerce from all parts of the UK. Discussions and informal cooperation take place at all levels. Government departments, for example, seek the advice of the Laboratory in formulating policies and drafting proposed legislation, particularly in matters relating to the environment, i.e. noise, electromagnetic radiation and atmospheric pollution. There is an exchange of advice and ideas with research departments in the universities, polytechnics and technical colleges. Visits, lectures and joint projects are organised as necessary, and details of the Laboratory's research activities are made available freely through publication in scientific and technical journals and NPL Reports, and through staff participation in national and international conferences. Moreover, members of staff at NPL are always available for consultation on matters relating to the Laboratory's interests.

In certain of its international activities the NPL has the formal responsibility of representing the UK. In discussions on the definition of fundamental units of measurement, and the adoption of international primary standards, for example, the NPL provides representation on all the appropriate international bodies. Nevertheless much of the Laboratory's contact with organisations in Europe and elsewhere is on the same informal basis as that within the UK. Many members of staff serve as individuals on specialist working groups and committees, and close links have been established with research groups throughout the world engaged in similar work. Staff exchanges form an important part of these arrangements. The contact and cooperation between NPL and other national standards laboratories is particularly close.

The principal national and international links are indicated in figure 128 (*over*).

In the field of primary standards, international agreement is the concern of successive General Conferences of Weights and Measures (CGPM), which comprise delegates from the member states of the Metre Convention. Their executive body, the International Committee of Weights and Measures (CIPM), prepares resolutions and executes decisions, as well as administering the International Bureau of Weights and Measures (BIPM). The CIPM is assisted by seven Consultative Committees, on all of which NPL is represented.

Direct links exist with the International Atomic Energy Agency, the International Commission on Radiation Units and Measurements and the International Commission on Illumination (through the National Illumination Committee of Great Britain).

In the field of calibration the Laboratory operates the British Calibration Service and is responsible for the periodic redetermination of the secondary standards of weights and measures, held by the Weights and Measures Service of the Metrology, Quality Assurance and Standards Division (MQS) of the Department of Trade. Through the MQS there are links with the International Organisation of Legal Metrology (OIML).

The NPL contributes substantially to the work of many of the committees of the British Standards Institution (BSI) and through them has links with

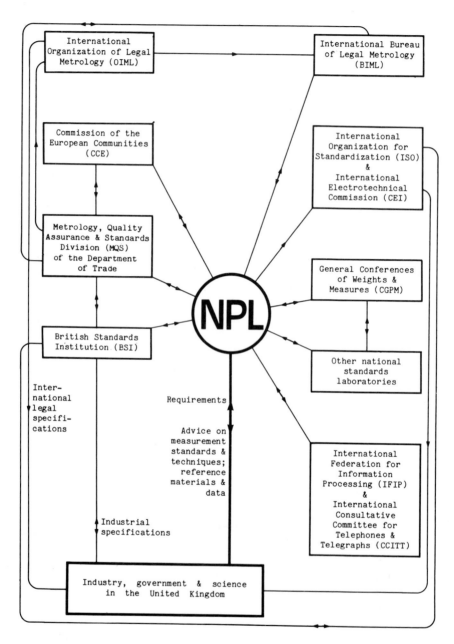

128   Chart showing the principal links between the NPL and other organisations.

the International Organisation for Standardisation (ISO) and the International Electrotechnical Commission (IEC).

The entry of the UK into the European Economic Community (EEC) brought NPL into contact with many institutions of the EEC. The organisation is complex but contacts with other national standards laboratories in the Community are closer than ever before. The Community Reference Bureau (BCR) plays a central role in coordinating standards and measurements and supports approved research in the laboratories of member states. The NPL is represented on the programme management committees of the Joint Research Centre (JRC) and on technical committees of the European Coal and Steel Community.

In the field of computing and numerical analysis the NPL is represented on the International Consultative Committee for Telephones and Telegraphs (CCITT) and the International Federation for Information Processing (IFIP). Standards affecting computer networks are organised through the BSI and the ISO. The Laboratory also participates in the work of the National Algorithms Group Ltd (NAG) and the Institute of Mathematics and its Applications (IMA).

Early in 1981 the Laboratory had six divisions: Electrical Science (O C Jones); Materials Applications (E D Hondros); Mechanical and Optical Metrology (P Clapham); Numerical Analysis and Computer Science (E L Albasiny); Quantum Metrology (M E Peover); Radiation Science and Acoustics (W A Jennings). P Dean was Director and P J Campion and R F Coleman, Deputy Directors. The Secretary of the Laboratory and head of Administration was R K Barnes.

At the present time the place of NPL in the overall scheme of things is much more clear than heretofore. Starting in 1900 as a semi-autonomous body controlled by the Royal Society, it had to create a place for itself in the national consciousness, to show that it could fulfil a national need and at the same time to ensure that its programmes did not offend other established scientific interests. As we have seen, this was successfully accomplished in the first two decades, mainly as a result of the untiring efforts of Glazebrook.

After World War I government control was tightened, but even under the DSIR there was a considerable degree of *laissez faire*. The programmes were still determined by a quite small minority interest—the various controlling committees, which, though certainly independent, responsible and reasonably representative, did not necessarily give the widest consideration to what was the overall best in the national interest. Programmes, many of them substantially open-ended, were often suggested by individual scientists and reflected the expertise of the staff as much as the needs of the community.

Since 1965 a succession of Governments have tried to establish tighter control. Open-ended research programmes were phased out and the

Ministry's Requirements Boards became the 'customers' for all the work, having to be convinced of the necessity for each piece of research and then allocating funds year by year with progress targets and conclusion dates set up in advance. The complexities of the science itself, the shifting pattern of needs, the restrictions imposed by the particular expertises of the staff, the existence of similar programmes being researched elsewhere and the need to avoid duplication, together mean that modern applied science just has to be controlled in this exacting fashion.

In the past the situation was not helped by the swings back and forth in purpose between academic research and industrial aid, while the exact nature of the role was never clearly defined. Now, however, the 'National Standards Laboratory' is undoubtedly the established role of the moment; perhaps this is the one it should have maintained throughout, certainly this is the one that its founders had in mind for it.

And what of the future? Here is how the Laboratory sees it:

> A steady continuation of the standards and measurement work undertaken by the NPL is essential to the industrial, scientific and environmental well-being of the UK. Nevertheless the detailed programme of the Laboratory must respond to changes in the nation's industrial structure and social priorities, and reflect as far as possible our probable future requirements for measurement capability and standards.

Unlike the primary standards used in the measurement of physical quantities, specification standards relating to the properties of materials, and those relating to the performance and quality of manufactured goods, have evolved largely within individual national frameworks in response to local requirements and conditions. Much greater international standardisation in this field is likely in view of the world-wide expansion in the use of equipment and industrial plant employing advanced technology, more particularly as much of this expansion is taking place outside the established industrialised centres. The ability to realise international specifications precisely and to ensure the compatibility of the UK's products with those from the rest of the world is essential if this country is to compete effectively in these expanding export markets.

Minimum requirements for product performance, of the type imposed on the motor industry by the exhaust emission regulations enforced by a number of countries, are also being adopted more widely. It is the responsibility of the NPL to ensure that appropriate standards and associated measurement techniques are available to assist the nation's export industries in complying with these specifications and requirements.

Standards relating to the environment and quality of life are achieving a greater prominence, and the Government is faced with increasing demands for the monitoring and control of pollution. Recent moves for European legislation to limit environmental damage now require that the UK should be able to monitor various forms of pollution, and provide reliable data for international discussion. Since sanctions may well be imposed upon those countries failing to comply with future legislation, such data may be essential to provide support for cases prepared to protect particular aspects of the national interest. The NPL is becoming increasingly involved in the development of measurement techniques and standards for use in this area, concerning itself not only with environmental pollutants but also with those in food and manufactured goods.

No major changes in the structure and organisation of standards and metrological work within the European Communities are likely for some years. Nevertheless, cooperation on a European basis will exert increasing influence on the Laboratory's programme planning, particularly in the development and proving of basic standards. Dissemination, essentially a regional matter, will remain the individual responsibility of the national standards laboratories. The total European effort in standards is not markedly different from that in the USA, and ultimate integration of the European facilities is unlikely to result in excess capacity unless considerable expansion occurs in the meanwhile.

Notes

1   Between 1945 and 1965 the following were in charge of divisions:
    Administration: E S Hiscocks to 1957, then H J Hadow
    Aerodynamics: A Fage to 1953, W P Jones to 1964, then R C Pankhurst
    Applied Physics/Physics: W F Higgins to 1948, B W Robinson 1964, then P J Campion
    Autonomics: F M Colebrook to 1954, R H Tizard to 1956, then A M Uttley
    Basic Physics: J A Pople
    Electricity: R S J Spilsbury to the end in 1958
    Engineering: G A Hankins to 1948, then D G Sopwith to the end
    Light: T Smith to 1948, L A Sayce to 1963, then J Dyson
    Mathematics: J R Womersley to 1950, then E T Goodwin
    Metallurgy: N P Allen
    Radio: R L Smith-Rose to the end in 1952
    Ship: J L Kent to 1950, J F Allan to 1957, F H Todd to 1962, then A Silverleaf
    Standards (Metrology): F H Rolt to 1953, then H Barrell
2   In the end this universality proved disadvantageous to users since, when the Basic Physics Division began to run down, miscellaneous groups from other divisions were quickly able to adapt it to their needs. Scientists in special-purpose buildings could not be so readily displaced, except at every great cost, or by groups needing very similar facilities.
3   The General Board and the Executive Committee, which had run the Laboratory since its foundation, was replaced at this time, after negotiations between the Minister of Technology and the Royal Society, by a Visiting

Board and a Steering Committee. The former comprised four nominees of the Ministry, 16 nominees of the Royal Society and one member from each of 16 technical bodies or societies. The 10 member Steering Committee had the responsibility of submitting annually to the Minister of Technology, and advising him on, a research programme with details of budget and staff required. The following year the Steering Committee appointed the Glazebrook Committee to advise them on measurement science, the Morgan Committee to advise on materials science and the Froude Committee to advise on ship research. In future the Director would be appointed by the Minister.

4   We can do no more than list them: E L Albasiny, N P Allen, A E Bailey, R G Baker, R K Barnes, H Barrell, P J Campion, R F Coleman, A H Cook, F G R Cook, J D Cox, D W Davies, P Dean, J Dyson, D A Everest, H A Gebbie, R J E Glenny, E T Goodwin, H J Hadow, E F G Herington, E D Hondros, B E Hopkins, W A Jennings, A Kelly, L W Nickols, J A H Paffett, R C Pankhurst, H H Pearcey, M E Peover, J A Pople, H Pursey, D W Robinson, A Silverleaf, O Simpson, S H Smith, A M Uttley, D H Whiffen and A Williams (see Appendix 1).

Among these, Allen, Campion, Dean, Goodwin, Kelly, Silverleaf and Simpson were promoted at some stage to Deputy Director, the list of which is completed by the names of those directly recruited—J K Foreman, J W Nichols and R G Voysey. For a period the whole organisation was divided into three groups—Measurements, Materials and Engineering Sciences, each presided over by a Deputy Director.

5   Now in the Science Museum, London.

6   A member of the former Mathematics Division, co-author of the programming language Algol 60 in the early days, contributed substantially to the subsequent Ada (1980).

7   Such was the constancy of these new standards that suspected fluctuations in the Earth's rotation were now revealed in detail, destroying for ever the astronomical basis for accurate time measurement.

8   Clinical thermometers averaged half a million per annum until the service was passed over to the British Standards Institution in 1962. Larger and more complex items handled in lesser quantities per annum included meteorological thermometers (10000), volumetric glassware (11000, falling within a decade to 3000), viscometers (500), hydrometers (1000), barometers (500). Taximeters continued at around 8000 per annum at the London Testing Station. As time went on the programme of Test House was extended to include standard cells (150), trilene inhalers (3000), watches (850), also sextants, Admiralty optical instruments and electric lamps.

9   Subsequent improvements in accuracy, here and in other national laboratories, enabled the CCDM in 1973 to define the speed of light as $299\,792\,458 \pm 1.2\,\mathrm{m\,s}^{-1}$.

10   In 1972 the CCE defined $2e/h = 483\,594.0\,\mathrm{GHz\,V}^{-1}$.

11   The first is in the Science Museum, the second in NPL Museum, the third is the present basis of the national time scale.

12   One of the NPL's most successful commercial projects, this has brought in several million pounds to the manufacturers over the years.

13   With special reference to building materials; but in 1948, for example, the conductivity figures for whalemeat were established.

14   In 1979 this was passed over to the Division of Quantum Metrology, where it was refitted for atmospheric pollution studies.

15   This pioneering instrument was loaned to Cambridge University in 1953 to work on determinations of geological age.

16   After the departure of the aerodynamics work these huge metal spheres (having walls 12 mm thick) were taken over in the late 1970s by the Division of Electrical Science for work on free field parameters. There they serve as electromagnetic shields in interference and antenna work.

17   The Basic Physics Division since its inception had been supplying the whole site with liquid helium.

Appendices

Appendix 1: Biographical Notes of Principal Characters in the NPL History

Albasiny E L: ed. Cambridge; joined NPL 1954; Supt Divn of Numerical Analysis and Computing (NPL) 1972; Supt Divn of Numerical Analysis and Computer Science (NPL) 1977.

Allan J F (1904–57): b. Brechin; ed. Dumbarton Academy and Glasgow Univ; apprenticed to ship builders and worked on ship model tank 1926–48; DSc (Glasgow) 1948; joined NPL as Supt Ship Divn 1948; died in office.

Allen N P (1903–72): b. Wrexham; ed. Burton-on-Trent GS, Sheffield Univ. and Swansea Univ. Coll. 1925–28; Asst Lecturer Birmingham Univ. 1928–35; Senior Metallurgist Research and Development Dept Mond Nickel Research Lab. 1935–44; joined NPL as Supt Metallurgy Divn 1945; FRS 1956; Deputy Director (NPL) 1966–67; rtd 1969.

Bailey A E: ed. Merchant Taylors and Sidney Sussex Coll. (Cambridge); various scientific posts in Government; joined NPL as Supt Divn of Electrical Science 1967; additionally Supt British Calibration Service 1977; rtd 1980.

Bairstow L (1880–1963): b. Halifax; ed. Halifax schools and Royal College of Science (London); joined NPL 1904; commenced aerodynamics work 1909; FRS and CBE 1917; appointed first Supt of Aerodynamics Divn (NPL) 1917; Air Ministry 1918; academic posts in aerodynamics 1920–45; finally Professor of Aerodynamics Imperial Coll. (London); knighted 1952.

Baker G S (d. 1949): Royal Corps of Naval Constructors; appointed Supt of National Experimental Tank 1910; rtd 1941.

Baker R G: ed. Bishop Wordsworth School (Salisbury) and Fitzwilliam House (Cambridge); research posts in metallurgy 1959–83; joined NPL as Supt Divn of Materials Applications 1973; returned to industry 1977.

Baker T W: joined Kew Observatory 1860; transferred to NPL Observatory Dept; rtd 1912 (52 years service).

Barnes R K: joined CRL 1955; Officer in Charge outstation near Harwell; transferred to Applied Physics Divn on return to NPL; Secretary (NPL) 1973.

Barrell H (1900–72): ed. Imperial Coll. (London); joined NPL 1923; DSc 1951; Supt Metrology Divn 1953; rtd 1966, but continued in an advisory capacity.

Bowley H: posts in industry; Ministry of Supply 1936; joined NPL 1947; Officer in Charge Test House (NPL) 1949–58; rtd 1960.

Bragg W L (1890–1971): b. Adelaide; ed. St Peters Coll. Adelaide, Adelaide Univ.

and Trinity Coll. (Cambridge); Fellow and lecturer at Trinity 1914; War Service; Nobel Prize 1915; Prof of Physics (Manchester) 1919–37; FRS 1921; appointed Director (NPL) 1937–38; Cavendish Professor of Experimental Physics (Cambridge) 1938; knighted 1941; Fullerian Professor of Chemistry Royal Institution 1953; rtd 1966.

Bullard E C (1907–80): b. Norwich; ed. Repton and Clare Coll. (Cambridge); Sc D 1948; research in earth sciences at Cambridge and Toronto Univs to 1950; appointed Director (NPL) 1950; knighted 1953; Asst Director of Research, Cambridge 1956; Reader in Geophysics 1960, Professor in Geophysics 1964–74.

Campbell A (1863–1954): b. near Londondery; ed. Derry Academy, Queens Coll. (Belfast), Edinburgh Univ. and Corpus Christi Coll. (Cambridge); various teaching posts 1887–1901; joined Electricity Divn of Physics Dept (NPL) 1901; rtd 1918 and continued private electrical research.

Campion P J (1926–   ): ed. Exeter Coll. (Oxford); NRC research Fellowship at Chalk River 1955; joined NPL 1960; Supt Divn of Radiation Science (NPL) 1964; Supt Divn of Mechanical and Optical Metrology (NPL) 1974; Deputy Director (NPL) 1976.

Carpenter H C H (1875–1940): ed. Eastbourne Coll. and Oxford Univ., Leipzig and Owens Coll. (Manchester); joined NPL 1901; head of Chemical and Metallurgical Divns of Physics Dept (NPL) to 1906; professorial posts at Victoria Univ. (Manchester) and Royal School of Mines (London).

Chree C (1860–1928) FRS: ed. Old Aberdeen GS, Aberdeen Univ. and Cambridge Univ.; Fellow Kings Coll. (Cambridge) 1885; Supt of Kew Observatory 1893; Sc D 1896; Supt Observatory Dept (NPL) 1900; transferred to Kew Observatory (Meteorological Office) 1912.

Colebrook F M (d. 1954): ed. City and Guilds Coll.; joined NPL 1921; Officer in Charge Electronics Sect. (NPL) 1948; died in office.

Coleman R F: ed. King Edward School and Coll. of Technology (Birmingham); DSc Univ of Aston; AERE 1954–73; Lab. of the Govt Chemist 1973–77; joined NPL as Supt Chemical Standards Divn (NPL) 1977; Deputy Director (NPL) 1981.

Constable E G: joined Kew Observatory 1873; transferred to NPL 1912; rtd 1925 (52 years service).

Cook A H (1922–   ): ed. Corpus Christi Coll. (Cambridge); Dept of Geophysics (Cambridge) 1946; joined NPL 1952; Supt Standards Divn (NPL) 1966; Sc D 1967; FRS 1969; Professor of Geophysics (Edinburgh) 1969; Jacksonian Professor of Natural Philosophy (Cambridge) 1972.

Cook F G R (d. 1975): joined NPL in charge of Hovercraft Unit 1969; Supt Divn of Maritime Science (NPL) 1972; died in office.

Cox J D: ed. Imperial Coll. (London); joined CRL 1948; Officer in Charge Divn of Chemical Standards (NPL) 1972–75.

Darwin C G (1887–1962): grandson of Charles Darwin; b. Cambridge; ed. Marlborough and Trinity Coll. (Cambridge); Lecturer in Mathematical Physics

(Manchester) 1910–14; MC in 1914–18 War; Lecturer in Maths Christs Coll. (Cambridge) 1919–22; Tait Professor of Natural Philosophy (Edinburgh) 1923–36; Master of Christs Coll. (Cambridge) 1936–38; knighted 1942; Director (NPL) 1938–49.

Davies D W: ed. Imperial Coll. (London); joined NPL 1950; Supt Divn of Computer Science (NPL) 1966; in charge of Computer Technology Unit 1977.

Dean P (1933–   ): ed. Hackney Downs GS and Queen Mary Coll. (London); joined NPL 1957; Supt Quantum Metrology Divn (NPL) 1969; Deputy Director (NPL) 1974; Under Secretary Department of Industry HQ 1976–77; Director (NPL) 1977.

Desch C H (1874–1958): b. London; ed. Birkbeck School, City and Guilds Tech. Coll. (Finsbury), Würzburg Univ; DSc (London) 1902; Metallurgy Dept Kings Coll. (London) 1902–7; Lecturer in Metallurgical Chemistry Glasgow Univ. 1909–18; Professor of Metallurgy Royal Tech. Coll. (Glasgow) 1918–20; Professor of Metallurgy Sheffield 1920; joined NPL as Supt Metallurgy Divn (NPL) 1932; rtd 1939; sundry advisory and committee work.

Dunworth J V (1917–   ): ed. Manchester GS and Clare Coll. (Cambridge); Fellow of Trinity Coll. (Cambridge) 1941; ADRDE during War; Demonstrator Cambridge Univ. 1945; AERE Harwell 1947; Head of Reactor Divn, Harwell and Deputy Director of Winfrith AE Est.; appointed Deputy Director (NPL) 1962; Director (NPL) 1964; rtd 1976; advisory and committee work.

Dye D W (1887–1932): b. Portsmouth; ed. Municipal Tech. Coll. and City and Guilds Tech. Coll.; apprenticed BTH; joined Electricity Divn of Physics Dept (NPL) 1910; FRS 1928; died in office.

Dyson James: ed. Queen Elizabeth School and Christs Coll. (Cambridge); research posts; Sc D 1960; joined NPL as Supt Light Divn 1963; FRS 1968; rtd 1976.

Eastland W H (1888–1959): joined NPL 1903; rtd 1953 (50 years service).

Essen Louis: ed. High Pavement School (Nottingham); London external degree 1928; joined Electricity Dept of NPL 1929; DSc 1947; FRS 1960; rtd 1966.

Everest D A: b. London; ed. John Lyon School, Harrow and University Coll. (London); lecturer in Chemistry; joined NCL 1956; Officer in Charge Inorganic Materials Unit 1966–67; Supt Divn of Inorganic and Metallic Structure (NPL) 1971; Supt Divn of Chemical Standards (NPL) 1975; Department of Industry HQ 1976.

Fage A (1890–1977): b. Portsmouth; ed. Portsmouth Royal Docks School and Royal College of Science (London); joined NPL 1914; FRS 1942; Supt Aerodynamics Divn (NPL) 1946; rtd 1953.

Foreman J K (1928–80): ed. Ashford GS and Medway Tech. Coll.; Chemical Inspectorate Woolwich Arsenal 1949–51; UKAEA Windscale 1952–66; Supt of Research Lab. of the Government Chemist 1966–70; Dept of the Government Chemist 1970–77; DSc 1976; appointed Deputy Director (NPL) 1977; died in office 1980.

Frazer R A (1891–1959): b. London; ed. City of London School and Pembroke Coll.

(Cambridge); joined NPL 1914; Deputy Chief Scientific Advisor Aerodynamics Divn (NPL); FRS 1946; rtd 1954.

Gebbie H A: ed. Edinburgh Univ; joined NPL Light Divn 1957; Officer in Charge Advanced Instrumentation Unit (NPL) 1966–67; NBS Boulder Co 1968.

Glazebrook R T (1854–1935): b. Liverpool; ed. Liverpool Coll. and Trinity Coll. (Cambridge); Fellow of Trinity Coll. (Cambridge) 1877; Lecturer in Mathematics Cambridge Univ. 1881–97; Senior Bursar of Trinity Coll. 1895–98; Asst. Director Cavendish Lab. (Cambridge) 1891; Principal of University Coll. (Liverpool) 1898–99; Director (NPL) 1899–1919; knighted 1917; Zaharoff Professor of Aviation, Imperial Coll. (London) 1920–23; served on numerous committees, particularly those directing the work of NPL and those concerned with aviation.

Glenny R J E: ed. Belfast and London Univs; English Electric laboratories and National Gas Turbine Establishment; joined NPL as Supt Divn of Materials Applications 1970; transferred to RAE 1973.

Goodwin E T (1913–   ): b. Wolverhampton; ed. Perterhouse (Cambridge); Lecturer Sheffield Univ. 1937; Cambridge Mathematical Lab. 1939; ASE Whitley 1943; Admiralty Computing Service (Bath) 1945; joined NPL 1945; Supt Mathematics Divn (NPL) 1941; Deputy Director (NPL) 1971; rtd 1974.

Gough H J (1890–1965): b. Bermondsey; ed. Regent Street Poly. and University Coll. (London); apprenticed Vickers Ltd 1909–13; joined NPL 1914; war service 1914–18; Supt Engineering Dept (NPL) 1930–38; FRS 1933; first Director of Scientific research at the War Office 1938; Director General of scientific research and development at Ministry of Supply 1942–45; industry 1945; rtd 1955.

Griffiths E (1882–1962): b. Aberdare; ed. University Coll. (Cardiff); joined Heat Divn of Physics Dept (NPL) 1915; FRS 1926; rtd 1953; continued scientific committee work.

Hadow H J: ed. Balliol Coll. (Oxford); gas industry; Chemical Defence Establishment 1940; DSIR HQ 1951; joined NPL as Secretary 1957; rtd 1968.

Hankins G A (1895–1950): ed. Royal Dockyard School (Portsmouth) and Imperial Coll. (London); apprentice H M Dockyard Portsmouth; war service; joined NPL 1917; Supt Engineering Divn (NPL) 1944; Director Mechanical Engineering Research DSIR 1947.

Harker J A (1870–1923): b. Alston; ed. Stockport GS, Owens Coll. (Manchester) and Univ. of Tubingen; work on thermometry at Kew 1898; transferred to NPL 1901; Head of Heat Divn of Physics Dept; FRS 1910; Head of Eskdalemuir Observatory 1913; Director of Research and Inventions Dept of Ministry of Munitions 1916–21; returned to NPL for a time, then rtd to consultancy.

Herington E F G: joined CRL 1946; DSc 1957; Supt Divn of Chemical Standards (NPL) 1965; rtd 1972.

Higgins W F (d. 1963): joined Physics Dept (NPL) 1910; Secretary (NPL) 1932–44; Supt Physics Divn (NPL) 1941–48; rtd 1948.

Hiscocks E S (1903–73): ed. Bishop Gore School (Swansea) and Univ. of Wales

(Swansea); Dept of Government Chemist 1926–39; Head of Technical Branch Raw Materials Dept of Ministry of Supply 1939–44; joined NPL as Secretary 1944; Director of UK Scientific Mission to North America and Scientific Advisor to UK High Commissioner Ottawa 1957; Director Tropical Products Inst 1960; rtd 1966.

Holder D W (1923–77): b. London; ed. Bec GS and Imperial Coll. (London); Aircraft and Armament Experimental Establishment 1943; joined Aerodynamics Divn (NPL) 1944; Head of High Speed Lab (NPL) 1950; Professor of Engineering Science Oxford 1961; FRS 1962.

Hondros E D: ed. Univ. of Melbourne; research posts; joined NPL 1961; Supt Divn of Material Applications (NPL) 1979.

Hopkins B E: joined NPL 1947; Acting Supt Divn of Materials Applications (NPL) 1968–70; Supt Divn of Materials Applications (NPL) 1977; rtd 1979.

Jakeman C (1874–1959): joined Engineering Dept (NPL) 1901; rtd 1936.

Jeffcott H H: joined Metrology Divn of Physics Dept (NPL) 1904; Professor of Engineering Royal College of Science (Dublin) 1909.

Jennings W A: Royal Northern Hospital 1946; Argonne Hospital, (Chicago) 1955; Principal Physicist, North London Hospital Group 1956; joined NPL 1966; Supt Divn of Radiation Science (NPL) 1975.

Jones O C: ed. Oxford Univ.; NRC Canada; joined Light Divn (NPL) 1960; Supt Divn of Electrical Science (NPL) 1980.

Jones W P: joined NPL 1935; Supt Aerodynamics Divn (NPL) 1953; DSc (Oxford) 1953; Director AGARD NATO 1964; Professor Univ. of Texas 1967.

Kaye W G C (1880–1941): b. Honley; ed. Huddersfield Tech. Coll., Liverpool Univ. and Royal College of Science (London); Trinity Coll. (Cambridge) 1905; *Kaye and Laby* published 1911; joined NPL 1911; war service 1914–22; Supt Physics Dept (NPL) 1922; FRS 1939; rtd 1940.

Keeling B F E (1880–1919): b. Bradford; ed. Bradford GS and Trinity Coll. (Cambridge); joined NPL 1901; Egyptian Survey Dept, Head of Helwan Observatory 1904; war service 1914; Surveyor General of Egypt 1919.

Kelly A: ed. Reading and Cambridge Univs; University posts Illinois, Birmingham, Northwestern Univs; University lecturer in metallurgy Cambridge 1959; joined NPL as Supt Divn of Inorganic and Metallic Structure 1967; Deputy Director (NPL) 1969; ScD 1968; FRS 1973; Vice Chancellor Surrey Univ 1975.

Kent J L P (1885–1973): apprenticed Portsmouth Dockyard; ed. Royal College of Science (London) and Royal Naval Coll. (Greenwich); joined NPL 1910; Supt Ship Divn (NPL) 1942; rtd 1947.

Lee E (1914–): ed. Manchester and Cambridge Univs; Admiralty Research Lab. 1939; Ministry of Defence 1946; Admiralty 1948; Admiralty Research Lab. 1951; Director of Operational Research, Admiralty 1955; appointed Deputy Director (NPL) 1958; DSIR HQ 1960; Deputy Controller of Research, Ministry of Technology 1964; Head of Research Services Dept of Trade and Industry 1970; Director Admiralty Research Lab. 1971; rtd 1974.

Macfarlane G G (1916–): ed. Glasgow Univ. and Technische Hochschule (Dresden); Government research posts (TRE etc) 1939–60; appointed Deputy Director (NPL) 1960–62; Director RRE 1962; Controller (Research) Ministry of Technology and Ministry of Aviation Supply 1967; knighted 1971; Controller (Research and Development Establishment) Ministry of Defence 1971.

May A: joined Kew Observatory 1899; transferred to NPL; rtd 1951 (52 years service).

Melsom S W (1879–1952): ed. Finsbury Tech. Coll. and Battersea Poly.; trained with Crompton Co.; war service; joined Electricity Divn of Physics Dept (NPL) 1922; industry 1925; rtd 1950.

Nichols J W (1919–): b. Godalming; ed. London Univ.; Royal Navy 1940–46; number of posts in government service; appointed Deputy Director (Maritime) (NPL) 1976; first Director of National Maritime Institute 1976; also Director Computer Aided Design Centre, Cambridge 1977.

Nickols L W: ed. Kings Coll. (London); apprenticed; joined NPL 1938; Officer in Charge Metrology Centre (NPL) 1966; rtd 1973.

Paffett J A H: ed. Taunton School; apprenticed Portsmouth Dockyard; Royal Naval Engineering Coll. and Royal Naval Coll. (Greenwich); Admiralty appointments 1945–62; Professor of Naval Architecture Royal Naval Coll. (Greenwich) 1962; Supt Ship Divn (NPL) 1967; Deputy Director NMI 1976.

Pankhurst R C: ed. Imperial Coll. (London); joined NPL 1939; Supt Aerodynamics Divn (NPL) 1964; Ministry of Defence HQ 1970.

Paterson C C (1880–1948): ed. Mill Hill School; apprenticed; Finsbury Tech. Coll.; Faraday House testing Dept; joined Electricity Divn of Physics Dept (NPL) 1903; Founder and Director of GEC Research Lab. 1919.

Pearcey H H: joined Aerodynamics Divn (NPL) 1952; Supt Divn of Maritime Science (NPL) 1975; Head of Research NMI 1976.

Peover M E: ed. University Coll. (London); joined NCL 1960; Supt Divn of Quantum Metrology (NPL) 1975.

Petavel J E (1873–1936): b. Streatham Hill; ed. Inst de Jeunes Gens (Ouchy), Tubinger Hochschule, Gymnasium Lausanne, Lausanne Univ. 1892 and University Coll. (London) 1893; exhibition at Royal Institution under Dewar and Fleming 1896–98; J Harling Research Fellow at Owens College (Manchester) 1900–03; lecturer in Meteorology (Manchester); FRS 1907; DSc (Victoria Univ.) 1908; Professor of Engineering and Director of Whitworth Labs (Manchester Univ.) 1908–19; scientific advisory and experimental work in the war years; Director (NPL) 1919; knighted 1920; died in office.

Pople J A (1925–): ed. Bristol GS and Trinity Coll. (Cambridge); Fellow of Trinity Coll. (Cambridge) 1951–58; Lecturer in Maths Cambridge Univ. 1954; joined NPL as Supt Basic Physics Divn 1958; FRS 1961; Carnegie Professor of Chemical Physics Mellon Inst. 1964; University Professor of Natural Sciences Mellon Inst.

Pursey H: ed. Merchant Taylors and Regent Street Poly.; ADRDE during war; industrial and educational appointments; joined NPL 1951; acting Supt Divn of Molecular Science 1970–71.

Rayment F J: joined NPL 1915; industry 1922–28; returned to NPL; rtd 1977 (56 years service).

Rayner E H (1875–1963): ed. Shrewsbury School and Cambridge Univ.; industry; joined NPL 1903; shared control of Electricity Dept (NPL) 1918; Supt of Electricity Dept (NPL) 1929; rtd 1940; continued in an advisory capacity at GEC to 1945.

Relf E F (1888–1970): b. Maidstone; apprenticed Royal Dockyard, Portsmouth and Haslar Ship Tank 1904–09; Portsmouth Tech. Coll. (evenings); scholarship to Royal College of Science (London) 1909; joined NPL 1912; scientific expedition to the Polar regions 1923–24; Supt Aerodynamics Dept (NPL) 1925; FRS 1936; Principal of Coll. of Aeronautics, Cranfield 1946–51.

Robinson B W: ed. Oundle and Cambridge; research at Royal Institution 1925–32; Lecturer at RMCS; RAE and MAP during war; Head of Instrument Section of the National Institute for Medical Research 1945; joined NPL as Supt of Physics Divn 1948; Supt of Applied Physics Divn 1958; rtd 1964.

Robinson D W: ed. City and Guilds Coll. (London); industry; joined NPL 1950; head of Acoustics section 1959, continuing in this post through all its changes.

Rolt F H (1889–1973): joined NPL 1912; MBE 1918; Supt Metrology Divn (NPL) 1946; rtd 1953; DSc 1954.

Rosenhain W (1875–1934): b. Melbourne; ed. Wesley Coll. and Queens Coll. (Melbourne), and St Johns Coll. (Cambridge); Scientific Advisor to Chance Bros glassworks; joined NPL as Supt Metallurgy Dept 1906; FRS 1913; rtd 1932; continued with consultancy work.

Sayce L A: Lecturer in chemistry Durham Univ. 1926; Asst Director Physics Research Admiralty 1946; joined NPL as Supt Light Divn 1948; rtd 1963; Head of Optical Methods Divn (NEL) 1963.

Sears J E Jnr (1883–1954): ed. Mill Hill School and St Johns Coll. (Cambridge); joined NPL 1910; Supt Metrology Dept (NPL) 1918; CBE 1920; Deputy Warden of Standards 1921–31; rtd 1946.

Selby F J (1867–1942): b. Catford; ed. University Coll. (London) and Trinity Coll. (Cambridge); Senior maths master Bristol GS 1892–1901; joined Optics Divn of Physics Dept (NPL) 1903; Secretary (NPL) 1918; rtd 1932; Secretary Advisory Committee for Aeronautics 1909–19.

Silverleaf A (1920–   ): ed. Kilburn GS and Glasgow Univ.; shipbuilding industry 1937; joined NPL 1951; Supt Ship Divn (NPL) 1962; Deputy Director (NPL) 1966; Director Transport and Road Research Lab. 1971.

Simpson Oliver (1924–   ): ed. Highgate School and Trinity Coll. (Cambridge); Admiralty Research Lab. 1955–56; Research posts at Cambridge, Michigan and in the Admiralty; joined NPL as Supt Basic Physics Divn 1964; Deputy Director

(NPL) 1966; Under-Secretary, Cabinet Office 1969; Chief Scientist, Deputy Under-Secretary of State, Home Office 1974.

Smith F E (1879–1970): b. Aston; ed. Smethwick Central School, part time Birmingham Tech. School, Royal Coll. Science (London) and Imperial Coll. (London); after a year of teaching, joined Electricity Divn of Physics Dept (NPL) 1901; Board of Invention and Research 1914–18; Supt Electricity Dept (NPL) 1917; FRS 1918; Director of Scientific Research, Admiralty 1920; Secretary of DSIR 1929; knighted 1931; twice acting Director (NPL); rtd 1939; 20 years in industry.

Smith S H: executive and administrative posts in Government; joined NPL as Secretary 1968.

Smith S L (1889–1958): ed. City and Guilds Engineering Coll. and Imperial Coll. (London); shipbuilding industry; academic posts in City and Guilds Coll.; Research for Royal Society War Committee; RAF; Reader in Mechanical Engineering London Univ. 1931; joined NPL as Supt Engineering Dept 1939; Director of Research, British Shipbuilding Research Assoc. 1944.

Smith T (1883–1969): b. Leamington; ed. Warwick School and Queens' Coll. (Cambridge); teaching at Oundle School; joined NPL 1908; in charge of Optics Divn of Physics Dept 1909; FRS 1932; Supt Light Divn (NPL) 1940; rtd 1948.

Smith-Rose R L (1894–1980): ed. Latymer Upper School and Imperial Coll. (London); Assistant Engineer, Siemens Bros. 1915; joined NPL 1919; Supt Radio Divn (NPL) 1937; Director of Radio Research (DSIR) 1948; acting Director (NPL) 1950 and 1956; rtd 1960.

Sopwith D G (1906–1970): ed. Manchester GS; training, Manchester dry docks 1922; Manchester Univ. 1925; joined NPL 1928; Supt Engineering Divn (NPL) 1948; Director of MERL 1951; rtd 1966.

Southwell R V (1888–1970): b. Norwich; ed. King Edward VI's School and Trinity Coll. (Cambridge); Fellow of Trinity Coll. (Cambridge) 1912; scientific posts in the Services 1914–18; joined NPL as Supt Aerodynamics Dept 1920; Lecturer Cambridge Univ. 1925; Professor of Engineering Science Oxford Univ. 1929; Rector of Imperial Coll. (London) 1942; rtd 1948; knighted 1948.

Spilsbury R S J: ed. Malvern Coll. and City and Guilds Coll.; joined NPL 1919; Supt Electricity Dept (NPL) 1940; rtd 1958.

Stanton T E (1865–1931): b. Atherstone; ed. Atherstone GS, Owens Coll. (Manchester); Demonstrator Owens Coll. 1891; Senior Lecturer Engineering, Liverpool Univ. 1896–99; Professor of Civil and Mechanical Engineering, University Coll. Bristol 1899; joined NPL as Supt Engineering Dept 1901; FRS 1914; also Supt Aerodynamics Dept (NPL) 1917–20; knighted 1928; rtd 1931.

Stiles W S (1901–): ed. University Coll. (London) and St John's Coll. (Cambridge); academic posts; joined Optics Divn of Physics Dept (NPL) 1925; FRS 1957; rtd 1961.

Strand R R: joined Kew staff 1907; transferred to NPL 1912; rtd 1957 (50 years service).

Sutherland G B B McI (1907–1980): ed. St Andrews Univ. and Cambridge Univ.; academic posts; Ministry of Supply 1940; Assistant Director of Research, Dept of Colloid Science Cambridge 1944; Reader in Spectroscopy, Cambridge Univ. 1947; Sc D 1948; Professor of Physics, Michigan Univ. 1949; FRS 1949; appointed Director (NPL) 1956; knighted 1960; Master of Emmanuel Coll. (Cambridge) 1964.

Sykes C (1905–): ed. Netherthorpe GS and Sheffield Univ.; joined NPL as Supt Metallurgy Divn 1940; FRS 1943; Supt Terminal Ballistics Branch, Armament Research Dept, 1943; Director, Brown-Firth Research Laboratories 1944–73; knighted 1964.

Tizard R H: ed. Oxford Univ.; joined NPL 1947; Officer in Charge Control Mechanisms Section (NPL) 1950; Supt Control Mechanisms and Electronics Divn (NPL) 1955; joined LSE 1956.

Todd F H: apprenticed to shipbuilding with Armstrong Whitworth; Armstrong Coll. (Durham); joined NPL 1928; seconded to Durham Univ. 1940; returned to NPL 1942; Chief Naval Architect, David Taylor Model Basin, USA, 1948; rejoined NPL as Supt Ship Divn 1958.

Uttley A M (1906–): ed. Kings Coll. (London); TRE 1940; joined NPL as Supt of Autonomics Divn (NPL) 1956; Professor of Experimental Psychology Sussex Univ. 1966.

Voysey R G: ed. Royal Dockyard School Portsmouth and Imperial Coll. (London); posts in industry and government; Scientific Counsellor, British Embassy and Director UK Scientific Mission to Washington 1966; appointed Deputy Director (NPL) 1970; rtd 1977.

Watson-Watt R A (1892–1973): b. Brechin; ed. Brechin High School and University Coll. (Dundee); Assistant to Professor of Natural Philosophy, University Coll. (Dundee) 1912–21; Officer in Charge Radio Research Station (DSIR); joined NPL as Supt Radio Dept 1933; Air Ministry research 1937; knighted 1942.

Whiffen D H: ed. Oxford Univ.; Chemistry Dept, Birmingham Univ. 1949; DSc (Birmingham) 1959; joined NPL 1959; Supt Divn of Molecular Science (NPL) 1966; FRS 1966; Professor of Physical Chemistry, Univ. of Newcastle 1968; Head of School of Chemistry (Newcastle) 1978.

Wilkinson J H (1919–): ed. Trinity Coll. (Cambridge); Maths research at Cambridge Univ. 1940; joined NPL Mathematics Divn 1946; FRS 1969; Professor of Computer Science Stanford Univ. 1977.

Williams A: joined NPL Divn of Radiation Science 1959; Supt Divn of Mechanical and Optical Metrology 1977; additionally Supt of British Calibration Service 1980; Department of Industry HQ 1981.

Womersley J R (1907–58): ed. Imperial Coll. (London); mathematical posts in industry; Government scientific posts 1937; Supt Mathematics Divn (NPL) 1945; industry 1950; mathematical post in US Air Force 1954.

Appendix 2: Calendar

Current events at NPL alongside world events in scientific, technological and general fields.

1900

NPL founded

Planck's quantum theory of radiation
First central battery exchange opened in England
First Zeppelin trial flight

1901

Bushy House accepted by the Royal Society for the Laboratory

Giorgi proposed the MKS system
First mercury vapour lamp
Marconi transmitted wireless — Cornwall to Newfoundland
Edward VII succeeded Queen Victoria
First motor bicycle

1902

NPL opened by the Prince of Wales
Fleming–Ediswan carbon filament lamp standard introduced

Heaviside layer proposed
Human voice transmitted (Fessenden)
Mercury arc rectifier invented
Rayon patented

1903

Work on wind forces on structures
Mercury standards of resistance

C T R Wilson's sensitive electroscope
Poulsen's arc generator
Krypton and xenon discovered (Ramsay)

1904

Research on tool steels
All electrical apparatus for the St Louis Exhibition tested and certified

Radium and polonium discovered (Mme Curie)
General theory of radioactivity (Rutherford and Soddy)
Diode valve (Fleming) and semiconductor crystal detector (Bose) invented
Photoelectric cell produced (Elster)
Rolls–Royce founded

1905

First measurements on current balance
MP of platinum determined as thermometric standard

Einstein proposed Special Theory of Relativity and theory of the photoelectric effect

Neon signs first displayed
First motor buses in London

1906

Resistance of iron and steel to direct reversals of stress investigated

Alloys of copper and aluminium investigated

Triode valve invented (Le Forest)
First Simplon Tunnel — the longest rail tunnel in the world
HMS Dreadnought launched

1907

Important electrical papers — on current balance, silver voltameter and Weston cell

Studies of superheated steam

Death of Lord Kelvin
Bakelite invented
Colour photography invented (Lumière)
First electric washing machines

1908

Magnetic observatory opened at Eskdalemuir

International Conference on Units and Electrical Standards visited NPL

Ammonia synthesised (Haber)

1909

Instructed to set up a special department for aeronautical investigations

Lorenz machine arrived

First electro-cardiograph
First cross-Channel flight by Bleriot
Ford's Model T Car

1910

50 m tape testing bench put into service

Meteorological work at Kew and Eskdalemuir relinquished

First time signals from Eiffel Tower
First roller bearings
Mount Wilson 100 in telescope completed
George V succeeded Edward VII

1911

William Froude National Tank opened

Roads Division of Engineering Department founded

Nuclear model of the atom suggested (Rutherford)
Amundsen reached the South Pole

1912

Transfer of test work from Kew commenced

Vacuum tungsten filament lamps introduced as photometry substandards

X-ray diffraction discovered (Laue)
First automatic telephone exchange in England
First sea-plane (Glen Curtiss)

1913

First British radium standard placed in charge of NPL

Magnetic measurements in connection with local railway electrification

Bohr's model of the atom
Gyrosope stabiliser invented (Sperry)
First diesel electric railway engine (Sweden)

1914
Large impact testing machine installed
Junior staff in Services, senior staff doing routine test work and committee work for Service Depts

World War I began
Panama Canal opened

1915
First lady appointed to scientific staff
Watch testing for Swiss industry

General Theory of Relativity (Einstein)
First fighter aeroplane (Junkers)
Ministry of Munitions established

1916
Gauge testing reached 10 000 per week
Glazebrook — scientific advisor to the Ministry of Munitions

DSIR established
Battle of Jutland
First tanks used in warfare

1917
Extensive new building for Aero Divn
Big increase in test work

Quebec Bridge across the St Lawrence — longest cantilever bridge in the world

1918
Responsibility for NPL passed to DSIR
Heating of buried cables

End of World War I

1919
Study of lubricating oils
R T Glazebrook, first Director retired
Duplex wind tunnel completed

Observations of total eclipse of the sun bear out Einstein's Theory of Relativity
Mass spectrograph established isotropy (Aston)
First transmutation of an element, by particle bombardment of nitrogen (Rutherford)
Atlantic Ocean flown for the first time (Alcock and Brown)

1920
Wave making facilities added to ship tank
1.5M clinical thermometers certified

First radio programmes put out (Conrad of Westinghouse)
Sub-machine-gun invented

1921
Two staff members killed in R38 airship disaster
Acoustics work begun

First medium-wave broadcast in USA

1922
Type approval of electricity supply meters taken over from Board of Trade
First participation in decennial comparisons of the yard and its copies

Hafnium discovered
Technicolor developed
First autogyro

1923

Ventilation of House of Commons studied

Lighting advice for new wing of Tate Gallery

Earth's magnetic field analysed (Bauer)

First mill for hot continuous rolling of wide strip steel

1924

Physical constants of metals and alloys at high temperatures

Transport of apples from Australia in refigerated ships

Wave nature of the electron (de Broglie)

Heaviside Layer measured (Appleton and Barett)

British Empire Exhibition, Wembley

1925

Detailed aerodynamic study of Bristol Fighter

Manoeuvring of ships

Foundations of quantum mechanics (Heisenberg and Schrödinger)

Penetrating radiation discovered in the upper atmosphere (Millikan)

Deep freezing process extended to pre-cooked foods

1926

Application of x-rays in industry

Melbourne Town Hall acoustics

Baird demonstrated television

Tetrode valve invented

Copper oxide rectifiers developed

First liquid fuel rocket demonstrated

1927

International temperature Scale put forward

High voltage facilities installed

Shortt clock introduced as time standard

Existence of 'anti-matter' postulated (Dirac)

Geiger counter constructed (Geiger and Müller)

Dirigible 'Italia' lost over NE Greenland

First trans-Pacific flight (Kingsford Smith and Ulm)

1929

Radio beacon for marine navigation installed at Orfordness

Transport of meat from New Zealand in refrigerated ships

First pentode valve

1930

Research on springs

Black body at FP of platinum introduced as a standard of light

Turbo-jet engine designed (Whittle)

Differential analyser (Bush)

Planet Pluto discovered

Crash of R101

1931

High current testing, up to 20 kA

Compressed air tunnel erected and put into use

Cyclotron devised (Lawrence)

Neoprene invented (Nieuwland)

ICI made petrol from coal

1932
Metre determined in wavelengths of a red line in the spectrum of cadmium
No 2 Tank completed
New high precision balance

Neutron identified (Chadwick)
Practical electron microscope produced
Foundations of radio astronomy (Jansky)
Sydney Harbour Bridge opened

1933
Specially designed acoustics building erected
Tests at 1 MV

Positive electrons discovered (Anderson and Millikan)
Frequency modulation invented
Fluorescent lamps introduced

1934
New radium standard
First high speed wind tunnel
Dye quartz ring oscillator

Induced radioactivity discovered (Joliot and Joliot-Curie)
USSR balloon 13 miles into the stratosphere
Descent 3028 ft below the ocean surface off Bermuda (Beebe)

1935
Vehicle noise studies
Short wave generation and propagation studies
Field tests on road surfaces

Polyethylene discovered (ICI)
Radio detection of aircraft demonstrated (Watson Watt)
Lower Zambesi Railway Bridge opened — the longest in the world

1936
Strength of welded joints
Essen ring quartz frequency standard introduced

Television broadcasting began in England
Edward VIII succeeded George V, abdicated and was succeeded by George VI

1937
Lithgow propeller testing tunnel installed
Air screw performance

First jet engine (Whittle)
Hindenburg disaster

1938
Liquid steel temperature measurement in industry
Aluminium and magnesium alloys

Nuclear fission discovered (Hahn and Strassman)

1939
Strength of materials
Determination of 'g' using reversible pendulum

World War II started
Possibility of splitting the atom of ^{235}U demonstrated (Joliot)
Transformation of hydrogen to helium in the sun explained (Bethe)
First flight of turbo-jet plane (Heinkel)

1940
Early electron microscope
Detection of buried bombs
Bombs on NPL site
Metallurgical problems with shells

Failure of Tacoma Narrows Bridge, USA
Cavity magnetron developed
Dunkirk, the Battle of Britain and the 'Blitz'

1941
Flax drier
First strain gauges
Magnetic powders
Location of radium on bombed sites

'Manhattan Project' for atomic research began
First junction diode
Colour TV demonstrated in USA

1942
Influence of wing sweep on flutter
Gas turbine discs
Moisture-proof packing

First controlled nuclear reactor built in the USA (Fermi)
Magnetic tape invented
Germans launched V2 rockets

1943
Noise from aero-engine test houses
Test of armour piercing shot
Airtightness testing
Magnesium alloys

Fully laden glider towed across the Atlantic in 28 h
First 'Liberty' ships

1944
New radio-sonde system
Sound insulation of houses
Large scale watch testing for services
Accurate comparison of radio signals and clocks

World's largest wind tunnel built in USA
V bombs on England

1945
Participated in Conference of Unification of Engineering Standards (Ottowa)
Mathematics Divn founded

The Atom Bomb

1946
Designs for the Severn Bridge
Radio meteorology

First electronic high speed digital calculating machine (Univ. of Pennsylvania)
Discovery of ^{13}C
Heathrow Airport opened to scheduled traffic

1947
Decennial comparison of Imperial Standards of yard and pound with their copies
Absolute System of electrical units replaced the International System

Reflecting microscope developed
Polaroid–Land camera introduced
Speed of sound first exceeded by an aeroplane

1948

International Temperature Scale revised

Hydraulics Research Organisation formed from Engineering Divn

Black body standard for realisation of the candela adopted

Transistor introduced (Bell Telephone Co.)

Bathyscaphe constructed (Piccard)

Long playing record invented (Goldmark)

1949

Test House set up

Regular production of pure iron begun

Pneumatic gauging

Diffraction gratings produced by optical methods

Cortisone discovered

Neomycin prepared

1950

NPL Jubilee

NPL News began publication

Velocity of microwaves determined

Kon-Tiki expedition

1951

Issue of *Notes on Applied Science* began

New determination of the ohm

'Flying spot' microscope devised

1952

Engineering Divn became independent MERO

Radiological Protection Service founded

Radio Divn became independent Radio Research Station

ACE Computer pilot model taken into service by Mathematics Divn

USA explodes hydrogen bomb

Keel laid for first atomic powered submarine

Queen Elizabeth II succeeded George VI

1953

Cutting from Newton's apple tree presented by Kew

Collins helium cryostat installed

Single crystals of pure iron

Structure of DNA (Crick and Watson)

First vertical jet lift aircraft flown

Cosmic ray observatory on Mount Wrangell

1954

International System of units (SI) adopted

Tests on sailing yachts

The maser invented

Solar battery invented (Bell Telephone Co.)

First VTO aircraft

1955

3.2 MV impulse generator installed

First long beam caesium standard

Hovercraft invented

Altitude record of 65 876 ft in a Canberra aircraft

1956
First shock tube
Solutions of differential equations
Pneumatic gauging

Neutrino detected (Los Alamos Lab.)
  and anti-neutrons discovered
Ion microscope developed
Image dissector camera developed
  (Mullard)
Transatlantic telephone service
  inaugurated

1957
Aerodynamics at hypersonic speeds
Automatic recording saccharimeter

First earth satellite (USSR)

1958
ACE Computer completed and handed
  to Mathematics Divn
Infrared Spectroscopy

Van Allen radiation belts discovered
Stereophonic gramophone recordings
US submarine 'Nautilus' passed be-
  neath the North Pole

1959
New ship tank opened at Feltham
Nuclear magnetic resonance

Synthetic diamond manufacture (De
  Beers)

1960
Helium tunnel installed
Orange radiation of krypton-86 adopted
  as the atomic length standard

Heart pacemaker developed at
  Birmingham
First reflector satellite

1961
High voltage work transferred to CEGB
First ruby maser in the country operated
Determination of the density of mercury
Glazebrook Hall opened

Gagarin (USSR) first astronaut to orbit
  the earth
Atlas Computer at Harwell

1962
Hovercraft principles studied
Zone refining techniques for metal
  single crystals
Direct measurement of molecular quad-
  rupole moment

Laser beam reflected from the Moon
USA launched Mariner spacecraft to
  Venus
First communications satellite (USA)

1963
Cryotron development for computers
The yard define as 0.9144 m and the
  pound as 0.453 592 37 kg

Existence of quarks postulated
Dish radio telescope built over a natural
  bowl in Puerto Rico
USSR puts first woman into space

1964
KDF 9 Computer installed
HCN laser discovered

Mariner IV (USA) and Zond II (USSR)
  launched to photograph Mars
Opening of the Forth Bridge and the
  Verrazano Narrows Bridge—the
  world's longest
Ministry of Technology formed

1965
NCL amalgamated with NPL
High speed marine craft

Britain agreed to adopt the Metric
  System
First space walk (USSR)
US space ship Gemini III manoeuvred
  in orbit and Geminis VI and VII
  rendezvous in space
Oil found in the North Sea

1966
Design of high speed aircraft
Tests to determine the optimum funnel
  design for the QE II

First un-manned landing on the Moon
  (USSR)
First weather satellite (USA)
Spacecraft landed on Venus (USSR)

1967
New measurement of 'g'
Hovercraft Unit joined NPL Ship Divn
Metrology Centre set up
Definition of the second based on atomic
  constants
New calculable mutual inductor

Mendelevium, the heaviest known nuc-
  leus, made
Isaac Newton telescope installed at
  Herstmonceux
First heart transplant

1968
International Practical Temperature
  Scale adopted
Divn of Electrical Science established

First manned orbit of the Moon (USA)
First undisputed reaching of the North
  Pole (US team)

1969
High voltage electron microscope
  installed
Josephson junctions applied to measurements of fundamental constants

First landing on the Moon (USA) and
  RT and TV transmission to Earth
Allende meteorite landed in Mexico
First flights of Concorde and Boeing 747
QE II maiden voyage

1970
1 MV electron microscope went into
  service
Slamming of ships investigated
Aerodynamics work transferred to RAE

Individual atoms photographed by
  electron microscope
Collapse of West Gate Bridge,
  Melbourne

1971
Long distance alignment by lasers
Ultra fine silica powder production
Propulsion and handling of large tankers

Largest steerable dish type radio tele-
  scope in the world installed in
  Germany
US spacecraft in orbit round Mars

1972
Traffic noise studies
Sea-going research vessel acquired

Stockholm conference on human
  environment

Mirrors of Herschel's telescopes reno-
vated and tested

Biological weapons outlawed

1973
Corrosion Advisory Service
Melting rocks
W European Metrology Conference
held at NPL
14th edition of *Kaye and Laby* edited by
NPL staff

Highest observatory in the world
opened near Denver, Colorado
Skylab launched

1974
Measurements on the Tokamak atomic
fusion power source
Structures at sea
Laser wavelength measurements

Largest telescope in the world installed
in the USSR
Sears Tower, Chicago, tallest building
in the world

1975
Primary pressure standards
Linac building completed and put into
service
Largest diffraction grating ever pro-
duced in the UK

Centenary of the Metre Convention
First link-up in space of USA and USSR
cosmonauts

1976
Auger electron microscopy
Computer verification of signatures
Ship and Maritime Science Divns
became NMI
Fail-safe devices designed for the chim-
ing mechanism of Big Ben

Concorde entered service

1977
Measurement of atmospheric pollution
NPL Museum set up in Bushy House
BCS became responsibility of NPL

Magnetic field of 300 kG (30.1 T) achieved in USA
World's largest tanker completed
New River Gorge Bridge, USA—the
longest steel arch bridge in the world

1978
Stratospheric water vapour measure-
ment by balloon borne radiometer
Ultrasonic standards measurements
began
Colour measurements at the National
Gallery

Highest sustained laboratory pressure
(160 GPa) reported from USA
International ultraviolet explorer satellite launched
North Pole reached solo (Uemura)

1979

Dynamic pressure measurement standards

Use of lead in free machining alloys

Rydberg constant measured

Fibre reinforced alloys

Spacecraft flying by Jupiter, spacecraft reached Saturn

Skylab destroyed on entering the earth's atmosphere after 34 981 orbits

1980

Microwave hazard monitoring facility operational

Force standards confirm weight of Concorde

National Testing Laboratory Accreditation Scheme (NATLAS) announced

Eruption of Mt St Helens in Washington State, USA

Appendix 3: Organisation of NPL

Organization of National Physical Laboratory 1900–1940

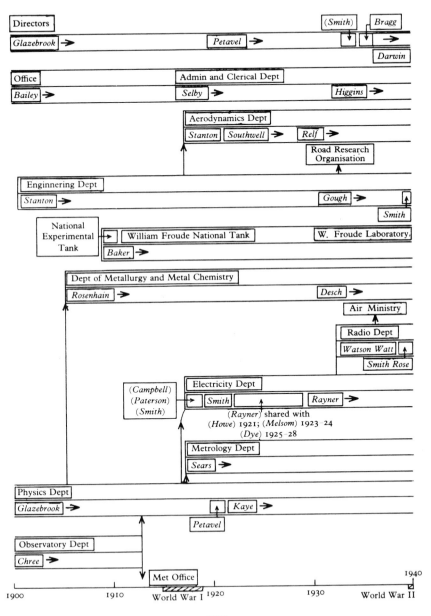

Organization of National Physical Laboratory 1940—80
(Physical & Mathematical Sciences)

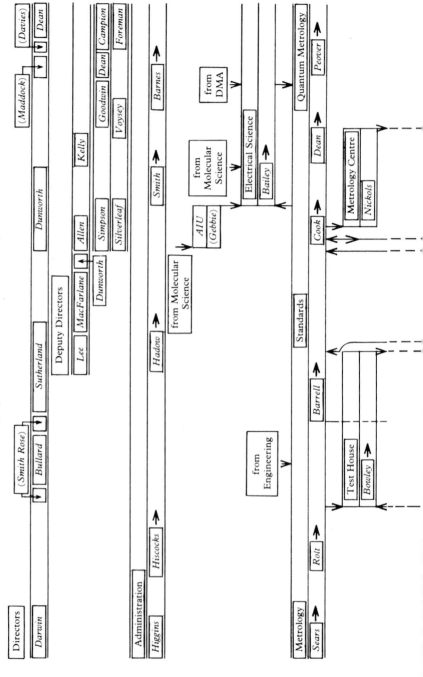

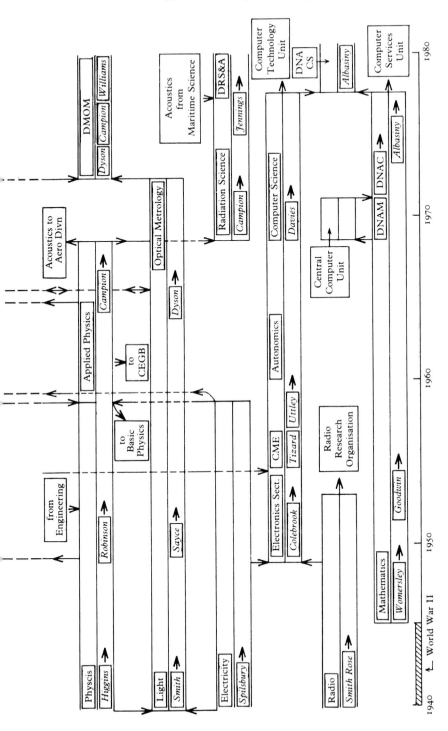

Organization of National Physical Laboratory 1940—80
(Materials & Applied Sciences)

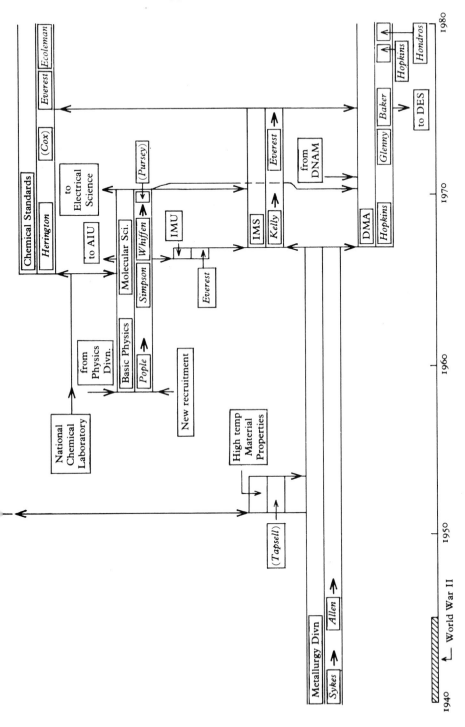

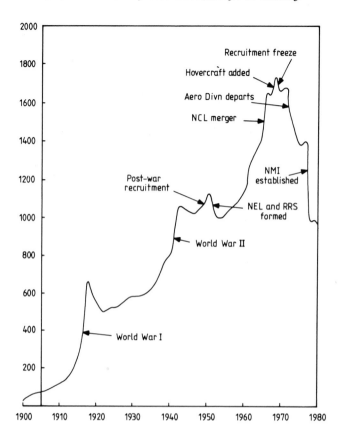

Scientific staff in post

Appendix 4: Highlights in the History of Standards

LENGTH

3000 BC Material length standards in ancient Egypt were based on the cubit, which may have been derived from earth measurements

The Yard

1305 A material end standard established during the reign of Edward I

1496 A material end standard established during the reign of Henry VII (Science Museum)

1588 A material end standard established during the reign of Elizabeth I (Science Museum)

1834 The current material end standard destroyed by fire in the House of Commons

1845 New material line standard constructed

1855 Its use legalised (Imperial Standard Yard) (Now held at NPL)

1900 Foundation of NPL

1922 NPL began to take part in the decennial comparisons of the Yard and its copies

1932, 1947, 1957 Further decennial comparisons

1963 The Weights and Measures Act defined the Yard in terms of the Metre— 0.9144

The Metre

1795 The Metre defined as 10^{-7} times the arc of the meridian between the North Pole and the Equator. The length was calculated from measurements made by J-B Delambre and P Méchain

1799 A material end standard legalised—the Mètre des Archives

1829 Wavelength of light suggested as a standard of length by J Babinet

1875 The Metre Convention held in France led to international agreement (not including Great Britain) on 'construction and verification with the best appliances of modern science of the new international standards of the metre and the kilogram'. As a result the Bureau International des Poids et Mesures (BIPM) was set up at Sèvres to act as the central organising authority, with the Comité International des Poids et Mesures (CIPM) and the Conférence Générale des Poids et Mesures (CGPM) to coordinate and plan the work

1884 Great Britain finally adhered to the Metre Convention

1889 The first meeting of the CGPM established a new material line standard, the International Prototype Metre, copies of which were distributed to member states. (Copy No 16 is held at NPL)

1892 First determination of length by optical interferometry by A A Michelson and J R Benoit

1897 Use of metric measures in trade became lawful in Britain

1900 Foundation of NPL

1926 Definition refined

1932, 1934–5 Determinations carried out at NPL by optical interferometry

1960 The metre defined by the 11th CGPM in terms of the wavelength of orange rediation of krypton-86 (1 650 763.73 wavelengths)

MASS

The Pound

1834 The standard Troy pound of 5760 grains destroyed in the House of Commons fire

1844 A material standard constructed — the Imperial Standard Pound Avoirdupois (7000 grains)

1844 Its use legalised

1900 Foundation of NPL

1922 Decennial comparison of the Pound and its copies

1932 Precision balance constructed at NPL for decennial comparison of the Imperial Standard Pound and its copies (capability of comparison to 1×10^{-6} g)

1947, 1957 Further decennial comparisons

1963 The Weights and Measures Act, 1963, defined the Pound as 0.453 592 37 kg (the UK Primary Standard of the Pound)

The kilogram

1795 The kilogram defined as the mass of a cubic decimetre of water at the temperature of maximum density (4° C)—soon replaced by a material standard

1799 A material standard legalised — the Kilogramme des Archives

1844 A material standard (called Kilogram E) acquired by the UK for comparison with the Standard Pound (now held at NPL)

1889 The International Kilogram established by first CGPM and copies distributed to member countries (Copy No 18 is held at NPL)

1900 Foundation of NPL

1967 The CGPM defined the kilogram as equal in mass to the International Prototype of the Kilogram

TIME AND FREQUENCY

The second, defined as 1/86 400 of mean solar day; long intervals determined by astronomical observation and subdivided by pendulum clocks

1900 Foundation of NPL

1931 Valve maintained tuning fork used as a stable source at NPL

1934 The Dye quartz ring oscillator used as a stable source at NPL

1936 Replaced by the Essen quartz ring source

1956 CIPM adopted one second as the fraction 1/31 556 925.9747 of the tropical year for 1900 January 0 at 12 hours ephemeris time

1964 CIPM recommended defining the second as the duration of 9 192 631 770 periods of the radiation corresponding to the transition between the two hyperfine levels of the ground state of the caesium-133 atom

1967 CGPM adopted the caesium standard

ELECTRICAL STANDARDS

1851 W E Weber proposed a series of absolute units based on length, mass and time

Units of resistance established by various material standards — coils of wire, columns of mercury etc

1863 A practical unit of resistance, the ohmad, advocated by the Committee of Electrical Standards of the BA

1864 J P Joule measured the ampere in terms of the force between two current carrying conductors

1873 L V Lorenz proposed an electro-mechanical method for standardisation of the unit of resistance

1892 The ohm defined by the BA Committee in terms of a column of mercury

1894 Material electrical standards set up in the Board of Trade — a Rayleigh type current balance, a Kelvin electrostatic voltmeter and a standard of resistance

1900 Foundation of NPL

1907 Absolute measurement of resistance by calculable mutual inductor at NPL

1908 The International Conference on Electrical Units and Standards adopted the International Ampere (based on a silver voltameter designed at NPL) and the International Ohm (based on a precisely defined column of mercury)

1908 The current balance, based on designs by W E Ayrton and J Viriamu Jones, used at NPL to measure the absolute ampere

1908 Weston Cell adopted as a standard voltage source

1914 Comparison of Absolute and International Ohms by Lorenz Machine at NPL

1920 Board of Trade material standards passed to NPL, where they still reside

1921 Sixth CIPM amended the Convention of 1875 to include electrical quantities

1938 Further comparison of Absolute and International Ohms by Lorenz Machine

1938 The ampere defined in terms of the force between two parallel conductors

1948 International System abandoned in favour of the Absolute System

1967 CGPM defined the ampere as the current which, if maintained between two straight parallel conductors of infinite length and negligible cross-section, placed one metre apart in vacuum, would produce between these conductors a force equal to 2×10^{-7} N/per metre of length

1967 Improved calculable mutual inductor designed at NPL

1970s Absolute measurement of resistance by calculable capacitor at NPL

1970s Use of Josephson junction as a means of reproducing the volt

TEMPERATURE

1641 First mercury in glass thermometer

1663 Standard thermometers available at the Royal Society

1665 Ideas for temperature scales put forward by Boyle and Hook

1701 Ditto by Newton

1724   Fahrenheit Scale proposed
1742   Centesimal Scale proposed by A Celsius
1887   CIPM adopted a gas thermometer scale — the Echelle Normale
1900   Foundation of NPL
1900   Constant volume hydrogen thermometer operating at BIPM accepted as providing a scale of temperature, disseminated by 'mercury in verre dur' thermometers
1927   International Temperature Scale adopted by the seventh CGPM — conforming as closely as possible to the gas thermometer scale by definition of fixed points between the BP of oxygen ($-183°$ C) and the FP of gold ($1063°$ C), and of interpolating means between them
1948   The International Temperature Scale revised in the light of researches in the intervening decades. 'Celsius' substituted for 'Centigrade'
1954   The kelvin, unit of thermodynamic temperature, defined as 'the fraction $1/273.16$ of the thermodynamic temperature of the triple point of water
1968   A revised scale — the International Practical Temperature Scale — introduced, defined between 13.81 K and 1337.58 K. The unit of temperature renamed the kelvin

AMOUNT OF SUBSTANCE

There is almost no history so far

LUMINOUS INTENSITY

1860   British Parliamentary Candle legalised for gas testing
1898   A G Vernon-Harcourt's 10 candle Pentane Lamp legalised
1900   Foundation of NPL
1902   Electric   carbon   filament   single   hair-pin   lamp   introduced   by Fleming/Ediswan
1909   One candle unit adopted internationally based on the Fleming/Ediswan carbon filament lamps
1912   Tungsten filament lamps introduced
1921   New International Candle agreed
1930   Black body radiator developed as alternative material standard
1948   Black body radiator for realisation of the unit, now called the candela, adopted internationally
1967   Candela defined in the SI system as the 'luminous intensity in the perpendicular direction of a surface of $1/600\,000$ m^2 of a black body at the temperature of freezing platinum under a pressure of $101\,325$ Nm^{-2}

National Physical Laboratory Units of Measurement

Quantity, unit, symbol and definition	Realisation and use at the National Physical Laboratory

LENGTH: *metre (m)*
The metre is the length equal to 1 650 763.73 wavelengths in vacuum of the radiation corresponding to the transition between the levels $2p_{10}$ and $5d_5$ of the krypton-86 atom.

The metre is maintained at the NPL through the wavelength of the 633 nm radiation from an iodine-stabilised helium-neon laser, illustrated. The reproducibility is about 3 parts in 10^{11}, equivalent to measuring the earth's mean circumference to about 1 mm.

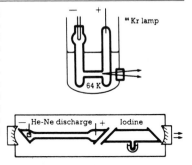

MASS: *kilogram (kg)*
The kilogram is the unit of mass; it is equal to the mass of the international prototype of the kilogram.
Note: This international prototype is made of platinum-iridium and is kept at the International Bureau of Weights and Measures, Sèvres, Paris, France, the British copy (No. 18) is kept at NPL.

Kilogram masses and sub-multiples of 1 kg, made from similar materials, may be compared on the NPL precision balances, illustrated, to about a microgram.

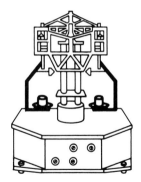

TIME: *second (s)*
The second is the duration of 9 192 631 770 periods of the radiation corresponding to the transition between the two hyperfine levels of the ground state of the caesium-133 atom.

The second is realised by caesium-beam standards, illustrated, with an uncertainty of 2 parts in 10^{13}—equivalent to about a second in 166 000 years. A uniform timescale, synchronised to 1 microsecond, is available virtually world-wide by radio transmissions

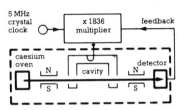

National Physical Laboratory Units of Measurement (*continued*)

Quantity, unit, symbol and definition	Realisation and use at the National Physical Laboratory	
ELECTRIC CURRENT: *ampere (A)* The ampere is that constant current which, if maintained in two straight parallel conductors of infinite length, of negligible circular cross-section, and placed 1 metre apart in a vacuum, would produce between these conductors a force equal to 2×10^{-7} newton per metre of length.	The ampere is realised at the NPL to a few parts in 10^6 by means of the Ayrton–Jones current balance, illustrated. The ohm is realised, using a Thompson–Lampard calculable capacitor, to 5 parts in 10^8. The volt is now maintained to 3 parts in 10^8 using the Josephson effects in super-conductivity.	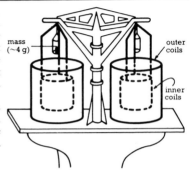
THERMODYNAMIC TEMPERATURE: *kelvin (K)* The kelvin, unit of thermodynamic temperature, is the fraction $1/273.16$ of the thermodynamic temperature of the triple point of water.	Temperature realised by triple-point of water cells, illustrated, at NPL are reproducible to ± 0.1 mK. Practical temperatures may be measured with uncertainties down to a few millikelvin, with platinum resistance and other thermometers calibrated at NPL, in the range 0.5 K to 3000 K.	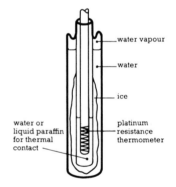
AMOUNT OF SUBSTANCE *mole (mol)* The mole is the amount of substance of a system which contains as many elementary entities as there are atoms in 0.012 kilogram of carbon 12. Note: When the mole is used, the elementary entities must be specified and may be atoms, molecules, ions, electrons, other particles, or specified groups of such particles.	The mole is not realised directly form its definition; it can be realised in various indirect ways by users of the concept of 'amount of substance'. The related Avogadro constant, the number of elementary entities per mole, is now known to about a part in a million.	 Space lattice of diamond

National Physical Laboratory Units of Measurement (*continued*)

Quantity, unit, symbol and definition	Realisation and use at the National Physical Laboratory

LUMINOUS INTENSITY
candela (cd)
The candela is the luminous intensity, in the perpendicular direction, of a surface of 1/600 000 square metre of a black body at the temperature of freezing platinum under a pressure of 101 325 newtons per square metre.

The NPL candela, illustrated, is realised with an uncertainty of about 0.5 %. International comparisons show a spread of ±0.8 %. The candela may eventually be redefined, for example as the luminous intensity of a source of monochromatic radiation of specified frequency in a direction for which the radiant intensity is 1/683 W sr $^{-1}$.

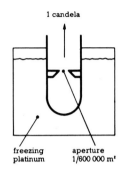

SI supplementary units
PLANE ANGLE:
radian (rad)
The radian is the plane angle between two radii of a circle which cut off on the circumference an arc equal in length to the radius.
SOLID ANGLE:
steradian (sr)
The steradian is the solid angle which, having its vertex in the centre of a sphere, cuts off an area of the surface of the sphere equal to that of a square with sides of length equal to the radius of the sphere.

The radian and steradian are supplementary SI units and may, as convenient, be regarded as base units or as derived units. NPL angle calibrations, illustrated, may achieve an accuracy of < 0.1 arc second. This would correspond to a navigation error of about 2 metres in crossing the Atlantic from New York to London.

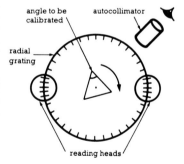

Appendix 5: Units and Standards of Measurement Employed at the NPL in 1928

Length and Mass

These depend on material standards, though there is a hint that length standards may one day be referred to the wavelength of a particular spectral line.

The Imperial Standard Yard and the Imperial Standard Pound are defined in the Weights and Measures Act of 1878. Copies of these known as 'Parliamentary Copies' are deposited at the Royal Mint, the Royal Society, the Royal Observatory at Greenwich and at the Royal Palace of Westminster.

The International Prototype Metre is defined by the 7th CGPM 1927. This and the International Prototype Kilogram and copies are kept at the BIPM at Sèvres. Copies of these have been distributed to the various countries which signed the Metre Convention.

The Imperial Standard Yard and Pound with one pair of Parliamentary Copies and the British National Copies of the Metre and the Kilogram, are in the custody of the Board of Trade, which also has a set of standards known as Board of Trade Standards.

The Board of Trade is responsible for intercomparison, but since the Superintendent of Metrology Department, NPL, is ex-officio Deputy Warden of the Standards to the Board of Trade, the NPL now carries out all intercomparisons on behalf of the Board.

In addition the NPL has its own series of length and mass standards, those of the metre and the kilogram being intercompared periodically with those of the BIPM.

The ratios of British and metric units were measured at the end of the 19th Century and have been given legal sanction by an Order in Council, 1898.

Time

The mean solar second is defined as 1/86 400 of the mean solar day. The solar day is the interval between successive transits of the centre of the sun's disc across the meridian. Time standards are established by time signals received from astronomical observations. Interpolation is by a Shortt clock which recently replaced the Morrison clock presented by Lady Galton in 1904.

Capacity

The gallon is defined by the Weights and Measures Act of 1878, the litre by the 3rd CGPM 1901. The ratio was given a legal sanction by an Order in Council 1898.

Density

This is defined by reference to the unit of mass and the unit of capacity and is measured by gravimetric methods or by the use of a range of standard hydrometers.

Barometric Standard

The value of standard gravity (at sea level at 45°N) has been defined by the Fifth CGPM as 980.665 cm s⁻².

There is no standard barometer at the NPL at present. The original standard barometers were left behind at Kew at the time of the changeover for use by the Observatory. The present working standard is a Fortin barometer which was compared with the Kew standards at the time of transfer and has since been compared with other standards. A new fundamental standard is approaching completion.

The Value of Gravity at Teddington

The best known absolute determination of gravity was made at the Geodetic Institute at Potsdam in 1898–1904. The value of gravity at NPL is taken as 981.195 cm s⁻², the average of a number of determinations all referred back to the original Potsdam figure. This refers to a bench mark on Bushy House wall (34 ft above sea level, latitude 51° 25′ 20″N).

Temperature

The NPL uses the International Temperature Scale adopted at the Seventh CGPM, 1927 based on the following fixed points — BP liquid oxygen − 182.97° C, ice point 0.0° C, steam point 100° C, BP of sulphur 444.6° C, MP of silver 960.5° C and MP of gold 1063° C.

For interpolation the scale is divided into four parts − 190° C to ice point — platinum resistance thermometer (quartic law); ice point to 660° C — platinum resistance thermometer (quadratic law); 660° C to gold point — platinum/platinum–rhodium thermocouple; above gold point — spectral radiation pyrometer.

The extensive calibration work on mercury-in-glass thermometers is carried out using mercury-in-glass standards calibrated against the above.

Radium Standard

The British Radium Standard is 21.13 mg of anhydrous radium chloride of high purity — certified in 1912 by Madame Curie, Professor Stefan Meyer and Sir E Rutherford. Allowing for decay this is assumed (1928) to be now 20.99 mg.

X-Ray Intensity

The standard is the International unit adopted by the Second International Congress of Radiology, Stockholm 1928.

Electrical Units

The International Ohm is defined as the resistance of a column of mercury of 14.4521 g mass and a length of 106.300 cm (realisation by NPL employs wire wound coils having a mean value of 1.000 03 ohm).

The International Ampere is that current which deposits silver from a solution of silver nitrate at 0.001 118 00 g s⁻¹ (there has been no recent realisation by this method at NPL).

The International Volt is defined by the EMF of a standard Weston cell—1.101 83 International Volts at 20° C, a value fixed at an International Meeting in 1910 (realisation at NPL by continuous construction of cells and intercomparisons with other standards).

Absolute units are to be introduced as soon as possible. (Scheduled for 1940, they did not actually take over until after World War II.)

The Absolute Ohm is realised periodically at NPL by the methods of Lorenz and of Campbell. It is measured to be 106.245 cm of mercury of standard density or equal to 1.0005 International Ohms.

The Absolute Ampere is realised periodically at NPL by the Ayrton–Jones Current Balance. It is measured to correspond to the deposition of 1.118 27 mg of silver per second i.e. it only differs by a few parts in 10^6 from the International Ampere.

Inductance

Standards of inductance are realised to a high degree of accuracy in CGS units by measurements of lengths and numbers of turns.

Capacity

Capacity is measured in terms of mutual inductance and resistance using a Carey–Foster Bridge.

Alternating Current Measurements

Links with DC measurement are established by measuring resistance, the value of which changes only a small amount between DC and a low frequency AC, and voltage by voltmeter.

Current is measured in terms of voltage and resistance; power likewise.

Photometry

The standard of candle power is the International Candle of the International Commission on Illumination, 1921, and is defined by incandescent lamps at NPL and in the USA and France. This standard is the same as the British unit derived from the Vernon–Harcourt Lamp.

The colour of the standard is that of the radiation from a black body at 1980 K.

Realisation at NPL is by secondary standards intercompared periodically with the above.

Appendix 6: *Historical Use of the Principal Rooms in Bushy House*

Room	1797	1832	1880	NPL Past	NPL 1980
SW wing	Ballroom	Morning room	Chapel	Chemical laboratory Electrical laboratory	NPL museum – site history
SE wing	Greenhouse	Library	Library	Nonmagnetic laboratory	Nonmagnetic laboratory
SE addition	—	Dining room	Dining room	Nonmagnetic laboratory (housing Lorenz machine and current balance)	Nonmagnetic laboratory (still with same items)
NE wing	Kitchen	Kitchen	Kitchen	Metallurgical laboratory and many subsequent functions	Electrical laboratory
NE addition	—	Domestic quarters	Domestic quarters	Domestic quarters, sundry scientific functions	NPL museum – apparatus
NW wing	Housekeeper's quarters	Servants' hall	Servants' hall	Thermometric laboratory	Offices
S room, main block	Dining room and small dining room	Drawing room	Drawing room	Thermometer testing	Senior staff common room
W room, main block	Great drawing room	Drawing room	Drawing room	Thermometer testing	Large conference room
E room, 1st floor	Picture room	Ladies-in-waiting sitting room	Duke's study	Director's office	Included in Director's private flat
W room, 1st floor	Ladies' dressing room	Bed room	Queen's bedroom	Director's laboratory	Included in Director's private flat
NW corner rooms	Sprial staircase	Spiral staircase	Spiral staircase	Mercury column	Lobby

Information from:
Soane Plan (1779)—Duke of Clarence about to move in
Phipps Plan (1832)—Duke of Clarence no longer in residence
Ministry of Works Plan (1880)—Duc de Nemours in residence (as taken over by NPL 10 years later)

Index

References to notes are indicated by a suffix n to the page number. References to figures are indicated by italicised page numbers.